Colorado
Flyfishing

Where to Eat, Sleep, Fish

Mark D. Williams

W. Chad McPhail

trails books
AN IMPRINT OF BOWER HOUSE

DENVER

BowerHouseBooks.com

Designed by Rebecca Finkel

Printed in Canada

Library of Congress Cataloging-in-Publication Data
Williams, Mark D., 1960–
  Colorado flyfishing : where to eat, sleep, fish / Mark D. Williams, W. Chad McPhail.
    p. cm.
  ISBN 978-1-55566-442-8
  1. Flyfishing—Colorado—Guidebooks. 2. Colorado—Guidebooks.
I. McPhail, W. Chad. II. Title.
        SH475.W55 2010
        799.17'5709788—dc22   2010018718

10 9 8 7 6 5

"Other places were scattered about the hemispheres. I have been in some of them, and...well, we won't talk about that. But there was one yet—the biggest, the most blank, so to speak—that I had a hankering after.

"True, by this time it was not a blank space any more. It had got filled since my boyhood with rivers and lakes and names. It had ceased to be a blank space of delightful mystery—a white patch for a boy to dream gloriously over. It had become a place of darkness. But there was in it one river especially, a mighty big river, that you could see on the map, resembling an immense snake uncoiled, with its head in the sea, its body at rest curving afar over a vast country, and its tail lost in the depths of the land. And as I looked at the map of it in a shop-window, it fascinated me as a snake would a bird—a silly little bird."

—JOSEPH CONRAD
(Marlow, from *Heart of Darkness*)

Contents

INTRODUCTION

"You forget what you want to remember,
and you remember what you want to forget."
—CORMAC MCCARTHY, *The Road*

"In culture after culture, people believe that
the soul lives on after death, that rituals
can change the physical world and divine the truth,
and that illness and misfortune are caused and
alleviated by spirits, ghosts, saints… and gods."
—STEVEN PINKER, *How the Mind Works*

"Ghosts are a metaphor for memory and remembrance
and metaphorically connect our world to the world
we cannot know about."
—LESLIE WHAT, interview, June 2002

We are teachers and writers. We are fishing buddies. The Mark and Mac Show.

We fish together, partly because each of us is pretty darned good at fly-fishing, partly because weird adventures worth writing about happen when we go on fishing trips, and mostly because we enjoy each other's company. We own hundreds of fishing guidebooks and dozens covering fishing the Centennial State, but saw a need for a different type of book.

Most fishing destination books break down chapters by rivers or fisheries. Most anglers go on fishing trips to a place, not usually a single river. They go to Lake City or South Fork or Salida. These anglers want to know where to fish around those home bases. Discovering which waters to fish around a place while thumbing through one of the conventional books is needle-in-a-haystack–level detective work for most anglers. If I fish the Rio Grande, what else is within an hour's drive? We resolved to group the thirty best home bases in Colorado and provide information to the reader-angler about where to fish in the area (and to have an excuse to fish all summer, every day, and a further excuse to include our adventures and meanderings). The structure of this book is that of a destination guide, grouped by home bases. But this book is also an armchair book. We believe that places are best revealed through experience, through stories. We are adventure magnets. We fish, and crazy things happen. So stories there are.

The two of us adventure magnets fished across Colorado for more than 55 days this summer, reacquainting ourselves with rivers and lakes and towns we'd been visiting for a combined sixty-plus years. Some of our favorite home bases were no longer as viable as we remembered. Some places that we had inadvertently overlooked or underestimated have transformed over the years into perfect home bases. We've each fished Colorado for decades, but we are also campers and backpackers. We are budget conscious. Motels over hotels. Cabins over lodges. Grill your own burger over five-star dining.

We include anecdotes and useful stories that illustrate the character of the home base, the fishing place. This isn't just a cut-and-dry informational book but also a sit-on-the-pot and dream-where-to-go book. "Let's see, if I stay in Pagosa Springs, I have seven medium rivers and ten lakes I can fish during my week's stay. And I want to see the road where the battery flew off Mark's trailer and bounced."

We are both Texans and, as such, might be called interlopers (and rightfully so), but who better to know about home bases than out-of-staters who come to these Colorado home bases for several weeks each summer (for twenty years)? Who fish these waters sometimes sixty to ninety days a year and need to know where to eat, fish, and sleep when they invade the state?

How did we decide which home bases to include? Aren't there more than thirty good home bases in Colorado? These all look like great home bases, but just for trout, not warm water species? How did we decide which home bases? Why not Denver? Why not Colorado Springs? Leadville? Walden?

1) It's all about trout fishing. Warm water species need not apply. We go to Colorado for trout, and that's what we know. We get enough warm water angling in our home state.
2) We wanted places you'd go to fish. Colorado Springs might have the South Platte fairly close, but you wouldn't go to the Springs just for a fishing trip.
3) We needed to know the places pretty well over the years.

4) The home bases needed to have several trout fishing options nearby. We wanted places that offered quality fishing at the home base and lots of different kinds of trout fishing rivers and lakes within an hour's drive.

5) The home bases needed to have good amenities. Even for camping-only places like Flat Tops or Grand Mesa, we wanted to find multiple options for camping, RVs, that sort of thing. If a home base didn't have as many amenities as, say, Breckenridge, then it needed to make up for it with a plethora of quality angling spots.

Some home bases we've included might be great for families, and you only get to fish as an adjunct. Some home bases are ideal for other activities like skiing, shopping, or hot springs. But all the places are good if you just want to fish.

We included Cuchara. We are aware that Cuchara's angling is not the best in the state. Cuchara made the list because it's close for Oklahoma and Texas and New Mexico, it's good for families, and anglers get choices of lots of little lakes and several small creeks—fisheries that are good for beginners to learn. Cuchara is attractive and unique with its coke ovens and dikes and Spanish Peaks and high country scenery. So it made the list. We're aware that there may be arguments over what should or should not have made the list. That's part of the fun of creating (or reading) a book like this. So bring it on.

Some of the stories may have been adapted and updated from magazine or newspaper articles or columns we've previously written. We tried to ensure that the majority of our material came from this summer rather than previous visits. No shortage of adventures. We had tons of material that didn't make the book, as it didn't fit a chapter or theme.

To wit: Johnny Cobb is a legendary wrestling coach in Texas—Hall of Fame, awards, coaching at Wayland Baptist after a lifetime of high school coaching. Cobb is a friend of ours. Cobb is a short, wiry fencepost of energy. He is fifty-something going on thirteen. He is learning to flyfish, and so far, he needs to stick with coaching.

This past summer he and Randy "Arkie" Denham and my brother-in-law Kenny Medling met up with us in Lake City. Arkie is a great spinfisher and fair-to-middlin' flyfisher. Kenny is a small-stream master and has been my fishing buddy for thousands of miles of river. Cobb is Barney Fife on the stream, oblivious to rules and courtesies and nuances and especially to stealth. For all his athletic prowess (for he is still an active senior citizen) he is a baby Rhino in the stream.

We were fishing the upper Lake Fork Gunnison, a mile-long stretch of the most beautiful public water in Hinsdale County, full of wide runs, big bend pools, gorgeous pocket water, and dark-blue holes. If we spread out, each of us could fish several hours, working each lie, the water in front of us calming down enough for the fish to feed again. We each took a section, but foolishly we let Cobb loose. Fish scattered as Cobb trounced through pools, splashed through runs, wading up to his waist in the water he should have been fishing. Cobb is a quick little sucker, too, so in a matter of twenty minutes, the river was frothed and useless.

Jump to an hour later on the last good public pool before we had to exit the river. I have cornered this one awesome flats, big pool section. Arkie and Kenny stand to the side whispering. Trout are rising at a drop-off, where the flats get deep and slam into the big rock. I had (and missed) two takes. I hear muffled giggling, and then out of nowhere Cobb is at my shoulder, casting wildly, walking up the stream and into the big pool. It was over in a flash. Arkie and Kenny were doubled over laughing.

"We called that one."

"You gonna clue Cobb in or am I?" Kenny is usually his co-conspirator on these things.

"I don't have the heart just yet. Look at how much fun he's having."

Cobb had doubled back a few hundred yards and was fishing his way back up to us at breakneck pace. Another trout broke the surface, but I knew that by the time I unstrung and cast to it Cobb would already be speeding through the pool.

"We'll tell him the rules before the next trip," Arkie advised.

I can't wait.

We had one of those summers you dream about. Imagine waking up somewhere different every morning and having your choice of lakes and rivers to fish. No deadlines. No worries or pressures of home. No phone calls or emails to annoy you. Just go fish somewhere. Go to bed when you like. Get up when you feel it's time. Build a campfire, grill some meat, drink a whiskey, smoke a cigar, shave whenever your beard says to. Bathrooms and showers and hygiene are but luxuries.

We improvised on our trip. We used a five-gallon bucket with a toilet lid and trash bags for our crapper. On the very last trip out this summer, we had taken in all the pots and pans to wash them, and we forgot to repack them—so we cooked bacon for the kids in a blue-flake metal pan and pancakes in a metal plate. I don't think either pan or plate survived the ordeal.

We showered when we could. Sometimes that meant yucky camp showers or pay-to-shower dives at RV spots. Other times it meant a river-soaked washcloth or a lemon-scented wetwipe. You'd be surprised how you can convince yourself you've "showered" if you fell in the river or got caught out in the rain. Additionally, when you've smelled yourself for three or four days, you really don't even notice that you stink. Only the other guy does, and that's how we'd know when it was time for a rinse.

We caught many more browns than rainbows, and we caught many more cutts and brooks than either rainbows or browns. We fished the high country whenever we could so we were bound to catch more brookies and cutthroats, but still we were trying to balance the equation the second half of the summer and catch more bows. Didn't happen.

What was cool about the summer was that we'd get to a home base, thinking in our head that we'd be there for, say, three days, but because of conditions (good and bad) those three days might turn into six or seven. By the same token, if we got our research done early, we could jet to the next place without worrying. It was a fishing trip, a buddy trip, a road trip, but it was also something else. Something quite different than we'd expected. We were both in search of answers, and we found plenty of them out there in the wild, on the rivers. We had themes that showed up throughout the summer. Myths were created, or continued.

Things get weird on the road. The invention of Harvey Pulmer (who blew up that damned dam back in '76) was the weirdest, and you'll see him pop up in a few pages. We make up songs, find slogans to use over and over again that are only funny to the two of us, gravitate toward the same music over and over (Amos Lee, Citizen Cope, and Gomez will never sound the same). We looked for signs, and they found us. Not just like the Kum 'N Go store, but metaphorical signs (dead birds, skulls, elk rib cages, talismans, that sort of thing).

We each had our special camp chair. If you're just camping for a weekend, your chair doesn't matter much, but if it's where you are sitting night after night, breakfast after breakfast, for fifty-plus days, your camp chair is important. You need a holder for your coffee in the morning and your cocktail in the evening (or maybe it's the other way around). You need it to be sturdy so it takes a beating and keeps on seating.

We had our essentials for spending a summer fishing across Colorado (it's fun to just write that sentence). Coffee and cigars and water and power bars and Early Times and camp chairs and polar fleece and skull caps. Those were tops on the list. Oh, and fire. Lots of fire. We carry the fire.

How we fish:
- We fish together, 98 percent of the time.
- We take thousands of photos. Daily.
- We walk. We hike. A lot.

- We start at point A and wade upstream, walk upstream for a long, long ways. We turn around at Point B and hike the long way back.
- We are guerilla anglers, locating the prime lies, the best pools, and we hit-and-run, always moving, exploring. Risk-to-reward ratio.
- A lighter rod is always better.
- If we can fish away from other anglers, we will.
- Big fish are great. Any-sized wild trout are better.

You'll see these elements, these credos, these themes repeated and evident throughout this book.

Typical day in the life of us, summertime, somewhere in Colorado

7:00, Mac's up first. Often by 6:00, but he's quiet until 7:00. I need my beauty sleep.

Breakfast. Consists of coffee. Mac boils water. We have number 2 filters and these little plastic filter holder-drip-things. We like rich dark coffee, the oily Italian Roast our favorite. We need no milk, no sugar. We sip then gulp down two 12-ounce cups each. Some mornings we each eat a banana, sometimes we eat a power bar or granola bar. Twice, we made pancakes. We are not hungry in the mornings nor do we want to waste the time.

7:45. We are dressed and doing odds and ends outside. The night before, we would have each sat on our bed and pored over maps, planning the next day. We have a loose plan but nothing that makes us think we're locked in. We don't like being locked in. As summer went on, we found ourselves camping nearer the water in more out of the way spots, so we drank our second cup of coffee in our camp chairs overlooking a lake or stream, no one around, and we'd watch the rises until we just couldn't stand it any longer.

Packing the Jeep with the day's needs. We kept some stuff in the Jeep all the time. Various rods, reels, extra fly boxes, wading shoes, caps, fleeces, rain jackets, a sack or two of lunch goodies, cigars, flashlights, cameras, and batteries.

8:30-ish: Let's go. We have a general plan in mind. Drive up to the trailhead and hike up the headwaters. Spend most of the morning and mid-afternoon. Hike back. Stop at a couple of tributaries along the way. Get pics of that lake along the road. Hit camp, eat a light snack, fish the tailwater for the evening hatch.

All day: Rain might have changed the plans. Maybe the fishing was too good to leave early from the headwaters. Perhaps the headwaters sucked (they rarely do, but they did above Trujillo Meadows Reservoir this year). Maybe we caught dozens by noon so we drove hard to a nearby creek we'd seen on the map and we got a great surprise.

Lunch? We kept jerky and crackers and a power bar in our chest packs. We carried water. We had cigars. No need for a true lunch.

Dinners were planned out, sometimes weeks in advance. Mark's wife Amy might make a huge dinner of pork roast and freeze it for us to take. Mac might make a super duper–sized helping of spaghetti and freeze it. We kept our frozens not in the fridge (because it didn't keep things cold and it drew too much power) but in a huge cooler. This thing worked well with block ice combined with cubed ice. We could keep food good for almost two weeks by only adding a second bag of cubes.

We might have lasagna, split into two large zip locks, dinner for each. We ate stroganoff, enchiladas, barbecue, boiled in hot water in the bags or defrosted throughout the day and ready for the pan at night. We sometimes had hamburgers wrapped in huge flour tortillas. Sometimes risotto, or our favorite, couscous. And sometimes Mac would sneak in a dash of curry powder when no one was watching, just to see if anyone could taste it. Sandwiches were a special treat instead of an every night thing like many fishing trip cuisines. We'd get fresh-baked bread, a couple of high-end sandwich meats—we tend toward salty Italian or French salamis and hams—an avocado perhaps or good cheese, grape tomatoes, that sort of thing. Spaghetti fresh, spaghetti bagged. We had steaks. Bacon. Ate at a diner—but not often. Olive oil was a must have. We went through three bottles this summer. It also served as our thermometer. When it was a thick gelatinous goo, we knew it had frozen hard in the Aliner that night. Semi-solid but still see-through meant about 35 degrees.

So then, when we'd get back from the day of fishing, all too often in the dark, we had our camp chores. I got dinner out, set up plates, poured drinks, cleaned up the Jeep, set out the chairs, downloaded photos to the laptop. Mac's the cook, *le chef.* He can turn Bisquick into a world class meal that even Tom Colicchio would love. He'd chop logs into his neat little firewood planks and we'd have a roaring blaze. We'd eat around the fire, scratching in our notebooks about the day's events. We'd share slideshows from each laptop of the fish we'd caught. *Great shot. We can use that for this article or that chapter.*

Then the after-dinner.

Planning. Talking. Debating.

Fishing destinations. Women. Books. God.

We favor whiskey and coke and red wine. We favor Maduro smokes. A campfire was a must. The after-dinner might go on for hours, might go on into the night. We talk about Notre Dame and Texas A&M football. We discuss the merits of Mark Danielewski's *House of Leaves* and Umberto Eco's *Foucault's Pendulum.*

Mac was divorced. About a year-and-a-half at this point. He and his ex-wife had been our friends for seven years, so while it was hardly unexpected by the end, it was a tear in the social fabric of our group of friends. Ever since, Mac has become a vanishing act from our houses and get-togethers. I see him mostly on fishing trips.

At Travis Middle School, where we met when we were first-year teachers almost a decade ago, back when Mac was closer to 220 pounds than the 170 he is now, all the female teachers thought he was handsome. I guess so. If he is, and I want to go on record saying that I have no opinion one way or another, he was well set to start a post-marriage dating life. Dude had more girls on a string than James Bond, even back then. This was our backdrop—his dating life—to the 55 days fishing.

A Band of Brothers thing. Neither of us served. We have guilt over that. We didn't experience war. But the Band of Brothers thing is a camaraderie-based, fear-based, conquering your fears sorta thing. Bonding. Overrated? Out of style? Not macho? Come on. If you're a guy, you have guy friends who mean a lot to you, the ones you say crazy things to and about—I love you man or I'd take a bullet for that guy—crap like that. Well, this summer was one of those kinds of summers. If you don't trust your buddy when you backpack six miles into the wilderness, you shouldn't be hiking with him. If you don't bond after spending 24/7 with someone in harsh conditions, close quarters for fifty-plus days, then you are a real masochist.

We had the best summer an adult should be allowed to have, and we hope that our exploits and energies are reflected in the experiences we had with each place. Thanks to our publisher Mira Perrizo, Amy Williams for all her support and research and beauty, Mark's mother Gwen and her husband Don Maroney, loyal dogs and fishing partners Princess and Piper, long-casting Yankee Jorgen Wouters, Mac's beautiful kiddos Savannah and Wesley. Thanks also to Columbia Northwest for the use of the Aliner, to Riverfields' owner Dave "Davo" Rittenberry and his generous support with gear, to Monic Fly Lines, and to all the fly shops and guides and tourist board folks who helped us with information.

Stuff All Anglers Need

- DeLorme topo maps
- An assortment of books and mags for where you're fishing
- Cigarette chargers of all kinds to charge GPS, phones, and gadgets
- Fleece, fleece, and more fleece
- Polarized sunglasses
- GPS of some kind
- Great-fitting wading boots and neoprene socks
- A great rod (not expensive, just great)
- A reel (any reel will do)
- Loads of the Top 10 flies we mention (page 267)

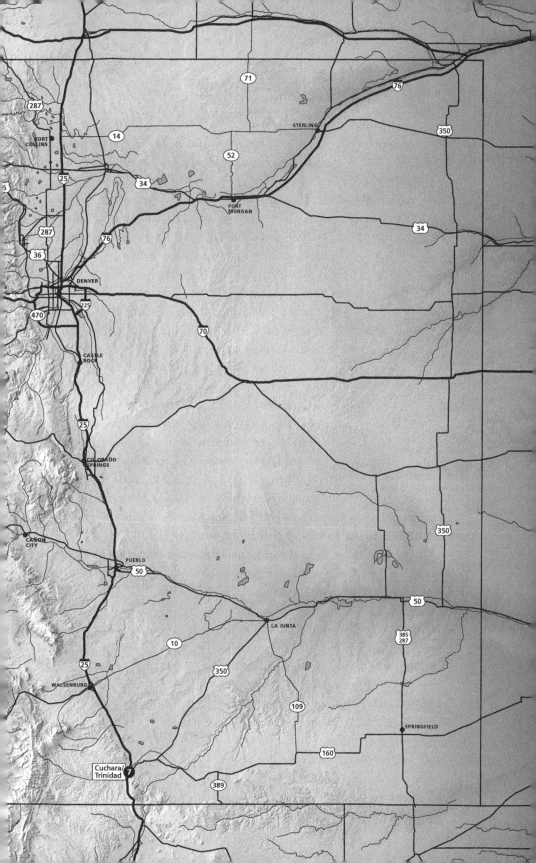

1 Aspen

The stickers for the Aliner became an obsession. Wherever we fished, we wanted a sticker. We liked stickers that were plain. Simple. Funny but not campy. Different but not stupid.

We collected stickers like weird, nerdy Star Wars fans collect Wookie figurines. It was weird at first. The trailer was on loan, a sponsorship thing. We didn't own it, but with every day in the easy, comfortable trailer we felt more like we did.

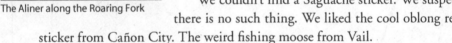

We have always been tent guys. When we get invited to lodges or cabins, we stay, but otherwise we like the tent-camp life. But it made sense to sleep in a more utilitarian mobile lodge for the summer trip, and we were digging it.

I am not a hoarder, but I'm close. I bring too many rods, reels, and fly boxes. I bring extra pillows, sleeping bags, fleece jackets. You name it, I bring it in duplicate. My friends call me Wal-Mark. The Aliner has three outside storage compartments. Several inside storage places. Cabinets, too. I was in outdoor gear heaven.

The Aliner along the Roaring Fork

We couldn't find a Saguache sticker. We suspect there is no such thing. We liked the cool oblong red sticker from Cañon City. The weird fishing moose from Vail.

The understated or unique stickers are what we like.

There's something about the stickers on the Aliner. Something about a public profession of where you've been, where you've sweated and passed through danger. Kind of like, with no disrespect, a soldier's medals. With each purchase, we made the application on the trailer a ceremony and ritual. By the end of the summer, I felt like I had to buy the damned trailer because we had forty-plus stickers on the thing. So I did. By the end of summer, we were addicted. Can't wait to see what stickers we get this next year.

As you may know, Aspen is one of the most luxurious, high-dollar resort mountain towns in the world. So you have

Aspen city limits

gathered that Aspen + tents = oddity. Aspen + trailers = oddity. Two guys with no money = oddity. We wanted to camp in Carbondale or Basalt—at a private campground because there are no public ones. We convinced ourselves that, since we've been out for six straight days with no shower, some hot water and cleanliness would be good for our spirits. No luck. No room at the inn.

Mac and I found that the rivers were up, the fish weren't biting for us, and we couldn't find a campground. So we camped at a high-elevation national forest campground above Aspen, on the upper Roaring Fork. It's as close as we'll ever get to being residents of this ritzy ski town.

Camping every night in a trailer in a campground away from cable, satellite, cell phone service, and usually running water is a different creature. Mac and I are digitally connected and love our laptops and the internet and television and movies and phone calls and texts. Neither of us even had a cell phone until two or three years ago because "no way in hell I'm gonna submit to this technological homewrecker." And then we got iPhones. Cool apps. GPS. Video. Camera. Internet. The Cult of Mac. The Apple Mac, not Mac our fishing buddy.

Top: Independence Pass; above: Weller Campground, upstream of Aspen

Independence Pass

We didn't camp 55 straight days this summer. We had breaks. So the break with our daily reality of the school year was a challenge but it was healthy and simplifying. Each campground without our electronic connection became a digital anchor. It's our other sickness. We got over it.

As you can imagine, campgrounds in this pricey neighborhood are few and far between. We found one up above Aspen at Weller Campground (after passing up Difficult Campground and going all the way to Independence Pass—and past Lost Man and Lincoln Gulch campgrounds). If you haven't ever driven from Aspen to Independence Pass, hold on tight. There's this one curve where the harrowing, curvy, narrow two-lane mountain road turns into a one-lane road. For no good reason. To the detriment of cars coming from both directions. Especially pulling a camper-trailer. It was scary as hell. Be warned—this may seem like a city, like civilization, but this is wild country and we've seen heavy snow on Independence Pass in mid-July, bears on trails, and angry barkeeps.

This campsite drew a perfect score from us. That's rare because one of our checklist boxes is a river within a stone's throw. The aspen stands enveloped our site in a mysterious green glow. We had only a short drive to park and fish the upper Roaring Fork.

Before we go on, there are some things you should know:

- You don't always have to be alike in order to be fishing buddies, but it helps.
- Sleeping within five feet of each other, night after night, especially when neither of you have bathed in days, well, that requires a fishing buddy mentality.
- Mac is an early riser, and I'm not. Felix MacUnger is a neat-freak, while Oscar "Williams" Madison is not. He's the better cook, but I'm not bad.
- We have traveled together over thousands of miles of road, fished together over thousands of miles of rivers. We've gotten to know each other pretty well over eight years. We can drive for several hours, and no one has to say a word. Sometimes, just a nod will do. He doesn't have to pee every hour like Amy does, so we can make good time on the road. If I mention the law of entropy or deus ex machina or Costa Brava or Max McGee, or use the words slake or cogent or cloying, he's there with me.
- Inside jokes remain inside jokes. I can trust him, he can trust me. Ditto if the other guy is off in the backcountry, farther upstream. We make sure the other guy isn't floating face down in the river. Face-up, funny. Face-down, save him.
- We like Fowles, McCarthy, and Hardy. Modern and postmodern American and British literature is our shared library. Movies like *Fargo, Waking Life, American Beauty,* and *Unforgiven.*
- We abhor the bro-hug, double-backtap. We shake hands like men.
- We favor gallows humor, dark jokes, risqué comedy, absurd references, and clever wordplay.
- We tend toward understatement, list-making, planning (with room for spontaneity).
- We are both novelists-in-training. Photographers for pay. High School English teachers.
- We like cigars, wine, scotch, bourbon, couscous, avocados, steaks, strong coffee.
- If one of us takes a spill, the other waits before he laughs. The guy might be hurt. When he isn't, there comes the locker room attack. The way it should be. When my beard is six days old and more gray than black, he goes with the Hemingway theme. When he wears his neoprene waders with that odd black fleece (the one that looks like a scuba top), I go with the Jacques Cousteau banter.
- Our *Sling Blade* imitations became a complete ongoing persona— Harvey "Harley" Pulmer. You'd have to hear Mac do him to get it. A cross between Karl Childers of *Sling Blade* and Christopher Walken.

Scary stuff. We have written a screenplay together that we plan to film ourselves. One day. Soon. *Three Wishes Road.*

This book is the culmination of something that began when we met at Travis Middle School. We discovered we were writers and anglers. One day we would write a book together. We tried to come up with something over the last decade, even wrote articles together, included his stuff in my books, but then this book finally came together. What better book than one that chronicles our crazy fishing trips? We are adventure magnets.

We've gone on lots of trips with Mac and his then wife. Mac and I talk all the time, let each other read the books and articles we're working on. He's like a brother. He tells me I'm like his much, much older brother. I know he'll be fine with me taking his last Royal Wulff #14. He knows I'll share my last granola bar.

It's nice that we both believe that wild trout are better than big stocked trout; that wet wading and chest packs and lightweight rods are inherently more fun than neoprene waders, loaded vests, and big flyrods. Good that he likes to backpack ten miles, set up camp, and still fish before dinner.

But most of all, we put up with each other's crap, which over three months' close quarters is essential to being a good fishing buddy. That and being a good angler who isn't worried if you catch more or bigger fish. We are about equal in that regard, so that helps. Being a fishing buddy, and for that matter co-author, is not an easy job. What's cool is that we both do a pretty good job of both.

Over the few days in Aspen, we did the usual on the Frying Pan and the Roaring Fork, but it was chicken and the egg. We didn't do well and weren't into it, or we weren't into it and we didn't do well. I've done well on both the Fork and the Pan over the years. My nephew, Chase, loves the Pan; he fishes there in the winter every year and then texts me pics of the 20-inch hawgs he catches. But not for us on this trip.

The Roaring Fork was up, not easily wadeable in its lower reaches all the way to Carbondale. Through town, it was clearing, and one evening we saw Pale Evening Duns darting above the water. No rises, no takes, we fish into when dusk becomes dark, empty-netted, hungry. All we have are memories of nice trout from years before.

On the Frying Pan, the Toilet Bowl was crowded. That's what they call the area immediately below the dam. We fished a stretch in the canyon, but got invaded by inconsiderate anglers who crowded our space on both sides. When

A falls on the upper Roaring Fork, above Aspen

Aspen 1

a guy with a BMW cast to the pool we were casting to, we left after catching only two average rainbows, not the lunkers we were looking for.

So we turned to the upper Roaring Fork. The water is clear but green-tea colored. The trout water is remarkable, pregnant with possibilities, ranging from stretches of long flatness to rumbling waterfalls, to runs and bend pools. We chose a run and bend pool. Our last full day found us entering the upper Roaring Fork not far from the campground. We'd fished a little lower on the stream, but too many splashing teens in bathing suits ran us off. We moved upstream and dropped in at a brushy section of steep canyon. Once in, the road and traffic disappeared. We did the usual—you fish, I fish.

Five brook trout each, two hours later. Fat squaretails, 8- to 10-inch copies. Then out of the blue, Mac tied into a long, heavy fish, and we were surprised that a cutthroat this big lived in water this small. Around that bend, we hit the Black Lagoon, this strange shaded place where the water was dark and mysterious, the shadows hiding whatever beasts lurk in this unusually deep one-hundred foot long pool. The Black Lagoon was so deep we couldn't wade through it, and in the shadows it was chilly, foreboding.

Mac plays a fish on the Roaring Fork.

We both cast on the other side of the shadow, just out of light's demarcation, but got no strikes. I went to a two-beadhead setup and cast again, slowly stripping in this lake-like pool. I almost didn't sense the take, it was so subtle, and with the darkness I couldn't see my indicator fly at all. I lifted, hard, set the hook, and the trout dived deep, then ran, and noisily crashed into the air out of the water. Thirteen-inch brook with dark green body, a real surprise, but we knew then, as Mac and I grinned at each other, that he was just a junior resident of the maelstrom. We two fishing buddies will be back next summer to try for the larger denizens of Grendel's watery lair.

You come to believe that Aspen is all beautiful people. We saw lots of stunningly good-looking people, but hey, not everyone was that way—we saw some fat folks, too. They were probably rich as Croesus, but we were skinnier. And you'll see lots of regular-looking tourists. If you get over the keeping-up-with-the-Joneses mentality, Aspen is fun, fresh, and frisky. Enjoy the gourmet

Along the Frying Pan

groceries and hotshot restaurants and elegant stores and cool, funky clothes. We were surprised by the traffic in town most any time of day. We were surprised by how many people are out running, biking, sunning (that one biki-ni-clad babe caught us taking a pic), chilling. Aspen is just a lot more crowded nowadays.

Aspen as a fishing home base is underrated. This is definitely a luxury vacation if you stay in Aspen or Snowmass. This can be a budget vacation if you camp nearby (which isn't easy, by the way, because of the limited number of campgrounds in the area). Basalt has grown into Aspen-Lite, a far cry from the two fly-shop town we knew not all that many years ago. Woody Creek lies north, between Basalt and Aspen, and it has a fun rep. The Woody Creek Tavern has a history of celebrities like Hunter Thompson drinking and relaxing there.

Aspen is known for its movie stars, artists, and writers. But Aspen grew up wild and woolly back in the early days. Sure—celebrities galore show up in Aspen, people like Jack Nicholson and Cher, and the millionaires moved out as the billionaires took over. So what if you're not filthy rich? Stay in a cool hotel or chic resort and enjoy the ride. Hey, we're writers, teachers. That Lamborghini on the corner costs three years of our combined salaries. So does the Ferrari in front of the Hotel Jerome. There's an undeniable shock and awe, rubbing shoulders with the rich and famous. Mac didn't like Aspen all that much, but he's willing to give it another chance. We both agreed that if you camp outside of the crowded nonsense, it's our kind of place.

So why is Aspen as a home fishing base underrated? Because of its proximity to so many big-name, gold medal waters. Frying Pan, Roaring Fork, Colorado, South Platte, Arkansas. The drawback? Lodging and meals are gonna cost you. By the way, we didn't find an Aspen sticker for the Aliner. We can only wonder if Aspen is too cool to have bumper stickers.

Favorite Places to Eat

You can't go wrong eating out in Aspen. Try the ribs at **Hickory House** (970-925-2313), where we enjoyed a feast, some kind of sweet deal where you pay 50 bucks and eat more food than any normal duo can handle, lunch with locals at **Little Nell** (970-920-4600), or grab grub at the grungy-but-good **Woody Creek Tavern** (970-923-4585).

Above: Hendricks has a feast in Aspen.
Right: The Hotel Jerome

Favorite Places to Stay

Weller Creek Campground, the classic and historic **Hotel Jerome** (970-920-1000), the hip **Sky Hotel** (970-920-6760). You can find Forest Service campgrounds south of Aspen on CO 82, but they are often crowed in the summer. You'll be hard pressed to find campgrounds in the area that don't require you to drive into the forest a bit. Lots of motels and hotels and bed & breakfasts in all of these towns around Aspen if you can't find or afford anything in town.

Fly Shops, Guides, and Tackle Stores

Taylor Creek Fly Shop (970-920-1128, www.taylorcreek.com); **Roaring Fork Anglers** (970-945-0180, www.roaringforkanglers.com); **Frying Pan Anglers** (970-927-3441, www.fryingpananglers.com); **Aspen Flyfishing** (970-920-6886, www.aspenflyfishing.com); and **Crystal Fly Shop** (970-963-5741, www.crystalflyshop.com).

Fishing Places Solid Choices near Home Base

Roaring Fork (Gold Medal Waters): Nowadays, the Fork has more folks in it than a shopping mall on Black Friday, and they're all fishin' and slippin' and slidin'. They're catching a few fish here and there, they're wearing their Orvis and Simms duds, and again they're slippin' and slidin' on the greased bowling ball rocks. These anglers are slinging woolly buggers from driftboats, but they're so far ahead we can barely see them—and, besides, there are a million pockets they just drifted past without hitting, so we've pretty much got the river to ourselves.

The Gold Medal Roaring Fork meanders down from her headwaters in the 12,000-foot Independence Pass, transforms into a canyon creek, becomes a twisting meadow stream before becoming a rough and tumble, floatable freestone river, un-dammed to its confluence with the Colorado River. This is wild country that in many places re-minds us of the Arkansas River.

A Colorado cutt from the upper Roaring Fork, above Aspen

You get a lot for your money on this stream. The Fork is only about 70 miles long from its headwaters to the Colorado, but the public access is plentiful and the fish are large and bountiful, some of the largest average-size fish (mostly rainbow and brown trout) you'll catch in a freeflowing river in the state. For the most part, the Fork is fished best by nymphing, not dry fly fishing. If you are a solid nympher or a big-nymph nympher or better yet a streamer-stripper, you'll have good angling. Get a copy of up-to-date regulations because sections of the river are flies/lures only with slot restrictions.

CO 82 east of Aspen follows the river to its headwaters near Independence Pass. **Frying Pan River (Gold Medal Waters):** Think chunky, trophy-size trout, canyon scenery. The fish are big, the canyon narrow, the river cold. Pound for pound, this smallish tailwater might be the best trout stream in the country. Some canyons have walls that rise so high and block out so much light that they suffocate, but the Frying Pan's red canyon walls have dancing light and colors, texture and depth, warmth and softness. These canyon walls comfort and insulate with a dazzling palette. The big plunge pool beneath Ruedi Dam is called the Toilet Bowl, and this wide, flat area is where the gargantuan trout you've read about live. They grow to obesity feeding on mysis shrimp that escape Ruedi Reservoir.

Think midges, in all shapes, colors, stages, and sizes. Year-round fishery. Limestone walls make for a fertile insect hatchery. The Pan has as varied and prolific hatches as any tailwater we've fished. The average size trout caught in the Toilet Bowl is four pounds. Designated a Gold Medal Water, the Frying Pan flows out of Ruedi Reservoir for 14 quality miles. Throughout the other 12 miles of the Pan, the rainbows and browns range from 12 inches to 16 inches, but the river holds an amazing amount of 16- to 22-inch trout.

The Pan gets crowded by fishermen anxious to cast into the feeding lanes or even sightcast for the big bows. Five-pound trout are as common as dollars in this section, so it'll be difficult to leave. Do it anyway. Spend an hour or two there, maybe an entire morning in the winter when the crowds are sometimes lighter, but move on. The Pan has so many different kinds of habitat, structure, and trout lies that you need to fish each section to see what it's like. You will find more cover, islands and submerged rocks, beautiful red sandstone walls cut by eons of erosion, and, in late spring and early summer, more stoneflies.

DIRECTIONS: From Glenwood Springs, travel southeast on CO 82 to Basalt. Take Frying Pan River Road, which follows the river. From Aspen, go west/north on CO 82 to Basalt and turn right.

Maroon Creek: You've seen the Maroon Bells, right? This is the creek that feeds the lake below those iconic peaks. Small rainbow trout in a postcard setting. Take Maroon Creek Road.

Castle Creek: Roaring Fork feeder creek. Castle provides 18 miles of decent angling for 10-inch rainbows and great vistas. Take FR 102 off CO 82. Watch out for private water, which is usually clearly marked.

Crystal River: Not always crystal clear—in fact, it gets downright cloudy at times. The Crystal is a large tributary to Roaring Fork, a

Mac angles in this dark canyon, just before the Black Lagoon.

nice option to get away from the crowds on the Fork and Pan. Still, the fishing is average at best, unless you like catching whitefish (plentiful up by Redstone and Marble.)

What we like about Crystal River is that it's in a pretty canyon (until it reaches the Roaring Fork River at Carbondale, which is not especially pretty scenery), that during fall and spring nice-sized rainbows and browns run up from the Fork, and if you get above the kayakers the river provides occasional hot and heavy attractor flyfishing. Plus, you get easy access, you can fish in winter on certain days, and the river usually has few other anglers. In the middle to upper stretches, you can catch some brook and cutts too.

Look for Penny Hot Springs north of Redstone Campground. Take CO 82 north to Carbondale and turn south on CO 133 (which runs alongside the Crystal).

Avalanche Creek: A brook trout haven with some nice rainbows and cutts. Flows into Crystal River north of Redstone (11 miles south of Carbondale) off CO 133. Turn east on 3E RD. Hard day hike or hard backpack trip, but well worth your time and effort.

For the Adventurer

Pine Creek: Here's a sleeper. A mile above Ashcroft, take Cathedral Lake Trail for 4 tough miles to fish for cutts. Day trip only—no camping.

Willow Creek and Lake: Feeder to Maroon Creek that is worth a day hike to the lake, where you can sometimes get into large cutts.

Woody Creek: A Roaring Fork tributary that is marginal at best but scenic.

Conundrum Creek: I'd love to tell you that this nearby creek has wonderful fishing, but it doesn't. We put it in here so you don't waste your time.

Hunter–Frying Pan Wilderness: Numerous options including Hunter Creek, which we like a lot.

Maroon Bells–Snowmass Wilderness Area: Snowmass Creek in the upper sections is a fun day trip.

Lake Creek (with North and South Forks, too)

Upper Frying Pan: Go up from Norrie on CR 4 / FR 504. Area is chockfull of small streams worth fishing (Chapman Creek, South Fork Frying Pan) as well as the upper Pan itself.

Blue Ribbon Fisheries not far from Aspen

Colorado River
Turquoise Lake
Twin Lakes
Arkansas River
South Platte River
Homestake Creek and Lake

2 Basalt

When I was a giblet, I always thought of dinner when I heard dudes speak of the Fryingpan and the Roaring Fork simultaneously. I mean, the Fork and Pan? C'mon.

Walking around, getting a feel for this place called Basalt where the Fork and Pan collide, it seems captured in stone, anchored to the very bedrock for which the town is named. These two epic rivers tumble through the White

The Frying Pan converges with the Roaring Fork in the distance.

River National Forest and converge here, in Basalt, in the very lap of this little village. I can hear the murmur of water no matter where I am standing in the historic section of downtown. She calls to you here, and that call never seems to cease. Water eternal.

It's as though time and erosion might have washed away a weaker settlement. But contemporary Basalt is grounded in recreating in the outdoors, a pastime that proves perpetual bliss. Here, it's all about having fun. Always has, always will be so. So don't rock the boat and fish here with an attitude. Be kind to these liquid ladies, and perhaps they will give forth their fruit.

Downtown is a marriage between old Victorian and contemporary architecture. The details of Basalt, right down to the streetlamps, reminisce of an era of trains, gold, and the old western gun fights John Wayne reenacted for us so many times on the silver screen. But miraculously, the town appears brand new, hand-crafted, hand-painted. Might as well still have the cellophane wrap and price tag attached.

It's a one-of-a-kind crossroads where old meets new in a way that no other Colorado town can pull off.

Basalt **2**

Favorite Places to Eat

Okay, so sometimes we treat ourselves to exquisite cuisine. At the **Cuvee World Bistro,** on Two Rivers Road, they serve these wild mushroom cakes over avocado pesto and roasted red pepper coulis. Neither of us even like shrooms, but this was paired with a Foris Maple Ranch Pinot Noir that we couldn't resist trying. **Riverside Grill** in Basalt Center Circle has a great view of the river with a casual approach and affordable menu.

We found **Darwin's Beer & Grill** by accident at 218 East Valley Road in El Jebel. It's only a few minutes from Basalt. It looked too cool not to at least have an appetizer. So we sampled the Mac and Cheese with Crab. And, dude...you should too. In El Jebel Plaza, **Atlas Pizza** makes some worldly good pie, and it's affordable. Order by name, and try "The Greek."

OTHER PLACES TO EAT: Bistro Basalt serves excellent French cuisine that you just can't get in other towns. **Smoke Modern BBQ** is a nice turn from all the trendy stuff. Meaty, saucy, yummy. **Tempranillo** serves Spanish-style food, including Paella. Great reviews, even from Spaniards! **Timbo's Pizza** serves—uhh—pizza. But it's something we wrote home about!

Favorite Places to Stay

Basalt Vacation Rentals is a website dedicated to finding you a home to rent for your stay in Basalt. The homes, cabins, and lodges range from $120 to

Historic downtown Basalt

$600 per night. You are sure to find something unique and comfortable. http:// www.vrbo.com/vacation-rentals/usa/colorado/northwest/basalt. **Best Western Aspenalt Lodge** is sometimes just a no-brainer, since it's riverfront accommodations. 157 Basalt Ctr. Circle, 970-927-3191, www.bestwestern.com. **The Green Drake** isn't just the name of a particularly important insect on the river. This fanciful motel is located at the crux of the Fork and the Pan rivers and boasts suites that will make you want to sell your home. 220 Midland Ave., 970-927-4747, www.green-drake.com.

Lodge at River's Edge has double occupancy cabins as well as enormous lodge rooms with five-and-a-half bathrooms and enough room for an entire family reunion. 600 Frying Pan Rd., 970-927-4991, www.lodgeatriversedge co.com. **Redstone Inn** is a rustic but classy turn-of-the-century Rocky Mountain resort. Redstone, CO, 82 Redstone Blvd., 970-963-2526, http:// red stoneinn.thegilmore collection.com/. **Taylor Creek Cabins** are owned and operated by Frying Pan Anglers. Find your own stretch of stream and own it all day with the help of one of Basalt's favorite guides. Contact Robyn at 970-927-9927, http://www.rent-cabins-colorado.com/index.html.

OTHER PLACES TO STAY: Avalanche Ranch, Redstone, CO, 12863 CO 133, 877-963-9339, 970-963-2846, http://www.avalancheranch.com/. **Crystal**

Dreams Bed & Breakfast, Redstone, CO, 0475 Redstone Blvd., 970-963-8240, http://www.crystaldreams get-away.com/. **Redstone Cliffs Lodge,** Redstone, CO, 433 Redstone Blvd., 888-652-8005, 970-963-2691, http:// www.redstonecliffs.com/activities.php.

CAMPGROUNDS: The Ruedi Complex offers four different campgrounds: the **Little Mattie, Little Maud, Mollie B,** and **Ruedi Marina,** which are all located in the same vicinity on Ruedi Reservoir.

Fly Shops, Guides, and Tackle Stores

Taylor Creek Fly Shop on the Fryingpan River (http:// www.taylorcreek.com/contact.htm); **Taylor Creek Fly Shop** on the Cooper Avenue Mall (970-920-1128); **Frying Pan Anglers** (http://www.fryingpananglers.com/ index.html); **Crystal Fly Shop** (http://crystalflyshop. com/id4.html); **Roaring Fork Outfitters** (http://www.rf outfitters.com/)

This old tree has been turned into fine art.

Other Stuff

There are a million places to rent and stay if the Fork and the Pan are going to be your trouteries. Look into staying in Redstone, Carbondale, or Snowmass for lodging if you can't find something in Basalt that you like or that fits your budget. The entire area is absolutely gorgeous. There are far too many lodges, rental properties and cabins to list here, so do a little legwork and you're sure to find exactly what you're looking for.

Fishing Places
Solid Choices near Home Base
Roaring Fork (Gold Medal Waters): On this day, rain and runoff have made the Roaring Fork a tainted, chalky mess for us—our pictures of the water turn out looking sepia tone. This is typical when rains come, as the canyons surrounding Basalt are not made of what its durable name suggests. Instead, the walls are of a more reddish sedimentary rock, rather than the black basalt boulders a newbie might expect.

The Fork around Basalt is your classic clearwater freestone stream that wears many masks as it rushes through north-

This informative sign is situated near the edge of the Frying Pan.

western Colorado. Sleek, wadeable sections punctuated by gouging rapids. That's what you'll see the entire length. Ever-changing, but somehow always familiar.

We're standing on a bridge overlooking the Fork, and I can see that look in my pal's eyes, even through those trendy reading glasses of his. I know what he's thinking, and I want no part of it. By now, we're Jedi. He's Yoda, I'm Mac Streamwalker. Sharing thoughts, anticipating the other's every movement, attempting to levitate trout from the stream.

"Okay." I interrupt his meditation. "Muddy Waters is a favorite bluesman of mine, too, but I don't like fishing in it. Even if it is a Gold Medal stream." (Fine! Color me spoiled. An entire summer fishing Colorado has made me a stream snob.) Williams' demeanor is stoic, unchanged. He's still contemplating putting in. So I devise a plan.

"Whoa! Did you see that snake down there?" I holler and point. "Where?" he asks, grabbing his camera instinctively. "Right there sliding back into those weeds! Right there! I ain't fishing in a river if there's snakes in it!" "Well, hell, me neither! I'm not tangling with a snake! Let's check the fly shop and see what they say about the Pan."

These machinations of mine are becoming far too easy.

Williams and I slip into a fly shop. I'm needing some floatant and Mark has misplaced yet another pair of clip-on sunglasses, but we're really looking for free stream info without getting too involved with guides and their lofty banter. Ironically, we immediately hear a Brit telling stories inside.

My first thought: *Robin Leach is about to get his trout on!* It's not an annoying London Cockney accent, thank the Maker, but more of a sophisticated "Queen's" English, and it's flowing out of him like hot Earl Grey in wintertime. It's the sort of soothing British accent two Texans like us find tolerable, even admirable. Perfect for making any bullshit story sound factual. (It's why Brits are often the voice of infomercials!) And also, it sorta makes you feel like you're out of the country. And that's always a bonus. Although, if you think about it, everyone in the Death Star has that dad-blamed British accent.

The Brit obviously works here. When we locate the source of this extraordinary vernacular, he is leaning back in a wooden chair, not at all in any sort of hurry, telling a potential patron looking for flies of today's water conditions. He rails on about the Fork:

A typical turnout on the Frying Pan

"If Ah were ew, Ah'd waite till la'er in the day. Ah'd fish the edges ov thah Rawring Fawk till layte. Or, jus go ovah an' fish thah Pahn. It-ull bay one helluva day on thah uppah Pahn t-day."

I don't remember, but I'm sure he said, "Gov'nah."

Through his London Fog, we come out thinking that fishing is hella good on the Fork despite high muddy waters, but only in the evening between tea and dessert. I peep around the leader and tippet display to see if Mark heard him. He peeps around the sunglasses display to see if I heard. Simultaneous smirks telegraph to the other our plan for the day. The Pan it is!

We purchase our accoutrements, grab two freebie stickers for the Aliner, and we're on our way back to the Jeep. Anglers are like ants, everywhere on the Roaring Fork, practically crawling over one another, trying their best to ignore the water's poor clarity. They've marched from all over the country to fish, and by God that's what they're gonna do.

Not us, though. Not here.

Frying Pan River (Gold Medal Waters): Up the Frying Pan, we pull over on one of seemingly a thousand available turnouts. BMWs and Ferraris parked in the dirt. No lie. Williams seems overjoyed to capture such pictures—it's like an oxymoron on film, American businessmen outdoorsing it from European sports cars. But who are we to judge? We teach our classes in flyfishing shirts. So what's the difference, right?

We both drop down into separate sections. Neither can see the other. I'm fishing my 5 wt. (probably an average choice weight for the Pan), and a hatch has infested the skies—something for which the Frying Pan is infamous. Mark chirps through the brush that he sees insects. Mayflies. By the billions. It's that scene from the movie *The Birds*, only miniaturized. I poise myself for tug-o-war.

Cast. Drift. No rise. Cast. Drift. Mend, mend, mend. No rise. *???*

Cast. Drift. Mend a bit. No rise. *WTF?* I think.

Cast. Drift. Mend. No rise. (**blink** **blink**............)

I scratch my head.

"Any takes?" Williams yells doubtfully. "Nothing!" I resound. "Going to a dropper!" he informs, though I'm already fishing with a red Copper John dropped 18 inches behind my dry with no results.

Another series of casts for me. Cast. Drift. Mend, mend. No rise.*???*

Cast. Drift. Mend. Still no rise. No spooked trout. No nothing.

"WTF?" I ask aloud this time.

Cast. Drift. No rise. (**blink** **blink**............)

Bored with the redundancy already, I find myself stringing up and heading to find the Curmudgeon. He's had good luck here so many times before. His nephew Chase caught 20-inch rainbows each of the last two winter visits.

This place is Gold Medal, after all. Emerging from the weeds, I find Mark already at the Jeep, eating pistachios. He's packed up and ready move on, and I don't mean to the next turnout. I mean, *move on*, as in driving on to the next home base. I can tell because he won't look me in the eye. I always know that when he comes off a river and he doesn't look me in the eye, it's time to move on. It's part of that intuitive language we possess, like Captain and Tennile had. Or Barney and Fred. Starsky and Hutch (the 1970s version, not the goofy 2004 remake).

I was surprised, but relieved as well. On our way, we talked at length about what we were leaving behind us. Two Gold Medal waters plumb full of trout the size and weight of antique bowling pins. Plus a picture perfect town where spectacular food, bawdy women, and 360 degree scenery could have kept us entertained for weeks.

But these two rivers require a certain amount of fidelity, loyalty, commitment. They're the temperamental women of waters, meandering feminine souls who have, over the span of time, learned not to give too much of themselves too soon. Disappointed by strings of misbegotten men, such as us, who practice impatience, intolerance, and insincerity, men who could not spend the time to listen, explore, and tap into the beauties they possess within.

It's true. Williams and I have become aquatically adulterous fly-fishing philanderers, guilty of a

A well-known stretch of the Roaring Fork close to town

great many cardinal sins, too many to count. No matter how many times we dip our toes into sacred rivers, no amount of water could wash away these two pescadors' pecadillos. For the first time all summer, we're left with dry hands, hands that still smell of the fresh, lemon-scented wipes we so frequently use to clean up after our nasty selves. No, today will remain with us for all days. Not one trout brought to hand.

Perhaps we deserved this denial. Our carnal unions with rivers are often brief whirlwind relationships of self-indulgence, taking what we want, often at will, pillaging these sensual bodies of water for whatever they'll offer us, all on a whim. Passionate rendezvous between mankind and moving, melted snow. And for this we offer our apologies.

If only we had the accent of a Brit. Perhaps then we could make you believe we cleaned house in Basalt. If only we sounded as smooth as hot tea, maybe then...

"But the old man always thought of her as feminine and as something that gave or withheld great favours, and if she did wild or wicked things, she could not help them."—excerpt from *The Old Man and the Sea*

Fact is, the recent rains and change in barometric pressure had put the fish down, and there was no amount of waiting we could do that day to bring them up.

Mark and I have both vowed to return to Basalt. No way will we come to the convergence of two Gold Medal streams twice and go home empty netted. Next time, we're hiring the Brit, and we're going for Moby Dick, whether he knows his Melville and Hemingway or not.

Crystal River: White marble slabs litter the canyon where the Crystal tumbles through Carbondale and Redstone. Some of the bigger fish, browns and bows, you will find near the Roaring Fork confluence in Carbondale. Upstream, though, the white stone-banked edges provide a haven for trout and also make for unique photo opportunities.

There are numerous places to access the Crystal. The parking lot at Days Inn at Carbondale will give you a place to start. The signage explains the access, and here you will have about 1/2 mile of stream. Satank Road access northwest of Carbondale offers fishing, too. Take CO 82 north and turn south onto Satank Road, drive until it ends, where there's a parking area. Fishing here is legal all the way to the Roaring Fork confluence. For Staircase Park, turn off CO 133 and drive behind the 7-Eleven and City Market, watching for Crystal Village. Turn in at the entrance, and then turn right on Oak Run. After about 1/4 mile, look for a walkway down to the river and a park. Fishing near and at the CDOW hatchery, on CO 133 about 1 mile south of Carbondale, is allowed. Otherwise, cruising upstream checking for turnout access on National Forest lands will pay off as well.

3 Breckenridge

From the last day of May until mid-September, Mac and I drove over 5,000 miles. We hiked hundreds of miles (maybe more, I don't know). We fished in dozens and dozens of rivers, camped in numerous campgrounds and forests. We were in wildernesses, near known bear haunts. We woke up several times to see bear tracks through camp. Bear scat sat near the trailer at Trujillo Meadows. But not once, all summer, did we see a bear.

What's weird is that I usually see several bears each summer, sometimes a lot closer up than I'd like to see them. On trails in the backcountry, crossing rivers toward the evening, in trash bins in campgrounds, crossing the road as we round a corner. I always see bears. I don't even have to keep an eye out for them, they just seem to pop up.

But not this summer. We saw deer, wolves, moose, marmots, coyote, but no bears.

We saw the coolest thing at La Jara Reservoir, where dozens of elk were bathing in the lake. We saw coyote, antelope, bighorn sheep, mountain goats, and two badgers. I thought that wolverines and badgers were the same critter, but they aren't. You'd much rather tangle with a badger than a wolverine. I spotted a badger in the Cochetopa River valley floor as I was walking back toward the car. I know little about these badgers, or whether they attack humans,

The beautiful city of Breckenridge

but I found out I was pretty darned fast in spurts, still. We also saw a fox with a marmot in his mouth crossing the highway outside of Steamboat Springs. No bears, though. I always want to see a bear until I see one. When the bear encounter is over, I have this weird feeling, a gut thing, an escape adrenaline rush that makes me feel a little more primitive. I know better, of course, but that's the feeling, nevertheless.

Before a week of fishing in and around Breckenridge, we'd known "Breck" like most Texans: a whirlwind ski adventure on a church trip, where the town is hoppin' and covered in snow, or fishing the Blue River north of Breckenridge while the wife shops at the outlet malls in Silverthorne. Boy, were we wrong. Breckenridge, even with all the traffic and people and stores, is right in the heart of fishing country and should be an ideal destination for many readers. The area—Dillon, Frisco, Silverthorne, and Breckenridge—is now one of our top home bases in the state.

Orvis meets Nike

Breckenridge is the ideal family fishing getaway. Once you get over the fact that you don't get the solitude of Lake City or Dolores or Platoro, once you realize that you can fish the river in the morning, a creek after lunch, and the evening rise on Lake Dillon, you don't mind walking the faux-Victorian, false-clapboard streets while the family shops in boutiques, specialty shops, and the inevitable souvenir shops.

My wife Amy is with us (and so are the dogs, Princess and Piper), and she remarks over and over "this is the perfect girlfriend getaway spot." It probably is, but hey, this is a fishing trip after all. My mother and her husband, Don, met

A metal angler catches metal trout in the Blue River.

up with us as well and went away thinking this is the kind of locale at which they'd like to spend a week or two. While they shopped in The Great Outdoors and the Polo Outlet, we fished fifty yards away in the Blue as it flows through Silverthorne. And we caught fish.

The Blue River in town is manicured, with trout-friendly lies created from manmade weirs and inserted boulders, but these artificial habitats hold fat healthy trout, and lots of them, enough that the Blue has been designated a Gold Medal Water. What's great about Breck and Frisco and Silverthorne and Dillon, four nearby (but slightly different in tone) mountain towns, is that you are always connected by a bike-hike trail that runs along the main river. If you like to bike, you can fish in places anglers normally wouldn't find easy access.

The negatives? Only two hours' drive from Denver, Summit County is crowded at times, but you can always find a long stretch of the Blue River with no one around. You can always find a high mountain creek to call your own. This is big country, after all. Not as expensive as Vail or Beaver Creek to the west, this isn't as cheap a vacation as South Fork or Creede, either. But there's just so much more to do that the money is well spent.

You never feel like you're in the wild when you're camping or lodging or eating or walking around Breckenridge. Even when you're fishing, you some-times hear the roar of I-70 traffic. But Breckenridge as a home base is about getting the full monty on a fishing trip: you can zip up CO 9 to the lower Blue or I-70 west to Ten Mile Creek or Gore Creek or Eagle River, all in less than thirty minutes. You can find great eats, budget or luxury, in all four towns. You'll discover history galore in this old mining town that is now celebrating its 150th anniversary. You can fish a Gold Medal Water or a tiny creek or alpine lake, or all in the same day. That's hard to beat for any home base.

Just some of the things we saw people doing this week: shopping, sailing, kayaking, hackeysacking, playing volleyball, picnicking, skateboarding, hiking, running, and riding the gondola—and seemingly everybody bikes.

The Blue River runs through Breck, Frisco, and Silverthorne, and the road follows this productive river on its northward course through Dillon and Green Mountain Reservoirs. We camped at Dillon Reservoir, and despite the fact that pine beetles have decimated the forests around the area, Dillon Reservoir is way cool. You have three other communities around Breckenridge, and you move from one to the other without really being able to tell when it's happening. The retail area in downtown Frisco is a tad cheesy, like they've tried too hard to make the faux Victorian fronts authentic. The town seems to be trying too hard to succeed, but the retailers we've met are dog-friendly and are about as sweet as any you'll ever meet. Silverthorne and Dillon complete the troika.

Above: Bubba Gump Shrimp Co. in Breckenridge
Left: There are no shortage of retailers in Breckenridge.

Favorite Places to Eat

Can you beat the **Mother Loaded Tavern** (970-453-2572)? Grilled PBJ? Get real. **Bubba Gump Shrimp** (970-547-9000) is enormously cliché, tremendously filling, a tad bit overpriced. Why go there? The shrimp is succulent, the people-watching divine, and the back patio overlooks the Blue River. Breakfast at this cool coffeehouse on the river—called amazingly enough, **Cool River Coffeehouse** (970-453-1716)—that serves awesome ham and Swiss croissants. Not much to look at, the Italian food–themed **Ristorante Al Lago** in Dillon (970-468-6111) serves delicious food. So many good restaurants, so little time.

Favorite Places to Stay

We have these high-roller friends who brag about staying at **Crystal Peak Lodge** (970-453-2333). Sure looks fancy. Your lodging options are amazing in this home base, ranging from staying in town, in Frisco or Silverthorne, up on the mountain. You can sleep at luxury resorts or find a private rental condo.

The best (and just about only) camping is around **Dillon Reservoir,** over 400 sites available. If you don't mind being a short drive from the towns, you can find camping along CO 9 north of Silverthorne. Lots of condos and town-homes and bed and breakfasts to choose from, so you'll have to fit your needs, but don't overlook the **Creekside Inn** (970-668-5607) along Ten Mile Creek in Frisco.

Instream weirs have improved angling on the Blue in Silverthorne.

Fly Shops, Guides, and Tackle Stores

Blue River Anglers (www.blueriveranglers.com); **Breckenridge Outfitters** (www.breckenridgeoutfitters.com); **Jackson Streit's Mountain Angler** (www. mountainangler.com)

The Blue River runs through Breckenridge.

Fishing Places Solid Choices near Home Base

River: I've fished the upper Blue, the Blue in front of the school, the Blue into Dillon, out of Dillon, north to Green Mountain Reservoir. It's all good. I have actually come around on the artificial-feeling chunky pools along the bike/foot trail in and around town. You may not know, but if you come to ski in the snow-cold winter, you can still catch huge fish in the lower Blue River below Dillon Reservoir. Tailwater. Fishable all year long. While the upper reaches are pretty and small and rehabbed, the real destination is the lower tailwater where the lunkers live. For novelty's sake, you can fish for nice trout near the discount mall in Silverthorne.

Yeah, the Blue doesn't feel like a wild river. It's not. You have to go to Breckenridge-Frisco-Silverthorne with the framework that you aren't on a hard-core fishing trip but a vacation with multiple options, and one of them is fishing a river in close proximity to the road. What's so great about the Blue? So close to any of these three towns (a river runs through them) that you can sleep in, shop, fish for a couple of hours, take in lunch, nap, fish for an hour, go biking, fish the evening hatch, go out to eat. Not much of this trout stream provides a wilderness experience unless fishing in plain sight of discount shopping centers and the cars zooming along the interstate is your idea of wild

Williams checks hatches and rises on the Blue River.

country. But the reason to visit the Blue is the big fish. The Blue has big fish, plain and simple.

The biggest browns are picky eaters and require drag-free drifts. The 10-mile stretch between Dillon and Green Mountain Reservoirs offers plenty of

Fishing near the outlet mall in Silverthorne

public access, and you can fish a small stretch all afternoon and not cover all the trout lies. The Blue has quietly become one of the most productive year-round streams in the West, with browns and rainbows growing to incredible sizes.

Ten Mile Creek: Doesn't look like much, but that's just the little bit you see from the road as you're zipping from Frisco to Copper Mountain. So much public water, so easily accessed, and yet hardly anyone fishes this quick mountain stream. The hiking/biking trail follows Ten Mile Creek. You get drop pools, rocky riffles, and pocket water, and you get trout that are not highly educated. (Nor are they large, but this is a freakin' river that runs right in the middle of everything!)

Dillon Reservoir: Amy and I stayed at Dillon for the first time in a decade, and things have sure changed. Because of the pine beetle infestation (and subsequent death of thousands and thousands of trees), authorities have simply removed the trees near campgrounds because of safety concerns. Looks like Siberia 1908. The reservoir is a solid choice for angling from boat or shore for rainbows and cutts.

Dillon Reservoir

For the Adventurer

Willow Creek: A feeder stream to the Blue around Silverthorne.

Green Mountain Reservoir: It ain't pretty, but it is productive. We tend to like rolling hills and everything the color of sage and putty, but that's just us. The lake holds trout, but most everyone seems to be fishing for kokanee salmon. From Breckenridge, travel north on CO 9 and you can't miss it.

Eagles Nest Wilderness (We like Eaglesmeres Lakes.)

Blue Ribbon Fisheries not far from Breckenridge

South Platte River
Gore Creek
Eagle River
Colorado River

4 HOME BASE
Buena Vista

It's early August. Mark and I are traveling north of Salida. The second time. We're in his four-door Wrangler towing the Aliner. Yet another trek. The windshield already looks as though we'd lived through a rogue horde of paint-ballers shooting yellow balls at us—so many bug splatters we can't see the road. It's noisy and sorta slow because there's one hell of a headwind in our grill. It's hot, and we'd stopped and had a single beer at this place back in Salida that I want to say was Benson's Tavern and Beer Garden, but I can't be sure. The woman in the tight tan dress walking her two dogs down the alleyway is all I can think of.

Okay, so anyways. We're on the road, like I said, US 285, heading north for Buena Vista, and for some reason that single solitary beer hits me. Suddenly, I have to pee. Badly. There's nothing out there but brush and telephone lines, and although I'm 165 pounds, I cannot pee behind a telephone pole and feel I'm hiding. I'm nervous like a little girl, squirming and dancing the jitterbug in the passenger seat while Williams coolly gnaws the tip off a cigar and spits it on the floor. "Don't tell Amy" he says, and I'm thinking, *She already knows, you tool.*

And there is the Arkansas River. Right over there. A volatile rush of raging roaring liquid, built up over ages, gushing outside my window, squirting

Summer days in Buena Vista are busy and festive.

between rocks and frothing up behind boulders, just mocking me, as though it were some epic urinal flow from the deep innards of San Isabel National Forest, or the *Terra Mater* herself.

Unable to stand it any longer, I inform Williams of my urinary dilemma.

"Boona Vista is like five minutes away. Can you wait till then?" I know Williams secretly hopes I can't. Seeing a buddy wet his drawers gives a man perpetual blackmail ammunition. The only thing more powerful a guy can have over another bro is if he accidentally goes number two in his drawers (i.e. upper Los Pinos, but I am not allowed to speak of this event).

"Boona Vista? I don't see a 'Boona Vista' on the map. C'mon hurry! Just get me somewhere."

"Well, it's spelled B-U-E-N-A, but pronounced *boona*," he proclaimed.

"Bullshit. It's pronounced *bway-nah*. I didn't spend three years of my high school life suffering through Spanish class, plus four more semesters in college just to intentionally mispronounce one of the easiest words in the Spanish language. Besides, if Ms. Zavala, Mrs. Mullin, or Mrs. Davidson heard me say boona, they'd beat me like a piñata."

It is at this point that Williams begins his cruelty.

"Look at that river." He peers over the top of his glasses. "That's a lot of water. Look at that view. Sure is a goooood view. Get it? Good view? Boona Vista?"

"DUDE! Shut up! Where is Buena Vista anyway? I'm serious!"

Williams toys with me even more. "Do you like those little fruit chewy things called Gushers?"

"Shut it, you tool. I want to fish! Let's get this done!"

"Remember that one soda pop in the yellow can? I think it was called Squirt."

"Williams! C'mon man, this isn't funny!"

"Honestly, though, I've always preferred Mountain Dew," he chortles.

"Enough already!" I command him to relax. Then, as always, like someone is playing an extremely elaborate psychological game with me, a sign appears on the side of the road. Not just any sign, but an honest to God, bona-fide, serendipitous sorta supernatural sign. The kind of stuff that only happens when Williams and I are together.

Williams sees it first. "Hey, Mac, look! Johnson Village! I bet you can find a place to pee there!" He laughs uncontrollably.

"ALL RIGHT, WILLIAMS! YOU WIN! PULL OVER!"

(10 minutes later…)

"Hey look, it's Buena Vista." My antagonist pronounces it properly this time. "Anybody gotta pee?" He's pretending we have the Brady Bunch in the back. "Last stop till Fairplay!" The smirk on his face is pure evil.

"Can we just fish, please?" I beg. "I just wanna fish."

"Yup. Sure. No prob. I got the perfect spot. It isn't far from here either. It's called Dry Creek. You should fare well there..."

I can see that this day is going to be a long one. After relieving myself, I spend some time sifting through our maps and guide books to hand-pick a grip of destinations. My episode actually bodes well for us. Like other prolific home bases, "Boona Vista," as the locals insist on calling it, will allow for a lifetime of exploration and trout hunting. Just don't get caught doing it with your pants down.

Favorite Places to Eat

Eddylines Restaurant and Brewery on Main Street is a "great brew pub right in the charming part of town known as South Main." Pizza, pizza, beer and pizza! **The Evergreen Café** at 418 US 24 seems to be the local favorite hot spot. Walk in and feel right at home. **The Global Café** at 222 US 24 has an eclectic menu but also caters to those who are also labeled as fuddy duddies with some old stand-by plates. **Gunsmoke Café,** situated at 12950 US 24, serves a well-rounded menu, but the best is the breakfast burrito smothered in green. Too much to finish in one sitting!

OTHER PLACES TO EAT: Buffalo Bar and Grill will be the place to have a cold one before hitting the hay after a long day of angling. **Coyote Cantina** freshly grinds their burgers and makes fine enchiladas.

Favorite Places to Stay

Point Campground, Cabins and RV Park (formerly Crazy Horse Resort) provides cabins, cottages, campsites, and even yurts for rent. Very cool, and only 5 miles north of Buena Vista. Buena Vista, CO, 33975 US 24, 800-888-7320, 719-395-2323, http://www.arrowheadpointresort.com/. **Cottonwood Springs Inn and Health Spa** won't allow alcohol on the premises, but offers a multitude of ways for you to stay and relax without needing to get tanked. A very therapeutic stay, in tents, cabins, or hotel-like rooms nestled in the high mountain natural ecosystem of the majestic Collegiate Peaks Range, bordered by Cottonwood Creek, and surrounded by the San Isabel National Forest. Buena Vista, CO, 18999 CR 306, 719-395-6434, 719-395-2102, http://www. cottonwood-hot-springs.com/index.htm. **Mount Princeton Hot Springs Resort** is a gorgeous natural oasis surrounded by towering peaks. A perfect recreational place to stay for the entire family. Amazing views and unbelievable accommodations. Nathrop, CO, 5870 CR 162, 888-395-7799, 719-395-2447, http://www.mtprinceton.com/.

OTHER PLACES TO STAY: A Bed on the Arkansas, Buena Vista, CO, 12753 US 24 & US 285, 800-497-7238, 719-395-6494, http://www.bedon thearkansas.com/. **Alpine Hotsprings Hideaway,** Nathrop, CO, 16185 CR 162, 719-530-1112, http://www.alpinehotsprings.com/location.htm. **Antero Hot Spring Cabins,** Nathrop, CO, 16120 CR 162, 719-539-8204, http://www.anterohotsprings.com/. **Arkansas River Rim Campground and RV Park,** Buena Vista, CO, 33198 N. US 24, 719-395-8883, http://www.colorado campgrounds.com/arkansasriverrimcamp/. **Chalk Creek Campground,** http://www.chalkcreek-campground.com/.

A good stretch on the Arkansas

Fly Shops, Guides, and Tackle Stores

ArkAnglers (http://www.arkanglers.com/); **Arkansas Headwaters Recreation Area** (719-539-7289); **Hi-Rocky Gifts & Sports Store** (http://www.hirocky.com/); **Keys to the Mountains** (http://www.keysto-the moun tains.com/colorado_fly_fishing.html); **Noah's Ark Whitewater Rafting** (http:// www.noahsark.com/); **River Runners** (http://riverrunnersltd.com/); **St. Elmo's Store** (http://www.st-elmo.com/)

Other Stuff

Buena Vista and Salida are like siblings. Not twins by any means, but they definitely share DNA, related by the blood of the Arkansas pumping through the San Isabel. And when the two moved out (Sal-eye-da and Boona) they didn't stray too far, so they still live just a few minutes apart on the same major river, where whitewater rafting is probably a bigger deal than fishing, but many of the guides and services will overlap, so be sure to see the Salida Home Base information when looking for shops, guides, activities, and whatnot. Do your research if you're coming to recreate with the entire family in order to find activities for everyone. That's what this place is about! Don't be afraid to raft, ride horses, hike a "Fourteener," get a cabin in the wilderness, have a drink at a pub. Do it up right! This place is a blast, and it remains one of the most affordable recreation areas in the state. Have fun. And remember. It's Boona, not Buena! (*Mark's note: he still got it wrong. It's Buna with a long u, as in stupid.*)

Fishing Places Solid Choices near Home Base

Trout Creek: There is actually a real place near Buena Vista named Dry Creek. Mark wasn't joking about that part. But we wouldn't suggest fishing it. Most places named Dry Creek are named that for a reason. Karl from *Sling Blade* might say, "It ain't got no water in it." Same reason as why Buena Vista's name holds true. What you see is what you get: a heavenly view of the Collegiate Peaks (Yale, Princeton, Columbia, Harvard, and Oxford Peaks, all of which are within casting distance of Buena Vista).

There really is a Johnson Village, too. Just 3 or 4 miles south of town, US 285 abruptly cuts back to the east, south of Buena Vista at Johnson Village and aims toward Antero Reservoir. This

Mac rigs up on the banks of the Arkansas, near Buena Vista.

is how we discovered Trout Creek. It follows you along the trip for an enticing scenic fishing experience. All the way up to Trout Creek Pass on the right-hand side of the road, the land will constantly stagger, from public to private, and back again. Pay close attention to the signage if you have a rod so you don't get a gun barrel in your face. This IS the Old West, still.

Arkansas browns aren't always easy to bring to hand.

Trout Creek fishing is remarkably good, but alders and brush will force you to be accurate like Robin Hood with your casting to have fun. You may find some larger fish than you expected, since some explorative browns and a few bows will leave the monstrosity of the Arkansas for the easier living conditions of slower water.

Chalk Creek: South of Buena Vista, the Chalk flows easterly out between Antero and Princeton peaks and is a fine creek to fish for brook, cutthroat, brown, and rainbow trout. Chalk is unbelievable and worth every effort spent to see its unique geology and fish-rich waters.

Also try many of the small feeder streams visible on the DeLorme topo map. Many hold huge numbers of trout, but they will most likely be small and slender. Chalk is home to 6- to 12-inch rainbows and brown trout starting above Mt. Princeton Hot Springs. Cascades area has some larger fish, and Chalk Lake just before the cascades gets stocked regularly.

Colorful native trout are the payoff for hiking into Collegiate Peaks.

Mark and Kenny used to fish Chalk all the time, and he told me that one time on the Chalk he had an errant cast that buried a fly deep into the back of his head, and he couldn't find Kenny, so he just yanked it out. Left a chunk of meat missing. A deep-tissue crevasse. I don't really believe him. Have you seen his ears? No way he could cast in any direction and not hook one of those satellite dishes.

Grizzly Lake requires a 3-mile hike from the St. Elmo turn-off. The lure here are the 6- to 14-inch brook trout, besides the scenery.

Cottonwood Creek past Cottonwood Hot Springs Resort is only a mediocre fishery for smallish rainbows and browns. Above Cottonwood Lake is not much better, but 10-inch bows will take a fly.

Cottonwood Lake is a popular and scenic speck on the map with a campground, which makes it a great spot for the family. About 10 miles west of Buena Vista off CR 306, it is easily accessible with just about any vehicle. Boats not allowed. Rainbows up to 2 pounds are caught here occasionally.

Cottonwood Creek above Rainbow Lake (which is private) to the crest of Cottonwood Pass will have brooks and browns up to 14 inches.

Denny Creek and Hartenstein Lake has 8- to 14-inch native cutts. Park at the trailhead on Cottonwood Pass Road, 2 miles above Rainbow Lake, then hike 3 miles on TR 1442 to the lake, fishing your way up.

North Cottonwood Creek can be found west of Crossman Avenue in town, and has 6- to 16-inch rainbow trout and brown trout along 8 miles of creek that ascend up between Yale and Columbia peaks.

Bedrock Falls and Pine Creek (10,400-12,500 ft.) has the Pine Creek Trail meandering beside the creek for 12 miles, gradually reaching into the upper basin surrounded by "Fourteeners." The creek has 6- to 14-inch natives and brooks.

Twin Lakes should not be confused with Silver King Lake at the end of TR 1459 (Pine Creek Trail). Twin lakes are several hundred feet below Silver King and hold 8- to 16-inch native cutts.

Clear Creek Reservoir is about 15 miles north of Buena Vista on US 24. Motor boats are allowed, and rainbow trout reach up to 30 inches.

For the Adventurer

Ptarmigan Lake is a breathtaking high-country lake about 6 miles west of Cottonwood Lake. The dirt road is hell, with the last 3 miles being 4-wheel drive only. But adventurers can hike the 4-mile path south from Cottonwood Pass Road. (Trailhead is 15 miles west of Buena Vista on CR 306. Hike 2.5

Twin Lakes, about 30 miles north of Buena Vista

miles past some small lakes up to the timberline.) Two-foot native trout are why you would want to go here.

Bear Lake: For native cutthroat trout up to 24 inches–plus, Bear Lake is another spectacular high-country lake that we do not recommend you attempt without DeLorme topo map and a keen sense of direction. Find North Cottonwood Creek, north of Cottonwood Pass Road. Work your way around the maze of Forest Roads until you find that you're on FR 365, which skirts North Cottonwood Creek. From there you will travel due west until a pack trail takes you north, up Horn Fork Creek, where you will hike about another 3 miles to Bear Lake. Take your alpine lake fly box until you locate what they want.

Hancock Lake (11,600 ft.) is actually closer to Salida than Boona Vista (ha-ha!), but the easiest way to get there is via Chalk Creek, then FR 295, then a 2.5-mile trek by trail TR 1422. Make the trip for the 6- to 14-inch natives and brooks.

Lost Rainbow Lake is an amazing find on the Main Range Trail, about 2 miles south of Pine Creek. For 6- to 26-inch natives.

Harvard Lakes are reached by hiking 2.5 miles north on the Colorado "Main Range" Trail from where it crosses North Cottonwood Road. Rainbow and natives reach 6–18 inches, with the larger trout in the lower lake near the base of avalanche fingers of Mt. Columbia, where you will definitely want your camera.

> **Mark and Mac Essential Survival Items**
> - A powerbar of any brand
> - Emergency poncho
> - Beer bottle/wine bottle opener combo
> - Water treatment tablets
> - Compass
> - Flashlight (headlamp)
> - Wetwipes
> - Ziploc baggies (wrap around cameras)
> - Beef jerky
> - Flagging tape

HOME BASE
5 Creede

I've kind of given up on Creede and Lake City. This is a difficult decision because my family has been coming to these two mountain hamlets since the 1940s. Amy's family since the 1930s. We have so many memories tied to the San Juans and these villages.

Things I remember:

Kenny fishing out of a raft, guided by Chris Gentry, broke his rod on the Rio Grande. Snapped it in half. We kept warning him not to get caught up in the willows as we zipped by. He caught a 20-inch trout on the 3-foot broom-rod he had left.

This Creede-area creek is found in a meadow near the park.

"Of course, it's been twenty years since I've been up there, but last time I fished Crystal Lake, my brother Glynn and I caught about fifty big, fat trout each. Never saw a soul," our father-in-law Fred Becker said as he motioned toward the mountains with his thick index finger.

We three young men glanced wide-eyed at each other at the news. We were in our late twenties.

"How far is it?" we asked.

"Best I can remember, it takes about an hour, maybe an hour and a half," Fred said as he turned and pointed again. "Just over that ridge."

Fred had never led us astray before—and he knew the lay of the land around Lake City, Colorado, better than most. He had been coming up to the San Juan Mountains since he was a child fifty years past. And he was one heckuva trout fisherman, too, always catching the biggest trout or the most trout. We sat around the rickety table in one of the Ox Yoke cabins on the Lake Fork Gunnison River dreaming aloud about the lunker brook trout we would fight in the morning.

I'm going to shorten this trip:

Rain, sleet, snow. Poor judgments on our part on clothing to combat such weather.

Can you say switchbacks?

Can you say steep?

Two fish total between three anglers.

We returned cold and wet at dark. "Dad, tell us one more time how long it took you and Uncle Glynn to get up to Crystal Lake?" David queried, his voice pitched.

"About an hour and a half, as I remember." Then Fred turned his cheeks in his big hand, got a twinkle in his eye, all of which seemed entirely too rehearsed, and revealed in mock astonishment, "Did I forget to tell you boys that Glynn and I used to go up to Crystal Lake by horseback? It's a lot quicker that way." Then he winked.

My former barber, who unexpectedly took a shot at antelope from the car as we drove through New Mexico, tossed his wedding ring into Love Lake near Creede because he and his wife had broken up, located his sawed-off shotgun after we had hidden his handgun, and pointed it at a car that cut us off. Oh, the good times.

Five hundred yards down in a canyon, the river twists and turns in big slow loops, forming deep pools against the granite cliffs and alternating shallow sandy, gravelly bars across from them. The biggest fish any of us had ever caught here was 20 inches long, maybe 4 pounds. Kenny and I saw a fish much bigger than that in what we call the Periscope Pool, this amazingly deep pool, dark green and bottomless, a stone vat of still water that holds between two sheer cliff-faces. We spotted this trout on two different occasions and each time he slowly sipped insects off the top and acted like he owned the place. Ten pounds easy.

Fred's been gone for eleven years now, but we all make eye contact when we reach bottom. It's a knowing thing, a brief payment of respect, a nod to the heavens.

Williams angles in the Periscope Pool.

Kenny talks about the Periscope Pool all year long. He dreams of catching the behemoth that haunts the waters between Scylla and Charybdis.

"Go on." He turned and quick-walked out of the water and up a trail that dropped down into Periscope Pool. Dave and I grinned and then turned upstream when he heard a big splash.

Dave was to my left casting across and upstream, working the tail, three or four feet from the cutbank. Trout had been rising the last twenty minutes and we each caught several. For an hour, we barely moved. Five or six times, we had double hookups.

Kenny was upstream of us in the Periscope Pool yelling something, but we couldn't decipher what he was saying. Maybe he had the big boy on and needed help or wanted to show off. Too bad. We're in the middle of a hatch, bucko.

At that moment, the big black bear, all 500 pounds of the monster, peeked through the tall grass on the bank and stared at us. Four feet away. Kenny continued to yell at us.

The big bear backed out, and the grasses swished and swayed. He stuck his head out again. He wanted to cross the river and we were in his way.

Kenny was hollering now, help me you bums.

Dave and I shot a quick look at each other—we'd love to buddy, but we have our own agenda right now. We looked right back at the bear. He snorted, wet, like blowing his nose.

We've seen lots of black bears while out hiking and fishing. We've had them in our camp foraging for food, destroying food bags and coolers and such. We've scared them off at distances of twenty, thirty yards. But neither of us had ever been close enough that if we fell forward, our noggins would drop right in the bear's lap. I'm not saying we were scared, but I am saying that this particular big bear four feet in front of us had our undivided attention.

David spoke first. "I sure wish Kenny would shut up."

I whispered back, "Me too." You can have all of my gear if he gets us, Kenny. I hated to let him have the 4 wt. Hexagraph, but I didn't have time to quibble.

The big black bear had us in a stalemate. He wanted to cross, but we were too knowledgeable and petrified to move. We wanted to move, but he was too big and ornery to let us. And Kenny was still calling for help.

The bear played hide and seek up and down the bank, peering out from the tall grass, lumbering upstream and trying again. He barked once, and we slid our feet backwards slowly. I know I'm not faster than the bear, but I might be faster than Dave.

The bear moved back ten feet off the bank and studied us.

"Get my camera out, Mark."

If I move, the bear sees me as prey. This is one big bear. But, if I get Dave's camera, I have to get behind him to get into the backpack, and then I've got a buffer.

Kenny angles from the bank of South Clear Creek.

I slowly moved behind Dave and got out his camera. Great. Dave's going to document on film our demise.

Kenny had stopped yelling.

Dave snapped off five or six shots.

The bear became bored, turned and waddled up the mountain.

And the fish stopped rising. Kenny came back. He had caught the behemoth and lost it when he couldn't land it.

It was now dark. Long walk back to the car.

Our brother-in-law David conned Kenny and me into riding the Alpine Loop from Engineer Pass to American Basin. On bikes. Swore it wouldn't take all that long. Safe. Fun. If you call all day on one of those two-wheeled death traps and flattening our bodies close to the ground when a lightning storm snuck over the mountain as safe and fun, I can set up a trip with him if you'd like.

A big cinnamon-colored black bear wandered into our compound in Lake City, above the Texaco, while all the children, ages one to twelve, were outside playing. Kids scattered like plastic figurines on an electric football table and all but one made it into one of the three cabins. No, the bear didn't attack, but it was a tense situation (hearts stopped, stomachs turned) when we realized not all the little chicks were rounded up. The bear left without incident.

After midnight at the compound, the same night the bear had been in the yard earlier in the day, we had tired from chatting on the front porch. Amy asked me to take the trash to the garbage cans. I lifted the lid, dropped in the bag when, to my utter surprise, an animal was startled and jumped straight out of the adjacent can. I thought something had me. I'm not gonna lie—the thought of the bear returning in the dark was in my mind. I turned to run and caught my toe and fell flat on my face. The raccoon scampered off into the night as my family roared with laughter. I just love it when they tell this story over and over and over every single family get-together.

The first time we drove back into South Clear Creek and looked down on the underfished meandering emerald stream. Fishing it was even better. That's all you're getting out of me on this one.

Mark's nephew Chase and his dog Franklin on South Clear Creek.

Fishing with father-in-law Fred for the last time. If you ever fish Big Blue, you'll see why it was his favorite river in the world. If you'd have fished it twenty years ago, you'd have thought it heavenly, what with all the cutts and good-sized brookies. The beaver ponds were quagmires, the mosquitoes dastardly, but the clean, cool cobalt stream meandered back and forth, hypnotizing, pregnant with opportunities, every bend another perfect pool or ideal flats. The river doesn't fish as well anymore, but we go back every summer because we know Fred loved it so.

Memories. I remember when my sister-in-law Debbie accidentally walked in the wrong cabin on my brother-in-law Kenny showering, and he was cool as a cucumber; the July 4th egg toss third place trophy that came home with Kenny and his wife Betsy; great ice cream shakes; that bear in the tree in the middle of town; and, as you can see, the list goes on. This is what place can do for you.

One last memory. The compound has three cabins, and David and his brood got one, mother-in-law Jane got the other, and we shared one with the Medlings. It was bedtime and everyone was in their rooms fixing to go lights out when Betsy, my pretty and funny sister-in-law, shrieked. Kenny and I bolted from our rooms into the living room to see Betsy holding a flashlight pointing out to the cars. I saw someone by the cars. Someone's trying to break into the cars! So Kenny and I, in our boxer shorts, run out of the cabin, yell at whomever is messing with our stuff to cease and desist (or something clever like that), and then dash onto the gravel. Big gravel, hard on the feet. We stumble-hop comically to the cars, look all around the vehicles, and find nothing.

We are amped. Betsy swore she saw a light moving around cars as she passed by the big picture window, but after a half hour we go back to bed. We hear Betsy laughing loudly in the living room. In between guffaws, I found out—deep breath, spasmodic laughing—it wasn't anyone—deep dry laughter—look. And she shone the flashlight on the window—it looked like there was somebody with a light moving around the cars. She turned off the light, and the perpetrators vanished. The flashlight, or more accurately, goofy Betsy, had caused the entire barefooted incident.

These 1950s-style cabins are found all over the Creede/Lake City area.

So why am I down on Creede and Lake City? Perhaps progress was inevitable. Money talks.

The last decade has seen creeping privacy, increasing wealth. What the locals called the Californication of these villages. These two towns were once havens for blue collar hardworking folks who came up for one to three weeks to fill coolers with brook trout and stocked rainbows. Every summer, when I go back to my old haunts, I find that somehow, someway, it's now posted private. Because the public water is shrinking, even though both Creede and Lake City have more public water than just about anywhere, the closest public accesses are hard-hit and the fish are smaller. Drive into Big Blue nowadays, and you won't catch cutthroats like you used to, and the brookies are stunted and overpopulated. The scenery, however, is San Juan exemplary, rugged and unique, pines and aspens, rushing rivers, really wild country.

Creede is a lot like Lake City. Small remote mountain village in the San Juans with wild woolly mining history, dead in the winter but frequented mostly by Texans and Oklahomans in the summer. These are typically families who return each summer, a family tradition. They stay in cabins, the same cabins they've stayed in each summer for years. They have fish-fry dinners and they hang wet waders on the front porches next to the 1950s-style metal chairs. The grocery markets are iffy outfits with limited offerings.

Creede 5

So why include Creede (and by proxy, Lake City) in this home bases book? Even though I've seen these two havens change over the years, you might not have and, as such, might not be turned off by progress. Progress is measured in small doses in Creede. No condos. No fake Swiss chalet neo-European

luxury resorts. In fact, you'll be hard-pressed to find lodging that meets up with Vail or Breckenridge or Eagle mid-level standards. If you want cabins, you better reserve them a year in advance because 1) they're popular and 2) they're disappearing because the owners, often Texans who loved the area so much they mistakenly bought a business, are often selling their cabin resorts off piecemeal to individuals.

You are not going to see very many folks because even when summer-full Creede isn't crowded. Walking up and down Main Street takes you past out-doors stores, fly shops, trinket shops,

Downtown Creede

historic buildings, cafes, coffeeshops, art galleries. The history of the mining town is impressive and woolly, ranging from the inimitable Soapy Smith to cigar-smoking Poker Alice to the outlaw Robert Ford who shot down Jesse James. Creede has a certain western charm you can't resist. Even though more of the rivers seem private, anglers will still have rivers entirely to their lonesome. This big primitive mountain forest is spectacularly wild and beautiful, under-fished, remote, and worth your time. I think Creede is ideal for families, for fishing buddies especially if you plan to stay a week or two. Go. Make some memories. I cherish the ones I have from Creede and Lake City.

Take in a view with your meal in Creede.

Favorite Places to Eat

Every summer we go back to Creede and Lake City, we see several cafés and restaurants closed or changed to something else. We recommend the **Creede Hotel** (719-658-2608), **Firehouse** (719-658-0212), and we love **Cascada Bar and Grill** (719-658-1033). Lake City: **Southern Vittles** (970-944-2010), **Poker Alice** (970-944-4100), where we eat breakfast and dinner several times each week when we stay in Lake City, and **Tic Toc Diner** (970-944-0444), which we don't like much, but everyone else does. The **Mocha Moose** (970-944-0334) is a nice coffeehouse.

Favorite Places to Stay

We always stay in cabins, and, so many cabins keep being sold off, you sure better check ahead of time and make sure. Remember that there are few places to stay that are going to rate high on amenities. Most are pretty basic. Around Creede: **Wason Ranch** (719-658-2413), **Cottonwood Cove** (719-658-2242), **Cascada Cabins** (719-658-1033). Go to www.creede.com and contact the Chamber of Commerce because they have listings for all the cabins for rent. Owners of lodging in both towns are amazingly friendly,

This sign was on a cabin in the Creede/Lake City area.

and if they don't have any rooms they will often know who does or will even call around for you. Around Lake City: **Town Square Cabins** (970-944-2236), **Wagon Wheel** (970-944-2264), the **Texan Resort** (970-944-2246). We hear good things about the **Creede Hotel** (719-658-2608) and the **The Old Firehouse** (719-658-0212)—they're both on Main in Creede and in the thick of the action—and you can't go wrong with any of the guest ranches around Creede or Lake City. **Broadacres Ranch** (719-658-2291) and the **4UR Ranch** (719-658-2202) are two of the finest fishing ranches in the state, and both sit on the Rio Grande. For camping, try **Thirty-mile Campground, Rio Grande Campground, Palisade Campground.**

Fly Shops, Guides, and Tackle Stores

Rio Grande Anglers, (719-658-2955, www. riograndeangler.com) and **Ramble House** (719-658-2482, www.ramblehouse.net) in

Rio Grande Angler in Creede

Creede; **Sportsman Fly Shop** (970-944-2526, www.lakecitysportsman.com) and **Dans Fly Shop** (970-944-2281, www.dansflyshop.com) in Lake City.

Fishing Places Solid Choices near Home Base

Rio Grande: The Rio Grande is the key to either place, Creede or South Fork. You could stay a week in a cabin and get out and fish a different part of the Rio Grande and never miss a beat, it's so good. The Rio Grande is a major western trout river, in great form, stunningly beautiful, good for wade-fishing or float-fishing. Consistent. The quintessential western trout stream.

Above: The Rio Grande
Right: Cool day on East Bellows Creek

I believe the mighty Rio Grande flows through the prettiest scenery in Colorado. The water is as clear as air, the air is clean, the mountains majestic, and the trout plentiful. And the river holds some whoppers. This is beautiful and rugged country, where the nation's second longest river begins its southward trek, the river swelling with tributary after tributary, surrounded by interconnecting trails and alpine lakes. Deep runs, big pools,

Top: We caught this cutt on North Clear Creek.
Left: We landed this rainbow trout in a Creede-area stream.

riffles, all kinds of water flowing through narrow canyons and broad valleys. You're in some of the most primeval scenery left in the lower forty-eight. One of the great things about this upper section of the Rio Grande is that despite its remoteness, despite its lack of angling pressure, the river is easily accessed by road and trail. If it's your first time to fish it, hire a guide and float it because by floating the river you can get to places bank anglers can't reach. The fishing generally begins to pick up in early May. After your float, wade-fish it and enjoy.

There is public land at both Rio Grande Campground and Marshall Park CG on both sides of the river, but in between is a mix of private and public land you would need permission to fish. From Willow Creek to 4UR Ranch, this is mostly private water. There is a public access at the old fish hatchery and at both Blue Creek and Palisade CG. At the Coller Bridge, there is parking and boat access, as well as pullouts along the highway both up and downstream. The public and private water of the Rio Grande between South Fork and Creede is well marked, so you'll be able to decipher where you can fish. From South Fork, CO 149 follows the river up to Creede.

North Clear Creek Falls

Top: Lake San Cristobal
Left: Amy enjoying a campfire at Lake San Cristobal

For the Adventurer

Upper Rio Grande: Freestone stream in wilderness setting with numerous tributaries. This is beautiful and rugged country. You'll be surrounded by dense forests and tall canyon ridges. Deep runs, big pools, riffles, all kinds of water flowing through narrow canyons and broad valleys. The upper river can be reached by traveling south on CO 149 from Lake City to FR 520 west (the Rio Grande Reservoir Road). Road Canyon Campground is located just west of the reservoir. FR 520 runs alongside the upper river for much of its course, and this forest service road is an often bumpy, rough dirt road, strewn with big rocks and deep potholes throughout. A 4-wheel drive vehicle is a must. From FR 520, anglers can reach the river and its headwaters by hiking the trails, of which there are many.

Goose Creek: Rio Grande tributary flowing north from the Weminuche Wilderness near Wagon Wheel Gap. Travel east from Creede on CO 149 to the

The Rio Grande at Wagon Wheel Gap

only road to the south before Wagon Wheel Gap, before Palisade Campground. Rough road, worth the trip. Long trip in and out, so consider camping. Goose Creek has excellent trout habitat for both native cutthroat and the flyfisher. Long stretches of open meadow, several beaver ponds as the creek spreads over grassy terrain. Upper Goose Creek (and Goose Lakes) can be reached by Fisher Creek Trail or Ivy Creek Trail.

Bellows Creek: Good fishing in both forks. Travel east from Creede on CO 149 to just north of Wagon Wheel Gap.

Río Grande Reservoir: Good fishing option for the day or overnight. Travel west from Creede on CO 149 to FR 520. Turn left (west) and travel for 12 miles to the reservoir. When the water's up, you can get into some big fish.

Road Canyon Reservoirs: The larger reservoir is the only one to mess with. It holds 140 acres, while the other only holds 4 acres. The larger Road Canyon Reservoir (elevation 9,275 ft.) is known for its big rainbows up to 18 inches, many over 4 pounds. The lake also holds brook trout, many of which reach 15 inches or bigger. Road Canyon Reservoir lies off FR 520 west from CO 149.

Continental Reservoir: An inconsistent producer, this reservoir is an irrigation lake, so the water level is up and down. When up, the fishing's good. Travel south from Lake City on CO 149 then west of FR 513.

Williams' mother-in-law angles a Creede-area stream.

Pole Creek: This cutthroat creek flows through a geologically interesting and colorful valley and consequently has plenty of eye-catching scenery, as well as casting room and a few rarely fished beaver ponds. A foot trail (TR 787) follows the creek for much of its course and can be accessed from FR 520 west from Rio Grande Reservoir.

Ute Creek: Tributary to the Rio Grande drainage, entering the Rio Grande Reservoir on its western side. The creek has good fishing in some awesome scenery. The three forks that make up the headwaters for Ute Creek are all excellent trout fishing destinations, mostly for cutthroats and rainbows, with some brook trout. Ute Creek Trail is a well-marked trail leading south to the creek's three forks. Each creek has a foot trail paralleling its course. The Ute Lakes are headwater lakes worth fishing for large trout.

Big Squaw and Little Squaw Creeks: Big fish, little water, high country solitude, some bushwhacking, some trails. Travel south from Lake City on CO 149 to FR 520.

Squaw Lake: Less than 10 acres, this is a productive side trip lake reached from TR 890 off of TR 813.

North Clear Creek

North Clear Creek: Less than a mile off CO 149, about halfway between Creede and Lake City, you'll see a sign pointing to North Clear Creek Falls. Go see it. The little creek winds through a treeless park before it plunges beautifully down a dark rugged chasm. The creek picks up Bennett and Boulder Creeks on its way to the Rio Grande as it flows past thick trees and heavy riparian habitat in the park. Clear Creek is a fair-sized stream perfect for setting up camp for a few days. From the three campgrounds along the stream (South Clear Creek CG, North Clear Creek CG, and South Clear Creek Falls CG), anglers can easily fish the main stem, the two forks of the creek, or the productive feeder creeks. South Clear Creek is a joy to fish if you have a high-clearance vehicle and can get back into the lower part.

Williams shows off his rainbow on the Lake Fork.

Brown Lakes: Travel west from Creede for over 20 miles on CO 149 (Spring Creek Pass Road) and follow the signs (FR 515).

OTHER FISHERIES WORTH INVESTIGATING: (I know I've listed a lot, but I know these great waters well and couldn't just leave them out.) Rito Hondo Reservoir, Rito Hondo Creek, Weminuche Creek, Twin Lakes, West Fork Cebolla, Cebolla Creek, Deer Lakes, Love Lake, Big Goose Lake, Fisher Creek, Ivy Creek, Deep Creek, Trout Creek, Trout Lake, West Lost Trail Creeks, Regan Lake, Miners Creek, Rat Creek, Embargo Creek.

Blue Ribbon Fisheries not far from Creede

Lake Fork Gunnison
Henson Creek
San Juan River (near Pagosa)
Piedra
South Fork Rio Grande

6 HOME BASE
Crested Butte

A great lonesome campsite in Spring Creek Campground

I'm writing this in the Aliner trailer-camper in the Spring Creek Campground while Amy is sleeping. Mac bolted for Amarillo to be with his kids for Father's Day. In his place for a research trip to Crested Butte, the much prettier Amy Becker Williams, my wife. She cooks better, smells better, and snuggles better.

So far on this trip, in the weeks before Mac sailed back home for a brief hey to the kiddos, we hadn't had much contact with the real world, often camping fifteen to twenty miles from any paved road, driving in on Forest Service 4-wheel-drive "roads."

We've been eating well for remote campers. Two weeks ago in A-Town, we pre-made chili, spaghetti and sauce, Tuscan soup, stuff like that, then vacuum-packed and froze it. We simply boil it when we get back to the Aliner. Delicious. We eat bananas and drink strong coffee for breakfast, snack on Ede's jerky and Clif Bars for lunch. We walk three to ten miles a day (to and along the streams), and if you've ever waded you know that wading a river mile is much more taxing than walking the track at your local high school. (Mac and I have both lost weight on this trip because of all the exercise.) After dinner, we build a huge fire and write down our notes, discuss the day's fish and missed fish and generally get louder as the fire gets roaring. Think *Blazing Saddles* meets *City Slickers*.

On to Crested Butte.

Amy and I saw the change coming. The Crested Butte that we knew, the one that was the last unrefined major ski resort in Colorado, the wild isolated hamlet, had changed right before our eyes and now rivaled Aspen and Vail for its development and eliteness. To be fair, Crested Butte is still a great getaway for family or couples because the town is: 1) romantic, charming, and quaint; 2) isolated; 3) has lots for the family to do; and 4) provides diverse fishing opportunities. Crested Butte is more than a downhiller's dream, a fat-tire enthusiast's delight, and a palette of wildflower colors.

Take a lazy stroll down Elk Avenue, past the false-front, clapboard shops and restaurants, and you'll feel like you are back in the Old West, and the

locals are friendly, helpful, and relaxed. The town has a funky, quirky reputation and fights progress at every turn, a town where bicycles often outnumber cars parked along the street. But the times, they are a-changin'.

So off the beaten path is this former coal-mining town, if you end up in Crested Butte, it's because you want to be there. Nestled under the surrounding Elk Mountains of central

The main drag in Crested Butte

Colorado, there are actually two Crested Buttes: The historic community of Crested Butte, designated a National Historic District, and the ski village of Mount Crested Butte, 3 miles away. The two are connected by a free shuttle bus service that runs every fifteen minutes. We like Crested Butte, don't get us wrong. It's just that we share it with so many other people now.

So here we are in June. Camping on Spring Creek without Mac, enjoying the best weather of the summer for much of the trip. No one else in the campground but one camper, and he's at the far end of camp. Amy tells me it's romantic. I reckon so, what with our evening meals with wine, the roaring fire, and the dramatic cliffs above us. We are enjoying late, slow mornings. Sipping hot coffee and hot chocolate, sitting in the sun, loosely planning the day, packing a bag with snacks and lunch.

Williams enjoys a great fire at Spring Creek Campground.

We can walk twenty yards to the creek. I take the dogs while Amy changes or cooks, and I'll catch 2 or 3 (some nice) and show the dogs, then stroll back to camp. We walk up the road a mile or two and fish this nice bend pool. Amy catches fish, I catch fish. Piper is always on the edge of the shore, wanting to enter the creek, but she nervously stays. We drive up a few miles, fishing along the way— some stretches are slow spring-creek like sections.

Back in Amarillo, during the real world, I teach English. High School, freshmen through senior. Alternative school. I see kids of all kinds, and at times it's disheartening to see the circumstances from which they come, the lack of normalcy in their lives. But every day they prove wrong my expectations, they triumph. Cylar Brown was sixteen when he came to my class. Cylar is an outdoorsman. He loves fishing. This much I learned his first day in class when I typically perform an informal assessment interview. Alternative education means that I can't use normal education methods and still expect these students to learn. They didn't learn in a traditional system, so it's insanity to think they'd do it now.

He saw a copy of my book, *So Many Fish*, sitting on my desk and commented, "My cousin has that book. Says it's pretty good."

"Yeah, that's cool. I wrote it."

I had the young man's attention.

Cylar did not know he was a writer. Most people think they know when they are, but Cylar was one of those for whom writing did not come easily. The ease with which you write has little bearing on if you are a writer or not. Cylar is a plodder, a muddler, and because he'd had little immediate success writing in the past, he was open to new writing techniques that fit his learning style.

After two weeks in my class, I saw him with a copy of *Southwest Fly Fishing*, reading an article I had written. I asked if he liked the magazine.

"Yeah, I wouldn't mind writing for an outdoors magazine one day."

"Well, why not now? Why not that one?"

Six weeks and lots of sweat later, he had crafted a pretty decent 500-word article. Sounds like it took long, I know, but writing for English class and writing for a sports magazine are two entirely different things. He added and revised every day. He read and re-read my articles. He didn't ask much, but when he did, he listened and implemented. He wrote about his favorite creek in the world, the creek he'd been fishing since he was a kid, a family legacy stream. Spring Creek.

He turned it in one day.

"I'm done."

I knew what he meant. Not only was the piece finished, he had exhausted all means to make this a great article.

"Now, it's time to learn how to write a query letter to the magazine."

His face dropped. He was tired of writing, and he was not excited about the prospect of being rejected by a national magazine. We wrote the query letter together, attached the article, and I had him finish it and hit "send."

An hour later, the editor of *Southwest Fly Fishing*, not knowing Cylar was sixteen, only knowing he was a colleague of mine, said the article was perfect and he'd like to purchase it. I ran down to Cylar's History class and pulled him out. Big white smile. He was a writer.

When the article came out, a local television station came out to interview him. Big star. The magazine was on the newsstands at the Barnes and Noble. His grandmother bought up all the available copies.

Here's what Cylar has to say about Spring Creek:

I know this creek where three things will happen when you fish it: 1) you will catch a lot of trout; 2) there's close to nobody on the water; 3) did I mention you'll catch a lot of trout?

Spring Creek is located six miles northeast of Almont on FR 742. From the start of this fantastic creek, lies an 82 acre reservoir (Spring Creek Reservoir) holding some good size (10 to 14 inches with some up to 20 inches) brooks, browns, and rainbows. At the south end of the reservoir starts the most fishable part of Spring

Creek, with a beautiful five to six mile tail water meadow section packed with little brooks and browns ranging from 6 to 12 inches.

The creek along the meadow section is about four to six feet wide with great cut banks and long smooth bends. One fly I recommend you get wet in this section would be a size 20 to 22 elk hair caddis; just something about floating that little fly along the cut banks drives the fish crazy. At the end of the meadow, the creek dips into a deeply forested area with two gigantic mountains on either side staring down at you. This part of the creek is fairly difficult fishing due to the massive pines that have fallen to old age, but if you have the guts to shimmy your way onto a tree suspended over the gushing waters and manage to dip your fly in what looks to be a promising run, this is the place for you. Below the meadow, the creek widens and picks up more water.

Spring Creek is one of those special streams that seems to create memories. Case in point: Me and Joe (Joe is my cousin, okay?) were on the way back to Gunnison from a Bob Dylan show in Telluride. It was about eleven at night driving through pitch-black rain with "A Hard Rain's A-Gonna Fall" still playing in the back of my mind. Not knowing what to do we kept truckin all the way through Gunnison (where Joe lived) and decided to stay at the Spring Creek Campground which is located on Spring Creek Road just off of FR 742 where the paved road ends and the dirt road starts. The campground is a great place for RV and tent camping, also a great place for the whole family to get out and have some fun. Wildlife is bountiful and you will see a range of animals including foxes, deer and the occasional trash-eating bear. The river from the south end of the campground down to Harmels, the little store at the beginning of Spring Creek Road, is all private. But the waters above the camping is where you need to focus for it is all fantastic public fishing.

Some of my most memorable fishing trips have come from this little eight- to fifteen-foot wide creek. Just above the second bridge starts what I like to call my little honey hole. Every time I pull up to this 300 yard stretch, I get butterflies in my stomach. It's full of long riffles, huge boulders and magnificent pocket water. I guess its knowing that I can fish this short strip of water all day and have a blast! Dropping a little 22 green midge off a big dry fly such as drakes, elk hair caddis, adams, etc. seems to be a magnet to fish lips. I would recommend you fish these waters with a 6-1/2 to 7 foot rod because trying to fish a 9 footer you would be in the trees and bushes more than the water."

Thanks Cylar.

Mid-July. Mac and I are back and looking to camp at any of the campgrounds along the Taylor River. We are out of luck. We don't want to camp around the

Top: Campsite on Willow Creek
Above: Williams fishes Willow Creek.

lake because it's cold and wet (imagine that), so we drive along Willow Creek. Got it. A singular primitive site. Free and overlooking the little creek and the big meadow.

We set up the Aliner with the door overlooking Willow Creek. No other campers within two hundred yards. We want a fire but it's raining. Imagine that. Later that evening, before dusk, a weird VW-type bus pulls up. The bus is odd because it's missing the middle. The middle is cutout (like the letter U) and three joes and a Vizla pop out of this monstrosity. The dudes are strange (posture, overkill angling attire, running to the river).

We worried that they were going to camp here, when there was so much open land. This could get ugly. They sucked. As quickly as they came, they left. As they did, one of the oddballs confided to us in his drawl, "Hey, if you'n wants to ketch'em, you gotta sneak right up on'em." Thanks Deliverance Boy. We went into spontaneous dialogue.

"Some people call this Kaiser Creek."

"I like to fish with the Kaiser Roll Cast."

"I bet Kaiser Soze would do well here."

"I'd like me some biscuits and mustard, uh huh."

Dirk Bosley with a beastly brown on the Taylor River

We were in full *Sling Blade* mode. The Harley Pulmer Show came next. Harley is a guy we created who rides motorcycles, has lived dreamily through drug-stupored decades, and is the root of whatever trouble is taking place. Mac does the voice best, and it sounds something like Karl meets Christopher Walken. Larry the Cable Guy meets Sons of Anarchy.

Willow is six feet wide and two feet deep, very little structure—flat on the topwater and bend pools and deep cut banks. Fish are rising regularly in front of us. We see fish rising all up and down the creek. We fished Willow and caught a few, but not nearly as many as we thought we'd catch—we'd seen so many rises after all. There are no lunkers in this small water, but there are lots of trout. And it is challenging because there are few spots where you can make a traditional cast, a cast that lays out, and you mend, you lift. Instead, you must cast across a grassy knoll letting the fly drop softly onto the bend, keeping the line and leader off the water then picking it up because of drag—high-sticking meets guerilla fishing.

In the morning, no hurry because it was cold and the water was cold. The roads were even icy, so we cooked pancakes and had Italian Roast coffee. We prepped to fish this so-called big fish mecca—the Taylor River tail water. I wrote in *So Many Fish* (Harper Collins) that I don't like the Taylor.

But I was ready that morning. We had this one guy who kept responding to our summer online articles in the Amarillo *Globe News,* who went by the name of harrytrout or some such moniker, and every week he'd complain that we had called a 12-inch trout "long and healthy." He would write sarcastically "ooh, gigantic trout. I didn't know 12-inch trout were considered large trout. Why don't you catch a big one?" That chapped our hides, and in fact we had been catching nice-sized trout. We each had trout in the high teens and a few in the low twenties.

For us, it's not about size but about experience. Look, we don't complain when we catch large trout. It's great fun. It's a super test of your skills. But we have both caught large trout over the years, and it was a trophy hunt—go to big rivers for big fish and it's like a safari. We are in a different phase of our fishing lives.

So that morning, I was ready for the hunt. Six wt. rod. Hexagraph. Nine foot. Big butted, soft-tipped, casts like a dream. Long leaders 6X and 7X. I loaded my small box, the tail water box, the one I first built in the '80s for the

Above: Floating the Taylor River
Left: This big brown is far from the biggest to be found in the Taylor River.

Top: Use long casts, mending, long drifts, and small flies on the Taylor tailwater.
Left: This angler plays a big trout on the Taylor River. He lost it a few minutes later.

San Juan River and have added to so much that flies desperately try to jump out when I open it. I found an empty fly box and filled it with odds and ends like muddler minnows, streamers, weird subsurface flies I've collected from around the world, from other tyers, flies that might be the only thing that will land that whopper.

The Taylor River tailrace is the mantelpiece fishery of this region, one of the finest big-trout fisheries in the country. The river immediately below the dam is the trophy water where you'll see shocked anglers holding trout as big as plump mannequins. The huge trout (measured in pounds, not inches) feed on the mysis shrimp that come out of the lake. It's a short stretch below the dam and crowded and slightly artificial. This is difficult fishing for behemoths with an audience watching from the bridge. Another Taylor River–area strange experience.

These lunkers are easily the most educated, dismissive trout of any I've ever fished, and that includes Henry's Fork and Silver Creek and the Test. There is precious little public water here, but that doesn't stop eager anglers from shouldering up in the 6/10 of a mile of perfect water. The fish are piggish and defiant. The last few state records have come from the Taylor: 23 inches long and 32 inches in girth. Or maybe it was the one that measured 40¼ inches long with a 29-inch girth. I don't know any more. This place is more like a freakshow, but it's like the carnival where you simply must go in and see the bearded lady.

While Mac was fishing, I was clicking pics. I saw a band of mountain goats with tags, perhaps twenty of them, moving down the mountain, eating. How cool is that? The tail water is about thirty to fifty feet wide. In some spots, it's fairly shallow, riffling over a bed of smaller rocks and sandbars, looping into dark-green deep runs and ridiculously black wide enormous pools. Before the private water, it rushes out of a flat slick pool the size of an elementary school and becomes a traditional western style river.

Fish are everywhere. Trout are easy to see, and we see them all right, huge floating logs. Not just your typical fat 15-incher that becomes a 17- or 18-inch trout during storyhour.

Bighorn sheep traipse by the Taylor River State Wildlife Area.

These fish were big and fat and memorable. We saw several that caused our mouths to open, that made us know we didn't bring enough weaponry.

Randy Fender (Montrose) and Dirk Bosley (Penrose) both caught trout over 22-inches and let us take photos. Mac caught a 6-pound brown. And then we both saw the clouds. We rushed to the car and jumped in just as the sky broke and the lightning and thunder attacked the area. It was a good day and, harrytrout, here's a big fish for you, buddy. Hope you like them french fried potaters, mmm.

Something to consider: anglers have two nearby excellent home bases near Crested Butte (and Gunnison). Both are good for a day or a few days. Almont and Taylor River/Reservoir. Almont is a cool home base where rivers meet, but unless you only want to fish, you're better off staying in Crested Butte and Gunnison.

Favorite Places to Eat
Teocalli Tamale (970-349-2005) for killer soft tacos, **Le Bosquet** (970-349-5808) for rustic world-class dining. Amy and I ate at **The Secret Stash** (970-349-6245)—not a coffee joint, but gets mistaken for it—with the dogs and

Top: Teocalli Tamale in Crested Butte
Far left: Stuffed peppers from The Secret Stash
Left: Pizza at The Secret Stash

enjoyed great wine and creative food, such as stuffed banana peppers and veggie pizza (best in town, so voted). **Django's Restaurant and Wine Bar** (970-349-7574) and **Soupcon Restaurant** (970-349-5448) are two other faves.

Favorite Places to Stay

If you plan to fish, stay in Almont at **Three Rivers Resort** (970-641-1303). If you want the Crested Butte ambiance, try **The Ruby of Crested Butte,** one of the finest bed and breakfasts you'll find in the state. 800-390-1338 (reservations), 970-349-1338, http://www.therubyofcrestedbutte.com/. You can stay in town, around town, or up at the ski resort town. We stay in condos when we go to Crested Butte, and we check with the chamber for information: www.cbchamber.com.

Fly Shops, Guides, and Tackle Stores

Almont Anglers (970-641-7404, www.almontanglers.com); **High Mountain Drifters Guide Service,** Gunnison, CO, (www.highmtndrifter.com); **Troutfitter Sports** (800-847-0244, 970-349-1323, www.troutfitter.com); **Willowfly Anglers** (888-761-FISH, 970-641-1303, www.willowflyanglers.com)

Beautiful country above Crested Butte

Fishing Places Solid Choices near Home Base

Taylor tail water: Year-round trophy trout hunting in a dusty canyon. Don't make a trip to go to the Taylor near Gunnison as your sole destination unless you are a masochist and you don't have much to do. Dirk Bosley of Penrose, Colorado, showed us how he and many others fish the Taylor River. Their setup starts with a Thingamabobber strike indicator, white, so it resembles an air bubble. They pinch on a bit of Mojo Mud tungsten putty half a foot or so below the indicator, and 18 to 24 inches below the weight they drift home-made mysis shrimp flies—and oftentimes a #20 to #24 dark midge pattern, like a Black Beauty or Mercury Midge, 18 to 24 inches below that. When it's not crowded along the edges, these guys cast upstream and follow their indicators,

Anglers line up to fish below the dam on the Taylor River.

walking down the bank, covering water, waiting for a hit. Otherwise, it's territorial angling. This is 7X tippet fishing, possibly even 8X, which we'd not seen until we visited the Taylor this last time. And you're gonna need a net.

Taylor River: You can reach the Taylor River pretty quickly from Crested Butte, twenty, thirty minutes tops. If you have time or inclination, hire a guide to float you down the river through the wooded canyon below the tail water. Wading is tough in the canyon, anyway. You have typical western habitat with riffles, runs, pools, overhanging limbs, but mostly you'll fish to water around boulders the size of Range Rovers. Rainbows, cutts, and browns, and not many of them you'll catch will be on the small side.

The upper Taylor is quick water, with easy wading, great character (riffles, runs, pocket water). Take a day to explore above the lake or camp on the river at Rivers End, Dinner Station, or Dorchester.

From Crested Butte, travel south on CO 135 to Almont (take Jacks Road cutoff to save time) and go up Taylor River Road.

Taylor Reservoir: Found 19 miles up from Almont on the Taylor River Road. Super spot as alternate day base or home base. Camping at both ends. Rainbow, brown, cutts, lake trout, and kokanee salmon. Also the predatory pike. A marina on the reservoir. A store at Willow Creek intersection with Taylor. Services of all kinds at Almont.

Working Spring Creek with a dropper rig

Slate River: The upper Slate is photogenic, but only offers average angling. You can find various stretches of the Slate open along its course, but the private signs will drive you crazy. There is a section in town near the high school. To reach the upper Slate, travel north on CO 135, and turn northerly (left) on Slate River Road, or continue north and you'll see another turnoff along the east fork of the river.

East River—see Gunnison chapter.

For the Adventurer

South Lottis Creek: That one creek off the road below the lake where my dog Piper ate cow shit. What a crazy dog. Decent side trip for a few hours fishing in a swift mountain stream for aggressive (but not prolific) trout. Along the Taylor River Road, you'll see the sign.

Taylor Reservoir marina

Lake Irwin: West of Crested Butte, Lake Irwin sits in the Ruby Range just waiting for you to come catch these high-country (10,500 ft.) jewels. No amenities, bring your own. Good day trip. Take Kebler Pass Road about six miles and turn at the sign.

Spring Creek Reservoir: Up Spring Creek Road 14 miles, which is a bumpy sucker, and has non-selective trout ready to strike. Nothing of much size, but a pretty spot to camp and fish. Take Taylor River Road then veer left at the sign.

Willow Creek: This is the small meadow stream where we camped near the reservoir and fought off the hillbilly van.

OTHER FISHERIES WORTH INVESTIGATING: Mirror Lake, Emerald Lake, Cement Creek, Coal Creek, Mill Creek, Brush Creeks, Illinois Creek, Texas Creek

Blue Ribbon Fisheries not far from Crested Butte

Gunnison
Black Canyon Gunnison
Lake Fork Gunnison

7 Cuchara/ Trinidad

What could be more paradoxical than dodging bullets while flyfishing? We're not sure, either.

So we top this hill just this side of North Lake, traveling south on CO 12 heading back to the campground on the North Fork Purgatoire on FR 411. Wes and Savannah, my kids, are pooped. Stalked trout all day on Bear Lake and area rivulets, and both had caught till they dropped. Brooks, browns, and I even caught a cutt in some fast water beneath a cavernous pool. We're exhausted. Not a peep from the back seat whatsoever.

In the distance, brilliant flashes of red and blue flicker at the crest of a hill. *Smokey and the Bandit* comes to mind. The entrance to the campground is halfway between us and these lights. We'll turn off before passing the anomaly. Wes is disappointed. He wanted to see some real action.

Suddenly, two sheriffs. Both standing firm. Drawn guns, loud negotiating, and nervous eyes draw our attention. A silver-colored SUV sits at the campground entrance where we wish to turn in. The driver's head seems to be their focus.

Williams slams on the brakes. Not just on the Jeep, but also on a half-finished four-letter word. He's surprised to see real live guns.

At this point, I realize the West hasn't changed much out here. I'm a gunfight virgin! So are my babies. What the hell have we gotten my kids into?

(...one hour later...)

Plate-like dikes slice through the wildnerness.

North Lake is spacious, scenic, and home to plenty of trout.

Hour-long stand-offs are boring as hell. This one ends in silence. And handcuffs. Wes is downtrodden. No shots. No blood. And that is a damn fine thing. Waiting in a ditch for an hour? Bor-ing. But sometimes, no action is all the action one can bear.

That day had certainly begun similarly silent, though not as boring. Out this way, the landscape hushes men. Alpine silences are what bring men like us out here, not bullets and bandits.

(...earlier that day...)

We leave out at 9:00 a.m. A mouse had jumped into our potty bucket outside the door and kept Wes and Williams awake all night thinking bears were about to eat them. They are both groggy. Grumpy. The drive allows them to wake and build up the tolerance needed to hear words spoken from other members of the human race. But that won't be till 10:30 or so. Quietude, for now.

Ancient, uplifted plates of rock now sit like exposed, vertical backbones of extinct dinosaurs. These dikes rise up from the earth like balanced knife blades on edge, cutting across time, as well as Colorado's southeast section between Cuchara and Trinidad. We stare out the windows. Eight eyes. One terrain. *Bedrock, this.* It captivates.

Wes and Savannah are mesmerized. Water cutting through the layered strata of millennia intrigues them. On these trips, they see all things through the fish's eye. Everything, exaggerated. Though, this landscape needs none. No one utters a word for miles. Words create limits. But impatience eventually overcomes them. They cannot wait to be immersed in the river. Obviously, age is irrelevant here.

Williams and I know Trinidad. It has a reputation. For fishier things than trout. But the kids know nothing of this. All they see is a small western town in a state of revived rejuvenation. New architecture mimicking the old. Old structures starved for the attention of new visitors. Despite our country's hard times, Trinidad is doing fine.

The town of Cuchara is worlds apart from Trinidad in many respects, though not far as the crow flies. The word means "spoon" in Spanish, and seems a strange

The rainbows that always hit flies make Bear Lake popular.

name for a town. The Cuchara Country Store is a fairly well-stocked general store and a good place to obtain a fishing license. A dive called The Dog Bar and Grill makes a fine slice of pizza. And the Timbers looks like a lodge and appears to make a great setting for a well-prepared meal for the fam.

Williams and I have heard good things about the River's Edge Bed and Breakfast located at 90 E. Cuchara Ave., but we passed on staying a night to check it out, as we are not willing to resort to snuggling unless three things are occurring simultaneously:

- we are in the deep wilderness (no less than ten hiking miles from another human),
- it is below 30 degrees and/or snowing,
- we are on the brink of death and there is less than a 4 percent chance of survival without combining our body heat.

(Bro Code Article # 77 states clearly and concisely that "Bros don't cuddle." However, it says nothing about snuggling.)

The waters glisten like diamonds and may not run as deep as you'd hope, but there are trout in all of them, and simple to catch.

Favorite Places to Eat

The Dog Bar & Grill (719-742-6366) is the focal point of Cuchara eateries, with a well-rounded menu that includes quesadillas, a Philly Cheese Steak, miraculous pizzas, and an Italian sausage slider that will fill up your tank. The outside deck is just plain cool.

OTHER PLACES TO EAT: **The Timbers** across the road offers a finer cuisine and adult beverages. After having been foreclosed, local investors are now in ownership, and The Timbers will be back for the 2010 summer season.

There are a couple of breakfast options in Cuchara. If you're staying at the **River's Edge B&B** or the **Dodgeton Creek Inn,** breakfast is provided for you. All these establishments are right in the retail village.

In the town of La Veta, the **Main Street Diner** on CO 12 opens at 7:00 a.m. with an excellent full breakfast and lunch menu. There's also **Sammie's,** and the **Ryus Ave Bakery.**

Cuchara—not much more than a few cabins and some friendly, rustic stores.

Favorite Places to Stay

The Cuchara Inn, Cuchara, CO, 30 Cuchara Ave. E., Suite A, 877-282-4272, 719-742-5310, http://www.cuchara.com/CchraInn.html. **River's Edge Bed & Breakfast & the Dodgeton Creek Inn,** Cuchara, CO, 40 Cuchara Ave. E., 719-742-5169, http://www.sangres.com/riversedge/. **Yellow Pine Guest Ranch,** Cuchara, CO, 15880 CO 12, 719-742-3528, http://www.yellowpine.us/.

OTHER PLACES TO STAY: **Cuchara Cabins and Condos** (for rent), Cuchara, CO, 877-722-2467, 719-742-3340, http://www.cucharacabinsand condos.com/cabins.html.

Campgrounds: Since driving from Trinidad to fish is not that economical or feasible, most of you will want to camp in one of the campgrounds closer to the town of Cuchara, as we did. There are three on FR 413 just northwest of Cuchara Pass on CO 12, and one on the West Fork of the Purgatoire at the end of FR 411. They all get very crowded, so call to see about reservations first.

Fly Shop, Guides, and Tackle Stores

The **Cuchara Country Store** will offer a very limited amount of flyfishing gear and other bait fishing accoutrement. 34 Cuchara Ave. E.,719-742-3450.

OTHER STUFF: Monument Lake Reclamation

From the *Trinidad Times Independent* (Randy Woock):

September 6, 2009

Fishing at [Monument Lake] will be prohibited and the lake will be blocked off during the "chemical reclamation" of the lake, which will continue until the project is completed and the lake restocked at an unspecified later date. However, the park's restaurant, cabins, lodge, and RV spaces are open and available for the remainder of the season. Robb said during a Thursday interview that "soft side" tents would not be allowed at the park during the near future, due to the fish kill possibly attracting bears. He also stated that the fish kill process could possibly take as long as thirty days or as few as fourteen.

Colorado Division of Wildlife (CDW) officials informed the city in November 2007 that white suckers, a type of fish alien to the lake, comprised an overwhelming [majority] of the lake's fish population to the detriment of the more-popular trout. It was theorized by the CDW that the white suckers may have been introduced into the lake by fishermen illegally using them as live bait. The CDW had been stocking the lake with extra trout as a temporary means of dealing with the alien fish.

In November 2007, CDW officials had suggested three more permanent options for dealing with the white suckers. The first involved doing nothing and allowing the white suckers to continue dominating the lake. The second option had involved introducing a natural predator of the white suckers to the lake. The third option involved dumping large amounts of chemicals into the lake, killing all the fish, and then restocking it with the desired species.

As of October 14, 2009, the chemical reclamation of the lake was complete and restocking of trout has begun. Mac revisited Monument Lake in June of 2010, and according to a resort employee, the initial addition of fish was in the range of 65,000 trout—50,000 kokanee fry, along with 15,000 rainbows and browns. Mac hooked into eight rainbows over the weekend, all but one 15-incher were in the foot-long range, having exceptional luck where the creek on the west side trickles in. Catchable rainbows are still being stocked regularly according to the online C.D.O.W. stocking report. Thanks to the Colorado Department of Wildlife, this fishery should rebound to the once stellar trout haven it was just a decade ago.

Cuchara/ Trinidad **7**

Fishing Places Solid Choices near Home Base

Bear, Blue, and North Lakes: Most flyfishers find themselves at Blue or Bear Lake, where rainbows are the stars and casting from the bank is effortless. Both are small lakes and see tons of anglers. But no one leaves without catching trout.

North Lake is our favorite still water here because it's bigger, the scenery is that of magnanimous mountains, and the fishing is fantabulous. It's the size of ten Blue Lakes, and the ratio of trout is the same. Perfect size for kayaking and float tubing. Woolly Buggers, damselfly nymphs, and beadheads around the edges draw the trout out of hiding.

Purgatoire River: The headwaters of the Purgatoire be-tween Stonewall and Weston is a fine place to put in and try your luck for rainbows. Here the water is obviously colder, and the trout are far more plentiful and responsive. Fishing near the adobe house bridge structure that crosses over the stream between Stonewall and Weston is scenic as well as productive.

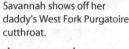

Another section is in the Bosque del Oso State Wildlife Area. To fish this section of the Purgatoire, from Trinidad go 18 miles west on CO 12. There is an entrance on the east side of Weston and another several miles farther west at the old entrance to the Golden Eagle Mine.

Savannah shows off her daddy's West Fork Purgatoire cutthroat.

Closer to Trinidad Reservoir is where the Purgatoire opens up. Beautiful water sifts through a lengthy canyon flanked by steep vertical cliffs. Step-overs, culverts, and gravely bottoms make it easy, even for kids. Rainbows and a few browns swim around these parts in search of flies. We caught both.

More tributaries support fishing, but traffic and brush make some of them pointless. Stick to the mainstays and leave with no regrets.

Cucharas River on the Yellow Pine Ranch: This ranch stretch will allow you to tangle with some nice browns on some of the best small-stream trout water in southern Colorado. Staying at the ranch is a pleasure in itself, but fishing the Cucharas here is an extra special treat. Fishing includes a regularly stocked pond ($3 per trout caught) and wild stream fishing limited to flyfish-ing, barbless hook, and catch and release.

The stream is characterized by freestone bottoms and undercut banks the trout love to hide in. Throw terrestrial patterns in warm months along the edges, or bushy attractor dries like a #12 Stimulator with a beaded Hare's Ear nymph about 18 inches behind. On any western stream, #18 Elk Hair Caddis and Irresistible Wulffs are deadly, but especially here.

The Yellow Pine Ranch is located just north of the town of Cuchara on CO 12.

"It was the secrets of heaven and earth that I desired to learn; and whether it was the outward substance of things, or the inner spirit of nature and the mysterious soul of man that occupied me, still my inquiries were directed to the metaphysical, or, in its highest sense, the physical secrets of the world." —MARY SHELLEY

Snowspur Creek. Most folks drive right past this little bubbly stream, or they park beside it as they take photos of Lizard Head Peak and never think about dropping in a line. That's fine with us, and it's good for this little creek. The less pressure the better. Why mention it? Most folks won't be sneaky or stealthy enough to fool many fish. Most folks won't believe that there are enough trout or big enough trout in a creek this small to even mess with. For those who have a modicum of skill and an interest in dry fly finesse fishing in tiny creeks, the rewards are sweet.

Case in point: we're traveling up from Durango by way of Dolores. CO 145, 54 miles from Dolores. We want to fish along the way as we head north to the Flat Tops, Grand Mesa, that area. We fished the upper Dolores for a

Complex bend in Snowspur Creek

few days, camping on the way, then drove up along Lizard Head. Mac had been back to take care of business in Amarillo for a couple of days and seemed refreshed, happier. I didn't prod because I knew that either over drinks around the campfire or through the slow daily grind, the reasons for his renewal would be revealed. This was a summer with a lot of questions for both of us, and so far the answers had come in bursts, in elegant sunsets or brilliant sunrises, along with tiny wild cutthroats and sizeable brown trout. We needed to know what was next for him after his divorce, why my novels hadn't sold, where we were in our lives. So here was another stream, another possible answer.

He had never fished Snowspur. We pulled into the parking lot and it went something like this:

"Pretty tiny, Williams."

"Lots of wild cutts, Mac. Bigger than you'd think."

"I'll get the rod."

"I'll get the camera."

And Mac proceeded to dap a #14 Elk Hair Caddis; second dap, bam, a fat 10-inch wild brown trout. In a thirty-foot stretch of twisting, skinny water, Mac caught 6 trout—2 browns, 2 brookies, 2 cutts, all between 8 and 12 inches. The cutthroats were spectac-

This brown was caught in Snowspur Creek.

ularly colored, loaded with purples and crimsons and greens. The brookies were outrageously orange, glaringly green. This dance continued for another thirty feet, then another angler appeared downstream fifty yards. And the sun came out. The fish quit taking.

"Give me five more minutes, Williams. Then you can have it."

"Getting some great shots. Take as long as you need."

There's this one freakish pool on this creek, a place you have no need to know its whereabouts. It's our pool. Now, we turned from this long narrow rocky stretch to where this amazing pool opened up. Most of the water on Snowspur is six to eighteen inches deep. This pool was three feet deep and maybe deeper under the cutbank. I didn't need to fish the creek. In a weird way, I was. That's how close fishing buddies become when they fish together all the time. When they share strategies and rods and flies and campsites and meals and bottles and smokes. And stories. Stories become legends. Myths. And this summer was fast becoming mythical. As British philosopher Allan Watts once said, "a myth is an image in terms of which we try to make sense of the world."

This was one of those pools you don't rush. We studied it while sitting on our haunches. No rises. No insect activity we could see. No feeding on the bottom. We judged angles, casting position, shadows. What a great empty-looking pool. But there just had to be a big one in there, the biggest in this stretch of stream.

"There just has to be a big one in there, Williams."

"I agree, Mac." Same thought.

The water entered the pool over a rock and dug into the dirt bend wall— that was where the big one lived. The first and only cast proved it. Mac lifted the rod tip and we stared at each other, gape-mouthed. The 3 wt. Sage might not be enough. Mutual thought. The brown rolled and dove for the undercut bank. Mac knew he had to horse him or he'd get caught in the rocks and branches. They battled, and Mac (and the 3 wt., the 6X tippet) won. The fish curled the rod so much, he was into the butt. Mac cradled the fat trout in his hands as I snapped pics, and then he released the trout. How big was the fish? Big enough, trust us. Big enough that we sat on the bank, stunned, for ten minutes, most of which was made up of our silence and smiles and head-

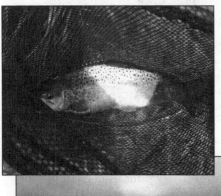

shakes. British fantasy writer Diana Wynne Jones once said that, "If you take myth and folklore, and these things that speak in symbols, they can be interpreted in so many ways that although the actual image is clear enough, the interpretation is infinitely blurred, a sort of enormous rainbow of every possible colour you could imagine."

Top: Feisty brown trout Mac caught in a battle on Snowspur
Above: Lizard Head Wilderness Area

We sat on the banks, our wading boots in the little creek, laughing and talking for another ten minutes, and we watched the sun-chariot turn from gold to sepia to ochre as it passed behind gray clouds, a symbol of some sort to the few hours we just experienced in a creek on a pass under a lizard.

Dolores is an up-and-comer, a real outdoorsy town. Everyone is lean, rides a bike, wears hiking shoes, seems to be tying down a kayak on the roof of their ten-year-old Subaru Outback. That sort of thing. Dolores is for active folks. A river runs through it. The Dolores River. If you travel south from Lizard Head Pass, you'll pick up the main stem of the Dolores River, and it follows the road into Dolores.

Amy fishes a feeder creek to the Upper Dolores.

A cool aspect of Dolores as a home base? You can fish the main stem of the Dolores in town. The city park is commonly pretty, and the river winds through it. The town is not overly blessed with coffee options (the Coffee House is pretty good) or restaurants, but that's changing every time we visit.

The Upper Dolores begins near Lizard Head Pass and rolls down, picking up little and medium streams as it courses toward the town of Dolores. Dolores is minutes from McPhee Reservoir, from the famous tail water section of the

Top: The Upper Dolores makes its way through a meadow.
Right: A brown, fresh from the Dolores River

Dolores River. We tend to see bears in the Upper Dolores, but didn't during our time there this summer.

At the end of the summer, Amy asked us this question: "You've been all over the state. If you had to pick three places you'd buy a lot and build a cabin, which home bases would you choose?" Unfair question. "I'm waiting." We huddled and discussed. Estes Park, Steamboat, Ridgway, and Dolores. "That's four." We're writers, not mathematicians.

That's how much we think of Dolores. You can feel that pioneers used to live in this small forested valley. You can almost hear the whistle of the Galloping Goose, which used to run on these rail tracks. You can imagine the Ute Indians who used to make this area their home. If you lived here, you'd surely learn to kayak the river, ride singletrack, soak in the Dunton Hot Springs, visit Anazasi ruins and museums.

Dolores is remote, uncrowded, pristine, in the middle of all kinds of things to do. It's not without some of the modern things you need, such as good cafés and restaurants, coffeeshops, groceries, but it's not a place where you're gonna find high-rise condos and faux Swiss chalet homes and all the trappings of a ski town. It's not a ski town.

I wouldn't bring the family unless: 1) they are anglers or 2) they like to be outdoorsy and ride bikes, hike, raft, kayak, that sort of thing. Dolores is

Dolores ⑧

ideal for fishing trips with fishing buddies or getaways with your significant other who likes to do outdoorsy things. You're two hours' drive from Durango, close to Mesa Verde National Park, twenty minutes from Cortez (the closest big town), not far from Telluride or Dunton. You have rivers to float, horses to ride, wilderness to explore. Dolores has just enough of an artists' community, enough hip coolness (or cool hipness) that while it tightropes being a 1962 Colorado town, it transcends it because of the amenities.

Favorite Places to Eat

Naked Moose Restaurant (970-882-7540), where breakfasts are hearty (but we've friends who like the burgers for lunch and dinner, and who rave about the ever-changing menu that includes steaks and seafood). **Old Germany Restaurant** (970-882-7549) if you like German food (we do) and Victorian homes (this place is in an old house). Go to **Dolores River Brewery** (970-882-4677) to get pretty good pizza and very good beer. **Dolores Restaurant and Café** (970-882-8016) is your typical western café with satisfying comfort food. **Dolores Bookstore and Coffeehouse** (970-882-7105) is a nice place to chill and catch some hot cuppajoe. **The Depot** (970-882-7500) is the best eating place in town, especially the shakes and burgers.

The town of Rico, at the edge of the Lizard Head Wilderness, is the heart of the Dolores drainage.

Dolores

Favorite Places to Stay

Dunton Hot Springs and Resort (970-882-4800, www.duntonhotsprings
.com) is an isolated spoil-you-rotten resort with luxury cabins and even more
luxurious amenities. How fancy is this ghost town-turned-resort? Some magazines have ranked it one of the top luxury hotels in the world. Actor Keith

The ghost town that was Dunton has been turned into a resort.

Carradine says that, "Dunton
Hot Springs is the finest ex-
ample of rustic luxury I've
ever experienced. It's a hedo-
nist's dream, combining five-
star cuisine with a mineral hot
spring in an atmosphere of
Rocky Mountain splendor."
What that means is that it's
beautiful, has amazing decor,
they take great care of you,
and you better open up the pocketbook, baby. Also check out: **Rio Grande
Southern Hotel and B&B,** 970-882-2125, 101 S. Fifth St., Dolores; **Lebanon
Schoolhouse Bed and Breakfast,** 970-882-4461, 24925 Road T, Dolores.

Fly Shops, Guides, and Tackle Stores

Dolores River Outfitters (970-882-3099); Will Blanchard, **Animas Valley
Anglers** (Durango) (970-259-0484, trout@gottrout.com); **Black Canyon
Anglers** (970-835-5050); **BootDoctors/Further Adventures** (800-592-
6883, 970-728-8954); **RIGS Fly Shop & Guide Service** (888-626-4460,
970-626-4460); **Telluride
Flyfishing & Rafting** (800-294-
9269, 970-728-4440); **Telluride
Angler/ Telluride Outside**
(800-831-6230, 970-728-3895,
www. tellurideout side.com);
**Telluride Sports Adventure
Desk** (800-828-7547, 970-728-
4477); **San Miguel Anglers**
(800-828-7547, 970-728-4477);
**Telluride Fly Fishing &
Rafting Expeditions** (800-294-
9269, http://www.tellurideflyfish
ers.com).

A prolific hatch on the West Fork of the Dolores
River

Dolores 8

This cutt was brought to hand from a Dolores-area stream.

Fishing Places Solid Choices near Home Base

The Dolores River tail water: Mark's wife Amy is an avid angler and professional writer. She had this to write about the Dolores, and we couldn't do it any better:

In talking with Will Blanchard of Animas Valley Anglers, he believes that in essence the Dolores is not a great tailwater fishery in the winter; in fact it doesn't act like any other tailwater. The river has suffered from low flows for a long time now, and Blanchard adds, "there's an awful lot of ice in a short distance and it can often be bank to bank."

In some years, the river is open and moving, the fish more plentiful and eager. The high-desert countryside below McPhee Reservoir is rugged and looks nothing like a setting for trout stream. This river was named Río de Nuestra Señora de los Dolores *(River of Our Lady of Sorrows). The Dolores in winter is for the adventurous angler, those fisher-folk who care as much about the beautiful rugged countryside, challenging fishing, and the trek as they do the quality of the angling. Even in open moving water, Dolores' trout are finicky and fickle.*

The fact that right below the dam fishers can usually find some open water gives a wee bit of hope to the wintertime wanderers. We've fished it several times when snow was on the banks and a bit of ice clung to rocks and had fish rise to our tiny offerings. If you are more into wandering, seeing beautiful sites, and getting some exercise then go ahead and tempt it—just be aware Blanchard warns, "the Dolores frustrates a lot of anglers."

Be advised that the forest service closes the access gate from December 1– April 1 for 4 miles below the dam. So, if you decide you're up to it, gather up your best winter patterns (think Baetis and midge) and maybe even your snowshoes and head out to a beautiful winter wonderland of the unexpected."

Sidenote from Mark and Mac: The Dolores looks like a freestone but acts like a petulant child. The Dolores River, with its nice riffles, horseshoe bend pools, undercut banks and deep runs, is a pleasure/nightmare to fish. The Dolores can often force anglers into technical fishing, similar to bigger tail waters. Think long thin leaders, tiny match-the-hatch flies, and careful casting with great mends. Then and only then do you have a spot of a chance of hooking up. Catching and landing is a whole 'nother story.

Solitary angling on the Upper Dolores

Upper Dolores River (a.k.a. Main Fork or East Fork Dolores): Amy's favorite drainage to fish in southwestern Colorado and with good reason, too. The upper main stem of the Dolores holds mostly rainbow, with some brown trout, and has good access, with CO 145 running right beside it. Anglers will find good fishing above Rico, from the headwaters at Lizard Head Pass down to the town of Dolores.

Between Lizard Head and the town of Dolores, the watershed is fed by a dozen feeder streams descending from alpine basins. Willing fish and magnificent scenery make the Dolores a Colorado trout-fishing classic. A great way to enjoy the Dolores is to fish right in town and upstream of town along the road.

Lizard Head Creek: This little meadow stream flows into Snow Spur Creek in the Dolores drainage. Travel south on CO 145 from Trout Lake.

Ground Hog Reservoir: A sleeper lake, and a big one (668 acres), stocked with trout. Ground Hog Reservoir lies 32 miles north of Dolores on FR 526 to a rough gravel road, FR 533.

McPhee Reservoir: This big watering hole located in a river canyon is the second largest body of water in Colorado. McPhee Reservoir is not the best fly fishing locale, but works as a nice home base from which to camp, boat the lake, and then fish the Dolores. The water stays cold all year long, very cold. McPhee Reservoir is best fished by boat because of its location in a canyon with steep-walled banks. The rainbow trout of McPhee average about 12 to

Above: Here the Dolores is wide and flat.
Right: A sign by the West Fork

WEST FORK RD NO 648
WEST FORK CAMPGROUND   1.5
WEST FORK TRAILHEAD NO 561 3

14 inches, some reaching 17 to 19 inches. The lake holds both trout and kokanee salmon. McPhee sees heavy stocking of catchable rainbow trout. Don't be surprised to occasionally catch a smallmouth bass.

West Fork Dolores: One of our favorite streams in the state. Except for a bit of angling pressure around the campground, there's never that many folks on the stream. You won't want to take the rugged road from Lizard Head Pass unless you have a high-clearance 4WD vehicle because it'll slow you down way too much. If you come this way, make sure to stop by Dunton and get some pics—it's a private resort and spa/springs now, but way-back-when Butch Cassidy used Dunton as a hideout. Aspens and cottonwoods share your views, the aspens hanging back with the pines covering the mountainsides while the cottonwoods give away the course of the river.

Fishing West Fork in the fall, with the brilliance of the aspens and cottonwoods, feels like you are in a surreal lighting experiment wherein the forest instead of the sun provides illumination. Catching fat trout is a bonus. You could make West Fork your home base by camping at one of three campgrounds along the stream. From Dolores, you drive north on CO 145, and after a few miles you'll see the turnoff where the West Fork comes into the main upper stem. FR 535 parallels the West Fork (more or less) for 30 miles and offers excellent access. This gem is a narrow feeder stream with rainbow, brown, brook, and the occasional cutthroat trout. Great dry fly stream. There are four campgrounds along West Fork of the Dolores River. All four campgrounds are on the river and are seldom full. Travel northeast on CO 145 from Dolores about 13 miles then turn north onto FR 535 (West Fork Road). Watch for clearly marked private land/water.

For the Adventurer

Fish Creek: Remote (but easy to access) freestone stream that feeds the Upper Dolores. Perfect for dry fly and small stream enthusiasts. Located in the Fish Creek State Wildlife Area and national forest, you have a decent trail that follows the stream for miles and miles. The creek isn't wide, just six to ten feet, but it is clear and cold and flows through both tight forest and open meadows. Near the trailhead, you'll find a bridge and some instream rehab, and in that big wide flat pool you'll always find fish rising. These improvements include weirs, arranged rocks, etc. Even with the rehab work, the stream is wild, the forest dark and green. You're in the middle of nowhere.

Fish Creek has long, wide pools in places; rocky choppy pocket water throughout. Fish hold in every available lie. They slash at any attractor dry, take most every beadhead nymph. You can work a twenty-foot stretch for a long time and still have fish hit your flies.

A pool on Fish Creek

You mostly catch rainbows, but also some browns. Nothing of size (but we have caught some relatively nice browns here), but it's a super day trip from Dolores. Drive north on CO 145, then you can cut off and go along the West Fork Road or on up CO 145 above Rico. Either way, you'll look for FR 726 (hard to see the sign). Turn on this road, go through private land, and you'll end up at a parking area.

Bear Creek: One of the best small streams in the drainage, Bear Creek enters the Upper Dolores River east of Stoner. Bear Creek averages about ten to fifteen feet wide and offers over 16 miles of dry fly fishing. The creek has abundant populations of rainbow, cutthroat, and brown trout (as well as big pools and waterfalls). The trout are small, 6 to 11 inches, but in the pools and beaver ponds and deeper runs you will occasionally be surprised with a trout in the mid-teens. Access to Bear Creek is from CO 145 and TR 607. You have to hike the trail to reach the river, but locating said trail isn't always easy and the first stretch of trail is private. The trail parallels the stream to its headwaters. You can also access Bear Creek by a steep trail from Mancos.

Taylor Creek: An average but pretty trout stream east of Stoner on CO 145. Taylor Creek holds rainbow, cutthroat, and brook trout and can be accessed by FR 545 for 5 to 6 miles upstream from the highway.

La Plata River: More creek than river, La Plata is a decent day trip in the spring. Fish above Mayday.

Mancos Creek: Concentrate on West Fork Mancos River for consistency, though the Middle Fork can surprise at times. Upstream from the town of Mancos.

Stoner Creek: Do it the right way. Take Stoner Mesa Trail, a challenging 17.5-mile, one-way hike to Twin Springs and Stoner Creek. Wild country with a small creek and lots of wild trout. Off of West Fork Road to Emerson Campground.

Barlow Creek: Good cutthroat and brook trout stream flowing into the Upper Dolores. You will find Barlow northeast of Rico, off CO 145 where it enters from the east. Barlow Creek can be reached on FR 578 south from CO 145, preferably by 4WD vehicles.

OTHER FISHERIES WORTH INVESTIGATING: Snow Spur Creek, Narraguinnep Reservoir, Priest Gulch Creek.

Blue Ribbon Fisheries not far from Dolores

Animas River
San Miguel River
Uncompahgre River

9 Durango

In the depth of winter,
I finally learned that within me there lay an invincible summer.
—ALBERT CAMUS

I have written about Durango more than any other place over the last twenty years. I have a cabin near Durango, in Bayfield, I love the area so much. This is one cool mountain town. The climate is ideal, there are fly shops and sporting goods stores on every corner, there are panoramic views, and all the residents are outdoors-minded. This is where high desert meets the mountains, where cowboys meet skateboarders. A western boomtown that has retained its blue-collar attitude. Within a couple of hours' drive, anglers can reach some of the top trout waters in the nation, including the Animas, San Juan (the upper and that sorta famous section in New Mexico), Piedra, Pine, Florida, and Dolores Rivers, Vallecito, Lemon, and McPhee Reservoirs, all sorts of high-country lakes and creeks. From any direction, you can find quality fisheries of all types.

We use Durango as a home base for most of our southwest adventures partly because we make forays into Arizona and Utah, and as such Durango is an ideal starting point, and partly because, like I said, I have a cabin there.

Walking down Main Street is just plain cool. The outdoors shops, clothing stores, bookstores, art galleries, cafés and restaurants and coffeehouses, the

Getting the Aliner ready at the cabin in Durango

Above: Hermosa Creek
Right: Amy casts into Hermosa Creek.

Victorian-style historic hotels Strater and General Palmer, the railroad depot. It's a must do. Fresh every time. Catch a cappuccino at one of our two fave coffeehouses and watch the people stroll down the sidewalk.

We have fished together for the last eight years. We fish the waters around Durango more than any other. The first time Mac fished Lime Creek, I bet him that if he'd use long casts and small flies, he'd catch 100 brook trout in the day. He kept missing trout and not landing many until he listened. We left after two more hours, during which Mac listened, cast long and carefully, and reached 50. Yes, we counted. We have a love/hate relationship with Cascade Creek, where we never come away fishless or without bruises from falling and slipping down. Thirty minutes north of Durango, East Fork Hermosa and Hermosa end up being our favorite day and overnight getaways without fail.

So to Hermosa Creek is where we head.

We set up camp at a primitive campsite on a knoll on the opposite side of the valley from the corral. You'll see the campsites to your left as you drive along the valley road and before you cross the creek and rumble into the trailhead parking lot.

A tiny creek flows right beside our site, plunging down the side of the mountain into East Fork Hermosa Creek. We wanted to keep our ice as long as we could, so we took our beer and cokes and set up a rock ring in the creek and deposited our drinks into the natural fridge. We set up a tripod of logs to hang our lantern and wet wading socks. We built a fire pit (one was there, but it wasn't up to Mac standards). For a week, it was our campsite, and we were proprietary about it. At that time, we didn't fix up camp vittles as well as we do now. We went the sandwich and soup mode back then. And we were drinking scotch back in those days, which, as you know if you drink scotch, creates hazy fuzzy warm dreamy episodes, especially when sitting around a big fire in the middle of a pine forest. But camping out for a week, overlooking a creek, fishing ten to twelve hours a day, settling into a rhythm, well, there's just something special about it.

Except for my big stupid tent. I don't know why I ever bought this beast. The tent is designed to sleep eight, but in reality it would sleep a battalion. You also need a battalion to erect the big stupid tent. The two of us were able to clumsily put up the big stupid tent in one frustrating hour. Not only is it so large and spacious that two people can't heat it at night but it's saggy and doesn't hold out rain well. I threw it away after that trip.

Mark and Yvonne Murphy (family friend and rooky flyfisher) fish the East Fork of Hermosa Creek.

We caught 1,000 trout that week. No, we didn't count, but it sure seemed like it. That's how good the fishing is in East Hermosa Creek. We fished East Fork near the corral, in the beaver ponds, in the small canyon, up at the meandering headwaters. There's this one stretch in the small canyon below the beaver ponds and campsites where the walls close in and the pools deepen. The greenery is different, almost tropical, spooky in fact, with fern-like plants and softy fuzzy moss and a canopy of limbs hanging over the water. We had always chosen to stop before we entered this shadowy den, but this time we moved up into the darkness.

Mac caught a small colorful cutthroat in a narrow pool that had a v-shaped groove cut into the riverbed. We watched as he released the fish and it swam back to the cutout, and we saw a dozen or more cutts holding in that relief. We caught half of them and waded up through bramble and fallen logs, finding oases and seemingly different ecosystems

We snagged this fat rainbow in a Durango-area stream.

in each compartment of growth. A definite *Heart of Darkness* feel to our movement up the river because each pool got more difficult to access, the canopy drew tighter around the pool, and the fish grew bigger and meaner. We were under a spell because the fishing was becoming difficult, hanging up flies inevitable. We had both forgotten flashlights and night was coming.

Afraid of meeting Kurtz, we fished one last pool, an amazingly large one that had rivulets and outlets and channels flowing in and out of it like arteries. I sightcast to a 12-inch cutt who obviously owned his lie, perhaps the entire pool, and he took the fly with confidence and, when hooked, fought with a ferocious disdain. He dived under a submerged bush and broke off before I could lift his head. We returned to camp, wet, muddy, smelling of damp earth, happy to be home.

In Hermosa Creek proper, a slightly different story. We had to work for every fish. We'd slip and slide and fall because the riverbed is uneven, rounded, oiled-up rocks. We enjoyed a week of fishing. Some days we'd hike way into Hermosa, hike until we were irritated we'd wasted so much fishing time. Sometimes we'd start fishing at the boundary and fish up until we were irritated that we'd fished up so far and that we were going to have to hike back in the ink-black night. You hear things in the dark.

> *He walked out in the gray light and stood and he saw*
> *for a brief moment the absolute truth of the world.*
> —CORMAC MCCARTHY (*The Road*)

So after seven days of amazing fishing, days of "I lost count," days of "did you see the colors on that cutt?" we fired up the small grill and cooked hamburgers for our last evening. Deer had gotten so used to us, they'd come down from the mountain and feed right on the edge of our camp before sashaying down the river below us. At night, the chilling eerie group barking of coyotes (we thought wolves, I'll admit, so boisterous and loud and different were the pro-

Yvonne gives her brook a kiss.

longed noises) sitting on the mesa behind us reminded us we were in the wild.

We'd done a lot of talking all week, beyond the usual "how 'bout them Cowboys" and "would you do this or that female celebrity." We had touched on Bill Bryson's *Short History of Nearly Everything*, imagined there's no heaven, figured out how to quit our jobs and write full time, and twice solved the problems of the world as the campfire flickered out—only to forget our solutions by morning.

The hamburgers were sizzling, the drinks were poured, the fire lit, and we were relaxing in our camp chairs, looking out at East Fork Hermosa, the gray silence of the evening settling over the valley. We both turned and we both turned back to each other when we saw it. To our right was one of those crazy once-in-a-lifetime sunsets similar to those we see in Amarillo, but when it's in the mountains it takes on a more fleeting, ethereal feel. The colors, gunmetal meets sanguine, a twisted cacophony of silver and red. We take photos (that do no justice) and then sit and watch the changing sky. We marvel at it like children looking through a kaleidoscope.

As if that's not enough, an elk herd is making its way from the opposite mountain to the little creek, feeding, drinking. Had we not been watching the stream, these shadows would have noiselessly slipped down the mountain, crossed the stream, and moved into the darkness of the forest. Fishing is not always about fishing, guys.

Mac and I have planned to camp in the same spot this next June. A week. In the Aliner, not the big stupid tent. Enjoying the days fishing and trying to see things in the dark.

Favorite Places to Eat

Durango, like Glenwood Springs and Telluride, has a tremendous ratio of size of town to great restaurants. The best Mexican food in town is found at **Gazpacho's** (970-259-9494), but if you have the time and the moolah to treat your wife and family to a special meal, there are none better in the West than the woodfire spit and grilled meats of **Seasons** (970-382-9790). A framed picture of my book, *So Many Fish*, is up on the wall next to Willie Nelon's mug at **Serious Texas BBQ** (970-247-2240) on the east side of town. Their pulled pork sandwiches are juicy and flavorful, better than any in Texas, in fact. Love that cherry chipotle sauce. Check out **Durango Diner, Carvers, and Old Tymers. Kennebec Café** in Hesperus is delightful. Try a local root beer from **Zuberfizz** (970-259-9600). Coffee is cool in Durango. Coffeehouses to try include **Durango Coffee Company** and **Steaming Bean,** both on Main Street. Microbreweries? Try cold ones from **Carvers** (970-259-2545), **Steamworks** (970-259-9200), **Durango Brewing Company** (970-247-3396), and **Ska Brewing** (970-247-5792). Carvers has a great covered patio and Steamworks is raucous, so your pick.

Main Street in Durango

Favorite Places to Stay

If you have been a bad boy (tsk tsk), make it up to your significant other by checking into the Victorian splendor of the **Strater Hotel** in downtown Durango (800-247-4431, www.strater.com). Amy and I love the Strater and its western-meets-European charm. If you have been a good boy (bully for you), you could get by with checking into the **Iron Horse Inn** (888-354-3143). **Blue Lake Ranch** is the coolest casita/lodge in the Southwest, and we highly recommend it (and the views and its gardens and food). Hesperus, CO, 970-385-4537, http://www.bluelakeranch.com/. You'll find cabins on the Florida River, around Vallecito and Lemon Reservoirs.

Fishing Places Solid Choices near Home Base

IN TOWN Junction Creek: Great early season, beat-runoff choice. Watch for joggers and hikers and kids and dogs. There are also trout, brook, and rainbow. Be prepared to have the kids or dogs jump in your pool.

The Animas River on the reservation

Animas River (Gold Medal Waters): A classic western stream. A must-fish. Great winter fishery. Fishable year round.

When the Spanish explorers came here, they named this boisterous river *Rio de las Animas Perdidas,* translated to mean "River of the Lost Souls." This wild freestone flows through awe-inspiring southwestern scenery, through wide valleys and steep canyons, past rugged mountains, continuing south from its headwaters on into New Mexico, one of the last free-flowing rivers in the West.

These athletic trout hide behind large boulders, camouflage on the cobbled river bottom, dart to take offerings from behind log jams. You can fish (and catch fish) all through town—lots of public access. Don't just fish at Purple Cliffs. Stroll along the Riverwalk and drop in at likely lies all along the way so you can hit some hardly fished water.

NORTH OF DURANGO Lime Creek: Fun mountain stream, perfect for beginning anglers, nirvana for flyfishers. Full of brook trout that rise willingly to dries, Lime is one of the finest small streams in the San Juans, amazingly productive for all the pressure it receives. North of Durango Mountain Resort on US 550.

Cascade Creek: You won't find many streams as slippery as this one. The rocks are round and slick, the water clear, fast, and cold. Great dry fly water located just north of Durango Mountain Resort.

Hermosa Creek: This creek is drop-dead gorgeous. The water gurgles and percolates around grey-white rocks, dumps and drops into plunge pools, slashes

Above: Fishing Hermosa Creek
Right: This brown was brought to hand on the Animas River.

undercut banks, wiggles and riffles, dances and dips. Dry fly nirvana. The trout are bigger than they ought to be in a stream this size. Hike-in wilderness stream ideal for teaching beginning flyfishers or for vets who want to catch strong wild trout and fish dry flies in a forested canyon creek. Access near the town of Hermosa or hike in from Hermosa Creek Trailhead behind Durango Mountain Resort.

East Fork Hermosa Creek: Little creek small enough in places to hop across, located on the backside of Durango Mountain Resort. This is great fly-fishing water, 2.5 miles long, meadow and canyon stretches, packed with small, feisty, colorful Colorado cutthroats high, and brooks and rainbows low. The creek can be accessed from US 550 north from Durango to Hermosa. Take FR 578 (Hermosa Park Road) west to Sig Creek Campground. The forest road parallels the little creek to the trailhead at the end of the road.

Animas—Train Trip: Experience wilderness angling unlike anywhere else in the Southwest by riding the steam-powered Durango-Silverton Narrow Gauge Railroad and getting dropped off in the middle of some of the wildest

Durango 9

The Durango–Silverton Narrow Gauge Railroad

country anywhere. You'll fish in deep green eerily clear waters, pools and pockets and chutes, and you'll angle for unseasoned trout that willingly take flies (especially dropper rigs). Rainbow, cutthroat, brook, and brown trout. This is a unique trip, and don't overlook the feeder creeks in this isolated wooded canyon river. You can do this on your own, but I recommend hiring a guide. You can fish until the afternoon Silverton train comes back, or spend the night (or two) and the train will pick you up.

EAST OF DURANGO Vallecito Reservoir: If you like to fish for pike, this is your destination. The lake has excellent populations of pike, brown trout, and kokanee salmon. Steep forested banks, stunning scenery, plenty of campsites and picnic places. Located 25 minutes east of Durango. Take CR 501 north from Bayfield.

Vallecito Creek: Great choice for spin or flyfishers for a half- or full day of angling for trout. Vallecito is within a 25-minute drive from Durango and provides stunningly clear water with lots of choppy, splashy runs and riffles, big smooth rocks, pocket water, and deep pools. If you have time, take a horseback or overnight backpacking trip up the river into the Weminuche Wilderness.

Los Pinos River: A.k.a. the Pine River. The lower stretches are private. In the upper reaches above Vallecito Reservoir, the river is public and at times productive, but you'll have to hike a good ways to get to open water. The deeper you hike upstream into the backcountry, the better the angling.

Lemon Reservoir: Easy to reach, lightly fished, Lemon Reservoir is best for those who want to putt around in a boat, lounge on the banks, or fish for cruising trout in the shallows. We're not talking great fishing here but the lake is pretty and close to town. East of Durango on CR 240 then CR 243.

Florida River: You fish the upper Florida River because you want to get away from it all and fish with dries and enjoy the rugged cliffs, pristine freestone water, and thick forests of blue spruce, aspen, and Douglas fir. If you want to fit in, pronounce the river's name correctly, Flo-ree-dah. From Durango, travel east on Florida Road (CR 240) for about 12 miles, then turn north on CR 243. You will shortly run into Lemon Reservoir and keep right on going to the north side of Lemon. Campgrounds on the west side of the river. A footpath follows the river on both sides for a good ways of the river upstream.

SOUTH OF TOWN Southern Ute Reservation waters. Overlooked opportunities to fish in solitude and catch some nice trout. Below Durango, the river flow slows, and it meanders through open meadows, coursing through reservation land. Anglers need to have a reservation fishing permit to fish this section. The fishing pressure is diminished, but the fishing for big brownies, if you can get flies deep to them or in the undercut banks, can be phenomenal.

Yvonne seems to think the water in the Florida River is cold.

Durango 9

Little Molas Lake—fishing in high-country lakes can be picturesque.

WEST OF DURANGO   Dolores River (tailwater, west of Durango, north of Cortez)

Upper Dolores River: (west of Durango, north of Dolores)

West Fork Dolores River

La Plata River: Nothing special, but it's a decent option in spring and early summer when other rivers are in runoff. West of Durango.

Mancos River: If you have time to reach the beaver pond sections of this river (mostly on the Middle Fork), you're in for a treat. Overall, the beauty of your surroundings exceeds the quality of the fishing, but Mancos is a river you choose for solitude or when the other streams are high and roily. The higher up you go on the forks, the better the fishing. West of Durango.

Blue Ribbon Fisheries not far from Durango

San Juan River, Aztec, New Mexico (45 minutes tops)

Piedra River (45 minutes east on US 160)

Chama River, Chama, New Mexico (1.5 hours)

San Juan River, Pagosa Springs (1 hour)

Rio Grande, South Fork (2.5 hours)

10 Eagle

Chance is always powerful.
Let your hook be always cast;
in the pool where you least expect it,
there will be a fish.
— *OVID*

Eagle is not our favorite home base, but it might be less about place and more about experience. Twice.

Sure, the scenery is spectacular. The fishing is great. Eagle has all you need in a home base. Good choices for lodging and eating. Proximity to numerous quality streams and lakes. So what is it we don't like?

Let me explain:

Mac borrowed my waders. Bad move.

I didn't know Mac well at that time, maybe a few weeks, and he was heading to a lake in the Eagle area to fish. He complained that his waders were

Eagle River near Eagle

leaking, so I offered to help him out. I had several pairs of waders, so it was no big deal. But what I did was not especially nice. I loaned him a pair of waders that I knew had leaks, one that had a camouflaged hole in fact, only detectable once you put them on. Dastardly right? But that's the way fishing buddies get each other some times.

Mac got to the lake, aired up his float tube and surveyed the cold gray skies. June by calendar but winter by Nature's decree. He pulled on the waders—a good snug fit, warm against the chilly wind whipping across the water. The flippers he brought—I no longer had flippers—were his then-wife's swimming flippers, ones he was sure would fit his feet. He was wrong. The flippers fit him (adjustably) in bare feet back home at the pool, but not with 5 mm. neoprene waders.

He got out his knife and duck tape and tried to Swiss Army those flippers to the thick neoprened feet. He finagled and sliced and taped, and before long he had rigged up the flippers to his feet, a comical angling penguin. Mac waddled to the water, dragging along the float tube and flyrod, and realized the

Matching the hatch on the Eagle River

oncoming ignominy and improbability of putting his butt into the float tube without falling on his ass.

He fell. Of course he fell. He was wearing absurdly small swimming flippers taped clumsily to thick waders while trying to back into the lake, into the float tube while holding a 9-foot rod. That's ridiculous. And ridiculously funny. More so because he is soaking wet in cold water and he hasn't even discovered the borrowed waders have pinholes and a cow-tongue flap.

Wait. There's more. He was in the float tube, embarrassed that the anglers on the bank had watched him walk, wear flippers (did I mention they were glow-in-the-dark-yellow?), and flop into the lake. Then the wind shifted and he was paddling into the wind, going nowhere fast.

When he was halfway across the lake, having spent all his energy, he realized that the coldness he felt in his legs was abnormal for 5 mm. neoprene waders. He flippered to the closest shore, where the day-glo flippers detached. They dangled from the leaking waders as he emerged onto the shore like a sea creature. Then and only then did he see the cow-tongue flap, see tiny water spouts coming from the little pinholes. He tossed the flippers in a nearby bush, yanked off the waders. Soaking wet, freezing cold, he slung the float tube over his shoulder and trudged back around the lake to his car and drove off.

I know all these details even though I wasn't there. Mac has told this story countless times, cursing me at the end. But you know what? Without the leaking waders, the story wouldn't be nearly as fun. You know, that story kinda makes Eagle one of my favorites, just not his.

BTW: When Mac read this as we were putting the book together, he wrote this back to me: "Williams, why don't you mention that there was a one-armed guy with a captain hook prosthetic rowing up and down the bank slaying the shit out of the trout! I couldn't catch jack."

The second reason:

It was near Eagle at a campground where Mac and I had our only argument all summer. Think about it. Fifty-five days in close quarters with the same person. Together 24 hours a day, 7 days a week. No bathroom or bedroom or study or living room to run off to. No television. We are fishing and cooking and hiking together all day long, planning and eating at night.

Look, I know close friends get into tiffs and passionate debates from time to time, but Mac and I had been lucky over eight years. Not once had we ever been in any kind of real argument. That's difficult for me with complete strangers, I'm so ornery. We usually agreed on most things, and when we didn't, we joked through the issue and moved on.

Cold night, clear with a big white round moon. We spent the morning traipsing around the area, fishing Lake Creek, Brush Creek, Gypsum Ponds. We drank early when we got back because it was raining, and then it cleared off and after dinner we drank some more. Whiskey and coke. Cigars. Too much.

It began like all evening campfire conversations. Recap the day's fishing. *You sure caught lots of brookies on that stupid Elk Hair of yours that has no damned hackle left. Would've liked to have seen that cuttbow in hand. Why is private water the best looking water?*

Remember that Mac was single and in the market again, and his stock was apparently doing well. I've been married twenty-one years, faithfully and happily, so it was vicariously fun for me to hear about what it's like in the dating world nowadays. I wouldn't want to go through it, to be sure. Mac had one woman he was seeing regularly (or more regularly than others), an out-of-town girl, and they decided to split up.

We got into a discussion about marriage. We both had our first marriages not work out. I figured the dissolutions occurred because of incompatibility. He assumed it was because of other reasons, and one of them was that the civil process, the act of government sanctioning a marriage, the public profession and ceremony of love, was a major factor in his unhappiness, and in mine, too. I disagreed. With fervor.

I don't know why I went there. I could sense that I ought to back off. We poured stronger drinks. Our voices became louder. He was drunk from Early Times, I was drunk from Early Times. Frosty became testy. I had a happy marriage, so it was easy for me to speak favorably toward the institution. He was happy where he was, and one rule we never violated, I violated. I made a judgment.

There was a moment, in the middle of the heat of the debate, a critical mass, where things went silent. The only sound was the prickly crackling heat of the roaring fire. If we both keep quiet, one of us will make a joke and we'll both laugh and the situation will be diffused. One of us could say, "you're a bastard. Fix us another drink." Or, "I caught more fish than you today, wussy." But we didn't say those things. We did say something, other things, temperature-raising things, and for another hour the tempest continued until it was too cold for the fire to warm us and we bitchily put up for the night.

It's funny how these things work. Any other friends who got this vociferous, made things this awkward, would have not

called for a week or two. We didn't have that luxury. We had weeks and months in front of us where we would be together 24/7. We didn't talk at all that next morning, but as we're in the Jeep, me driving, going up Brush Creek, Mac grins and predicts, "Bet I catch more fish than you today."

"Bet."

We found a pullout next to a nice pool and got out and fished upriver all day long. He did catch more trout than I did that day. Don't tell him, but I let him. You believe that, don't you?

Top: We took this heavy-bodied rainbow from the Eagle River.
Above: The Eagle River around Edwards

Favorite Places to Eat

A good place
to eat in Eagle

Eagle Diner (970-328-1919). Nothing fancy, good prices, comfort food. **Moes BBQ** (970-337-2277) seems a little chain-y, but we haven't eaten there yet, so what do we know.

Favorite Places to Stay

AmericInn Lodge & Suites (800-634-3444, http://www.americinn.com/hotels/CO/Eagle); **Hitching Post Bed and Breakfast** (http://www.hitchingpostbnb.com/).

Fly Shops, Guides, and Tackle Stores

Fly Fishing Outfitters (970-845-8090, http://www.flyfishingoutfitters.net/); **Gore Creek Fly Fisherman** (970-476-3296); **Mountain Angler** (970-453-4665, http://www.mountainangler.com/home/index.php); **Taylor Creek Fly Shop** (970-927-4374, www.taylorcreek.com): **Crystal Fly Shop** (970-963-5741, www.crystalflyshop.com); **Minturn Anglers** (970-827-9500, www.minturnanglers.com).

Fishing Places Solid Choices near Home Base

Eagle River (Gold Medal Waters): Gore Creek joins the Eagle River, and then this underrated year-round Gold Medal river flows west until its appointment with the Colorado River near Dotsero. The Eagle is a freestone river, medium-sized, flowing for 70 miles, often overlooked by anglers choosing to fish nearby Colorado, Roaring Fork, and Frying Pan. The Eagle has a lot of private water, so keep your eyes peeled, but there is ample public access along its flow. You talk about slippery wading, finicky fish, dangerous floating, lots of beautiful water. That's the Eagle. Oh yeah, did I mention big, athletic trout?

Long, light leaders are necessary most of the time

The Eagle River

It's not exactly wilderness fishing, but the Eagle is profound.

with these picky fish. Brown and rainbow trout (some brook and cutthroat trout in the upper section, but mostly little brown trout) are your targets, and you might even see some loaf-of-bread-sized trout feeding, but unless you have a great cast, drag-free presentation, and the right fly, it's not going to happen.

You might see some automobiles and a few bridges, so it is not always a total wilderness angling experience, but the river is sentineled by mountains and trees, which light up in electric colors in autumn. Hire an outfitter for a float trip—the Eagle is too tricky unless you know it well. From Denver, travel west on I-70 to US 24/US 6, which runs beside the river. Lots of campgrounds along the river.

Brush Creek: Our kind of angling. Small stream, tight casting, wild trout, no other fishermen. Mac got stuck to his knees in a beaver pond. (I'll grant you that since he's so short that's not much punkin. But watching him struggle as though in quicksand was delightfully delicious.) It looks like Brush Creek might be the next in a long line of streams that were once great and then got developed. Great.

Sylvan Lake: State park up West Brush Creek with 42-acre lake. Good weekend getaway or day trip.

For the Adventurer

Gypsum Creek: The ponds outweigh the stream in terms of quality. The upper Gypsum is fun for small brookies. Along the headwaters, consider hiking to Sourdough, Red, Lost, and Ragged Lakes.

Homestake Creek and Lake: Wilderness stream with lots of eager trout and few anglers. See the Vail chapter for more information.

Lizard Lake: East of Marble on FR 314. (It becomes the crappiest road in Colorado at some point, but they call it Crystal River Jeep Trail. Had we been wanting to four wheel for fun instead of getting to the lake, it might have been fun.) Lizard Lake has tons of brook trout, wind, and pretty scenery.

Yule Creek: Another Marble-area fishery, another tough 4WD road, Yule has fun dry fly fishing for cutthroats and headwaters lakes.

OTHER FISHERIES WORTH INVESTIGATING: North Fork Crystal River, Geneva Lake, and Camp Hale Pond.

Blue Ribbon Fisheries not far from Eagle
Frying Pan
Roaring Fork
Crystal River

Best Packable Foods for the River
- Beef jerky
- GU Energy Gel
- Payday Candy Bars
- Power bars/cereal bars
- Dried fruits
- Sunflower seeds
- Nuts
- Granola
- GORP
- Tuna in a pouch

Grizzly Creek dumps into the Colorado River.

11 Estes Park

This town is comfortable, *like grampy's argyle cardigan from the '40s* I note upon driving through Estes Park. *Kitschy…in that nostalgic slash vintage sort of way.* Stringing the length of Fall River are various village-like shops, eateries, pubs. It's alive, and cute as a button.

Even though there are several local coffeehouses we could have chosen (Coffee on the Rocks sits on Estes Lake, where elk visit regularly, and Kind Coffee has two locations in town for caffeine bingers like us), we find the ubiquitous Starbucks and down our respective Americanos while overlooking the clear riffles of Fall River. The weather whispered *perfection* in our ears. Trout whimple in the pockets of our minds. Fishing is in our blood, like trout are in the river. It's times like this when I reflect upon the readings of my younger days when I was far more impressionable.

Carl Jung said, "In all chaos there is a cosmos, in all disorder a secret order." At no time in my life have I ever found a more precise meaning for those simple phrases than here. Yes, Estes Park is quite possibly the perfect place for laidback outdoorsy types, though especially for anglers fishing the east side of Rocky Mountain National Park (since the west side is more easily fished when home basing out of Grand Lake). The historic Estes Park village is cozily nestled up against that other park…the *Rocky Mountain National* one. So it's easy to fall in love with.

John Gierach familiarized literate fly anglers with magnanimous rivers near Estes Park, like the Big Thompson and St. Vrain. But many more waters circumvent E.P., and they deserve anglers' full attention.

For info on backpacking into the backcountry for rare Greenback cutthroat trout, we head into RMNP Ranger Station. One gal spins yarn about the flood in 1982. "'Round here, it's called The Tale of Three Steves," she smirks. We lean in. "Story goes, a man named Steve was camping in the backcountry the morning of the catastrophe. The former dam gave way. A wall of water swept through the canyon and the man was swept away in his sleep. Another man named Steve was also in the area. He heard what resembled a plane crash, recognized the dam had burst, and phoned the city of Estes Park to warn of disaster. Yet a third man named Steve, who worked at Estes Lake, had the presence of mind to release water from Estes Lake dam, allowing more room for the floodwaters, thus saving the town."

The only mountain village in the Rockies we've visited that seemingly has more candy stores than Estes Park is West Yellowstone. Not many other mountain villages or valleys in the Rockies are as beautiful, I know that. Longs Peak stands watch over the bustling hamlet. Elkhorn Avenue is the main drag, loaded with the aforementioned candy stores, sporting goods, cafes, souvenirs, art, clothing, punctuated by an amazing number of pedestrians, who, if you stop to listen to them, come from all over the world.

There's a Swiss Chalet theme that wears thin pretty quickly, but after a day you quit noticing. There's too much else to do here. Estes Park is number one on our list of home bases from which to fish, and the main reason, other than you can reach an amazing number of fishing spots, is that there is so much else to do other than fish. That, and a river runs through it.

Estes Park has Alps-style condos, golf courses, modest cabins, luxury lodges—the full gamut. The town has the Fall River, which flows into the Big Thompson River, with a riverwalk that winds right past patios and homes and businesses. Lake Estes is on the east side of town. The village is close to major metro areas like Boulder and Denver and Fort Collins. The town has a dry climate. Nice sunny summer days, cool by comparison to lower elevations. You'd think Estes Park would be draped in snow all winter, but it's not. Amy calls it romantic, almost European faux-chalet chic. While in Estes Park, go see the Stanley Hotel, the one the Stanley Steamer founder built, the one that was in the movie *The Shining.*

Estes Park is a great home base to combine downhill biking or mountain biking or horseback riding or bird watching or river rafting. Most anglers will enter the park, but that big expanse is not your only fishing option. You can fish right in town. The Big Thompson below Lake Estes is minutes away (closer if you stay right there). The

Top: Fishing in Estes Park is possible on the Fall River in certain parts of town. Above: Greenback cutthroat are Estes Park's pride and joy.

first 8 miles are catch and release only. Great guides and shops here, and here you really need them if you're new to the area or the sport. This is a high mountain valley village. More shops than should be allowed in a town like this—300 or more. A resort town that has maintained a small-town feel. Amenities galore.

Estes Park is ideal for families; also great for fishing buddy trips, romantic getaways, long cabin stays, on-the-lake vacations, shop and fish weekends, adventure in the backcountry, etc. It's our perfect home base, the one that stands out above all others.

Favorite Places to Eat

We found ourselves eating breakfast at **Ed's Cantina and Grille** at 390 E. Elkhorn Ave. "The Scramble," with fried potatoes, eggs, and sausage is no less than delectable. Sabroso! Ed's restaurant décor is inviting and warm. It's 10:00 a.m., mind you, and patrons are having beers already. We are still clearing the sleep from our eyes. "Laid back, huh," Williams remarks with a grin. I agree.

Ed's Cantina is well worth the stop for breakfast or beers.

The Egg and I at 393 Elkhorn Ave. is extremely popular for breakfast and brunch. This dig tends to be most visitors' favorite eatery for breakfast. It was so crowded, we went across the street to Ed's. Either will knock your socks off. **The Rock Inn Mountain Tavern** at 1675 CO 66 not only doles out great steaks and delicious appetizers, but happy hour here is a blast and the live jams in the evenings keep the atmosphere pumped.

OTHER PLACES TO EAT: Poppy's Pizza right on the Big Thompson River in Barlow Plaza. **Estes Park Pie Company** is perfect for grabbing a chunk of pastry or pie after a meal or to accompany

The Trailblazer and Huevos Scramble at Ed's Cantina.

your cup of Starbuck's coffee while you sit and watch the rippling flow of the Fall River. Both are on Elkhorn Ave. close to Ed's Cantina.

Favorite Places to Stay

Hermit Park (Larimer County Open Space) is 2 miles southeast of Estes Park on US 36, with 28 campsites at $20/night, a group campsite for $150/night, and 13 rustic non-electric camper cabins, with 4 padded bunk beds (bring your own linens or sleeping bags), table with benches, covered front porch, propane lights and heat, 2-burner propane cook stove (bring your own cookware), picnic table, fire grate (bring your own firewood), and port-a-potty for $80-$100/night. Minimal water is available, so fill your tank before arriving. Two cabins (Blue Bird and Big Gulch) are ADA accessible and open year-round. 800-397-7795, http://rockymountainnationalpark.com/places/hermit_park.html.

Estes Park Condos offers another decent option. http://www.estescondos.com/rates.html. **Nicky's Resort** was newly remodeled in 2004. Estes Park, CO, 1360 Fall River Rd., 866-464-2597, 970-586-5377, http://www.nickys resort.com/Index.html. **Swiftcurrent Lodge** has something going for it that no one else can duplicate—it's the first lodge on the Big Thompson as it filters out of Rocky Mountain National Park. Magnificent waterfront cabins and lodgerooms with privacy and intimacy. Estes Park, CO, 2512 CO 66, 888-639-9673, 970-586-3720.

OTHER PLACES TO STAY: Alpine Trail Ridge Inn, Estes Park, CO, 927 Moraine Ave., 970-586-4585, http://www.alpinetrailridgeinn.com/. **Boulder Brook on Fall River,** Estes Park, CO, 1900 Fall River Rd., 800-238-0910, 970-586-0910, http://www.boulderbrook.com/. **Mary's Lake Lodge,** Estes Park, CO, 2625 Marys Lake Rd., 970-586-5958 , http://www.maryslake lodge.com/. **Stanley Hotel,** Estes Park, CO, 333 E. Wonder View Ave., 970-586-3371, http://www. stanleyhotel.com/. **Wildwood Inn,** Estes Park, CO, 2801 Fall River Rd., 970-586-7804, http://esteswildwoodinn.com/.

Fly Shops, Guides, and Tackle Stores

Kirk's Flyshop is the finest, most well-rounded outfitter store we've ever encountered. Not just in Colorado, but anywhere. 230 E. Elkhorn Ave., 970-577-0790. **The Estes Angler** (970-586-2110, http://www.estesangler.com/); **Lake Estes Marina** (970-586-2011, http://www.estes valleyrecreation.com/marina.html); **Rocky Mountain Adventures** (800-858-6808, 970-586-6191, http://www.shoprma.com/); **Scot's Sporting Goods & Fly Fishing Shop** (970-586-2877, 970-443-4932, http:// scots sportinggoods.com/).

Other Stuff
Several things
There is far too much water around Estes Park for this to be a comprehensive chapter.

You'll find all you need here on Elkhorn Avenue.

To home base in Estes Park is simply a dream come true, and we assure any angler a helluva great trip if you so choose to stay anywhere near here. Our suggested fisheries are nothing more than our first recommendations and our favorite stops along this massive outdoor playground. Feel free to explore other publications that are more focused on the area to find just how much water surrounds Estes Park.

Home basing in Estes Park rather than camping inside RMNP will allow for access to many creature comforts, such as impeccable lodging, mouth-watering restaurants, and a shopping experience unlike any other. As well, many of the fisheries listed in the Rocky Mountain National Park chapter may overlap with this one. Either place is magical, and both are arguably in our top five favorite bases. So if roughing it is more your style, we suggest that you home base inside RMNP. If you desire all the amenities of home, but want to fish killer water as well, Estes Park is the absolute perfect place to do that.

Greenback cutthroat are only found in this tiny area of the world, most of which are protected within the boundaries of Rocky Mountain National Park. It is well worth the trip to do some species-specific fishing that you simply cannot do anywhere else in the world. These fish are remarkably easy to catch, and their colors are unlike anything you've ever seen on any other freshwater species of trout. Please practice catch-and-release tactics and make every effort to handle these rare and delicate trout with utmost care.

Fishing Places Solid Choices near Home Base

Fall River: Spilling through Rocky Mountain National Park, Fall River offers some of the best fishing around here, especially in Horseshoe Park. There are also numerous public fishing points on the Fall in the town of Estes Park as well. Watch your backcasts. Rumor has it that nothing more than a #12 Parachute Adams is necessary to rack up big numbers of browns, greenback cutthroats, rainbows, and brookies.

Middle fork of St. Vrain Creek: The middle St. Vrain holds small-to-tiny cutthroat. We hiked upstream past the Peaceful Valley Campground and Camp Dick and flicked short lines and shorter leaders into tiny pools. Williams and I played a game we called "I betcha can't catch one smaller than this with a fly bigger than this!" These glorified minnows grow tiresome. And with a glance at the DeLorme, there are literally a thousand other lakes, ponds, and streams on our map to scope out in the area. We become overwhelmed.

Glacier Creek also fishes well using a Parachute Adams #18, Stonefly Stimmie #16, Deer Hair Ant #16, Parachute Ant #18 or a Parawulff Adams #18, trailed with a Copper BH Pheasant Tail #20, copper-beaded Micro

Mayfly #20, transparent #16, or a Mighty Mite #20. Yes, you might tell from its name—the water is cold. Be prepared!

Lake Estes, outside of town, kicks in for fishing after ice out at the inlet and doesn't require the trip and fee to get into RMNP. But several alpine lakes on the west side of the park need exploring.

Ypsilon Lake fishes almost as well as Lawn, but is a much shorter hike. Ypsilon was named for the "Y-shaped" valley in which the waters comes to rest. Same patterns and techniques as Lawn Lake, but expect smaller fish and more angler traffic.

Big Thompson River: This is definitely our *go to* fishery. Once thought extinct, greenback cutthroat were discovered in this very river. We pounce on greenbacks where some unnamed feeder creeks dump in. Fly shops ask us to keep secrets, too! The Moraine Park section of the Big T is our favorite for stirring up chunky rainbows around the undercut edges of the meadow.

For the Adventurer

Roaring River: Williams and I love stories like The Tale of Three Steves. So we had to see the area of the Lawn Lake disaster first hand. The hike takes us along the Roaring River—6 miles. My favorite fly at the time is a Lime Trude, and I don't mind flicking it into any type of water. The Roaring Fork hustles down abraded sediment slopes chock full of sand and stone, so pockets and pools are the majority of the structure, and all the way up greenback cutthroat and brook trout dance in front of us when they decide the Lime Trude is their favorite fly as well. A 3 wt. rod is perfect for this piece.

North fork of St. Vrain Creek: South of Estes Park on CO 7, the North St. Vrain Creek is a designated Wild Trout Waters from the confluence with Horse Creek downstream to Button Rock Reservoir (8.5 miles). Here the trout are wily and willing, but a foot trail is almost non-existent. We chose not to fish the "North" because details about accessing it are sketchy at best. However, a man who wished to remain unnamed says he's descended 1,000 feet near the town of Riverside off of FR 920. The fishing was amazing for browns, and he spoke of how easily the 14- to 16-inch trout rose to nearly any presentation.

Lawn Lake: This cool drop of water resting high up in RMNP is pinched between the feet of Mummy and Fairchild Mountains. This is no destination for the out of shape or faint of heart since the elevation gain and lengthy trek nearly insist on an overnight stay. Nearly any dry pattern like Royal Wulff's or Lime Trudes chilling on the surface will attract a greenback. Charlie's Hoppers around the edges are a blessing to fish as well. Find underwater structure such as boulders or drop-offs, and just let the fly sit. Be sure to take gear for sudden rain or snow showers and high winds.

These rare greenback cutthroat attack with slow ambition. Watching them take a fly is like watching William "The Fridge" Perry of the Chicago Bears bumble bee his way into the end zone back in the 80's. It's the sort of slow but heavy hook set one might expect when fishing for something like whale sharks in the ocean. (Fishing for whale sharks is illegal, so don't go trying this. This was only an analogy, so don't go saying you heard you could fish for whale sharks from Mark and Mac because it simply isn't true.)

The Big Thompson can be hella-good fishing at nearly any point on the river, but some favorite places for sure-bet hook-ups are around Moraine Park and along the Fern Lake trail. Here you'll find a vast open meadow where undercut bank fishing is all the rage. Small dry flies like #18–20 Parachute Adams, Red Quills or even caddis patterns, often trailed with an assortment of colors of Copper Johns, are good setups when pitched against the grassy edges. Repeated attempts on the edges may drag a monster rainbow or fat brook trout like you've never caught in the park before.

OTHER FISHERIES WORTH INVESTIGAT- ING: Sprague, Dream, and Spectacle Lakes, if time permits.

Best Chest Pack Going

We've tried everything out there to hold our junk while fishing the river—vests, fanny packs, fly wallets, bandoleers, Wal-Mart bags. They all work, they just all have their problems. We've been experimenting with nearly a dozen chest packs. The San Juan by Fishpond is by far the best thing we own. It's compact enough that it doesn't get in the way, yet big enough for all our accoutrements. It's cool looking, because orange is cool. It opens up into a usable work table, and it has a removable foam fly patch, so it essentially becomes your fly box. It sits on your chest just the way it needs to, and the thing is tough as Evel Knievel. For what it cost, it's definitely a fine flyfishing in"vest"ment!

12 Fairplay

In fishing, as it is in life, tragedy often strikes and alters our plans. Williams' pop died that first year we'd met. The sheriff had to locate Mark (a man the officer had never seen in his life) in Cimarron Canyon to tell him that his father had passed away. Somehow the sheriff found him. Williams had to drop everything and leave for home immediately. The trout would have to wait for another day.

Once, my son Wesley and I were fishing at Latir Creek near Vermejo Park in New Mexico. Wes was five—already casting and landing Rio Grande cutthroat trout on his own. We'd set up camp right on the river, and we used a tiny pool as our refrigerator to cool our sodas.

Wes had just caught a nice rainbow behind a rock. He'd read the water and cast all on his own. I jumped up and cheered for him once he got it to the bank; I was so proud. A few head of cattle were spooked at my antics and started a little mini stampede. We both chuckled, I took a hero shot, we were on top of the world. But it was short lived.

A man in a rusty bucket of a truck appeared and asked if I was Mr. McPhail. I said I was, paralyzed with trepidation. I sensed an unsettling foreboding in his eyes. He said, "Your baby girl is sick. You need to call your family." Forty miles down a dirt road later, Wes and I found out over the nearest

South Fork of the South Platte River

payphone that Savannah's temperature was 103 and her lymph node under her left ear had swollen to the size of a giant grape. It needed to be drained. She had already endured open-heart surgery at the tender age of one, so this was urgent. We drove back forty miles to camp, packed up in forty minutes, and drove home so I could be with my daughter in the hospital. The trout would have to wait for another day.

Fact is, if you travel enough, if you're away from home enough, receiving that dreaded message is inevitable. And when you get it, it scares the hell out of you and tears your heart out at the same time, because the guilt of being away from home racks you with every mile traveled back to your family.

"Your baby girl is sick. You need to call your family."

"Your baby girl is sick. You need to call your family."

It still echoes in my mind.

About a week before arriving in Fairplay, Williams' stepfather, Don, had been having a few spells of being short of breath, dizzy, uneasy. He had just begun repainting the deck at the Durango house, and he could just tell something wasn't right.

Mark's mom, Gwen, and his wife, Amy, were with him on the project. They called and said he was complaining about his breathing, and at that point, that's all it was, mere complaints. We'd left the three of them in Durango just a week or so before, and when we drove away, everything in the world was fine, normal, safe.

Then the call.

"Mark, Don is in the hospital." And without batting an eye, we made an abrupt about face and returned home. We left the lakes and streams and Fairplay as they lay.

Of course, they were happy to see us kids back in town; there's something about Mark and I that seem to comfort those in distress. Our most challenged students tell us this constantly, not with words, but through action. We listen. Give advice. Pretend to like their music. Write them short uplifting notes. Attend their rite of passage ceremonies and eat their terrible brownies they bake us. He and I are those two teachers, the dads many never had, whom the kids trust, to allow into their worlds. They allow us in when their world is an amazing place to be. But also, they need us there when those worlds are falling apart. Our presence, collectively and individually, have a way of making those around us feel that everything is going to be okay. Even when it may not be.

Our plan, before we got the call:

• Travel into Fairplay (which we had just accomplished).

• Set up camp somewhere centrally located (which we were about to do).

- Continually check the weather (because our ultimate goal was to fish Fairplay, then roll into Rocky Mountain National Park when the weather "window" broke—perfect for a three-day backpack excursion).
- Find fun and interesting things to do with the family around South Park.
- Fish the middle fork of the South Platte at Tomahawk and at Cheesman Canyon.
- Fish the Gold Medal Waters of Tarryall.
- Fish Antero and/or Spinney Mountain and/or Elevenmile Canyon Reservoir.

On the way, Williams was telling me all his South Platte stories, and after all his exaggerations I was telling Williams of a time when I had first fished below Cheesman Dam. I'd ventured down Gill Trail back in the stream's heyday when things were good, pre–*A River Runs Through It*. This was the time when flyfishing in the West was still relatively a mystical, dreamy pastime and seemed nothing more than a wives' tale, an era when the streams were empty of all things but bugs, trout, and a handful of seasoned flycasters.

I had approached a pool, deep and thick with opaqueness, not from silt or runoff but from depth. I had come upon it quietly, in predator mode, to see what might be in it. I could see a trout, most likely a rainbow, pushing 30 inches, just sitting. No movement. At first I believed it to be driftwood. But its shape was too true. It was a trout. I tied on a #22 Royal Wulff. I took twenty min-

Kenny angles in the South Platte River.

utes to tie it on, it felt; my hands were shaking from the adrenaline. I'm sure putting the crosshairs on a thick bull elk does the same. I finally lay it subtly atop the film, just in front of him. Like a cat, he literally crept up to it from beneath, then smashed it like he was angry at it for landing there. I was an unaccomplished flyfisher at this time, but an experienced angler. I had terrorized fish for decades. But when the line went taut on this one, I knew I was out-matched. Several seconds of insane fighting shook me to the core, then this trout leapt from the water several feet, like in a Sea World show, and smacked himself upon a rounded boulder on the bank. Dazed and confused as Hunter S. Thompson, the fish simply slid down rock and into the pool, where it dove deep and broke me off. "This was my first cast of the day!" I insisted.

Williams counters with his own storytime. He and his brother-in-law, Kenny, used to fish the South Platte area in their younger days, near Tomahawk. But the river got to where it was always too crowded, and they stopped going. "But this one time," he was laughing hysterically before he even began his tale, "me and Kenny were camping in the Park. Colorado experienced some sort of weird freakish weather phenomena and we had hundred mile-an-hour winds. It nearly blew the pop-up over. Kenny and I nearly had to cuddle that night, for the second time! But we didn't." Williams also added that Kenny fished the South Platte without a shirt on like white trash once. But there are no pictures to prove this occurrence, so it can't be held against the man.

This is a fair-sized brown for the South Platte River.

South Park is just another one of those areas with too much to do and too many waters to fish, where an overwhelming grab bag of activity can make you "Ack a Fool." One water distracts you from another water. *This* stream keeps you from fishing *that* lake. The lake keeps you from checking out the tail water. Alma, Deckers, Hartsel, Fairplay—they all serve as ample home bases because there is so much water. Decisions, decisions, decisions. Just pick, and roll.

Anyways, had we been able to stay and play, had we not gotten the call, had we had more time and pitched up camp, the following were our planned and mapped out waters to visit. And yes, *this* would have been magnificent. But, those trout will have to wait for another day.

Favorite Places to Eat

Alma Natural Foods at 135 North Main St., just a few minutes north of Fairplay in Alma, is a natural food store downstairs, coffeehouse upstairs. Open 7:00 to 7:00, with indoor/outdoor seating, stunning views, homemade baked goods made onsite, superb coffee, stupendous breakfast burritos. Supplies for hiking, biking, and camping.

Beary Beary Tastee Bakery at 600 Main St. in Fairplay is a quick place to grab breakfast—homemade bagels and breads made without eggs or milk for the vegan in your caravan. You'll also find sandwiches, soups, salads, and handmade sweet treats, plus award-winning scones and "Colorado's best cinnamon rolls." **Millonzi's** on 501 Front St. in Fairplay serves fried oysters and fried artichoke tapas to get the appetite raring to go. After that, the Raviolli Millonzi and Eggplant Parmesan are nice entrées. Their unique salad dressing is homemade. There's a versatile wine list, and the owners are also the chefs, Tim and Jenifer Mallonzi. True Italian.

OTHER PLACES TO EAT: Brown Burro Cafe is also on Main St. in Alma. Expect unhurried service, but quaint and cozy surroundings. Breakfast and lunch only, from 6:00 to 2:00. Huge breakfast burritos and crispy, tender chicken fried steak. **South Park Saloon** is also in Alma. Good place for a brew after a long day of fishing. They grill up hamburgers, steaks, and Mexican dishes, too. At 10,580 feet, the **South Park** is the highest saloon in America.

Favorite Places to Stay

American Safari Ranch Resort ain't your typical Safari. This Old West ranch takes good care of you, cowboy style. With log cabins and resort rooms, horses, fishing, cowboy golf (???), and more. Also, a 20 percent discount on all inclusive packages just for mentioning the "Colorado vacation directory website." Fairplay, CO, Off of US 285 near milepost marker 189, 719-836-2700, http:// www.coloradodirectory.com/americansafari/. **Mountain Comfort Bed & Breakfast** opened its doors in 2007. Former school teachers Ernie and Sandy Dumas created a magnificent lodge feel with laid back charm. If you're going fishing/hiking/biking near Breckenridge, Fairplay, or any points in between, book a room here. Rock fireplaces, jacuzzis, unmatched views and amazing rates. Alma, CO, 52516 CO 9, 719-836-4517, 719-839-0028, www.mountain comfortbandb.com/. **Riverside Inn Hotel & Fishing Resort** offers 50 rooms and sites on the water's edge. Rather nice facility and a stocked pond on the property. Fairplay, CO, 249 US 285, 719-836-0600, www.riversidefairplay.com.

OTHER PLACES TO STAY: **A Wolf Den Bed and Breakfast,** Twin Lakes, CO, 5430 CR 10, 719-486-7262, www.awolfden.com. **Hand Hotel Bed And Breakfast,** Fairplay, CO, 531 Front St., 719-836-3595, www.hand-hotel.com. **South Park Management,** Fairplay, CO, 800-731-3755, 719-836-3755, www.southparklodging.com/properties.htm.

For even more lodging options, visit the **South Park Trout** website (http:// www.southparktrout.com/ute_trail_river_ranch.html). Go to the "streamside lodging" button. Here you will find several ranches/lodge homes/cabins available for rent.

Fly Shops, Guides, and Tackle Stores

Yer Flies Open Bugs & Bullets (719-836-2229) in Fairplay; **Alpine Ski**

& Sport (866-908-7547, 800-356-4992, http://www.alpineskiandsport.com/fishing.shtml); and **Mega Mountain Magic** guided fishing trips 719-486-4570, evenings: 719-486-8236, http://www.leadvillecoloradohorsebackrides.com/) in Leadville; **South Platte Outfitters** guide services (303-647-0409, http://www.southplatteoutfitters.com) in Deckers; **Colorado Trout Hunters** professional guiding services (http://www.coloradotrouthunters.com/Rates.html) in Morrison; **Jonah's** tackle and gear (719-836-0289) in Jefferson; **Angler's Covey** (719-471-2984, http://www.anglerscovey.com).

A wise man named Gary Nichols has built an incredibly important relationship between South Park ranchers and the flyfishing community at large. His website (http://www.southparktrout.com/) is a testament to his dedication to trout, rivers, and the people who love and respect both. His work proves an invaluable tool for "trout terrorists" like us visiting South Park looking for public water with "private" characteristics. In cooperation with many ranchers with rivers running through their private land, they have opened up small "public tracts" on pristine private water, available for regular guys like us at VERY reasonable rates, some as low as $35 a day per angler, with most at $60 per day. (When I say "regular guys like us" I mean everyday ordinary guys like us—nothing about our digestion was intended.)

OTHER STUFF

If you are in Fairplay, Alma, Decker, Jefferson, or anywhere in South Park, you are only minutes away from the outdoor playground of Breckenridge. The drive up CO 9 from Fairplay to Breck is a wonder to me, a transportational engineering achievement. That this highway even exists perplexes me. God, how anyone could focus on getting such a tough job finished in such a laid-back setting like this is simply mindboggling to me. Flanked on both sides by monolithic ranges—Fourteeners on the west, with liberal views of Mount Democrat, the liberating Mount Lincoln, and the thought-provoking Quandary Peak. To the east, there's Pike National Forest and all her peaks; Little Baldy, Mount Silverheels, and Red Mountain. Too much, I say!

Within those ranges, folks find themselves overwhelmed at times with so much outdoor activity they don't know what to do next. Whitewater rafting, canoeing, kayaking, hiking, backpacking, rock climbing, snow skiing, mine tours, dog sledding, snowmobiling, snow shoeing...the list never ends, really. It's a rich landscape carved out by time, weathered by water, wind and ice, pushed up by forces unimaginable.

So maybe this piece has begun to encroach on the home base of Breckenridge a little. I think that's okay. The point I'm trying to make here is that no matter where you home base, there is another home base nearby,

Mark D. Williams and W. Chad McPhail   131

and their boundaries are vague and tend to overlap, bleed into one another, coalesce, as do waters, activities, and cultures, and ultimately fun. Find a place to home base that suits your purpose, whether it's to get away from every last mutha on this green planet and seclude yourself Thoreau-style, or rent a tiny oaken box of a room with your two overly gassy brothers just to try and bag a few double-digit trout. Feel free to move about from base to base, town to town, water to water, and experience what the diverse state of Colorado offers us all—a real chance to connect with our delicate, fragile Earth.

Fishing Places Solid Choices near Home Base

Spinney Mountain Reservoir is one of those sprawling, wide-open, big-sky lakes with a fair amount of boating and angling action. But the reason it's popular is because of the trout that have been cultivated here. Spinney Mountain trout are lengthy, fat, and they fight!

Out of Fairplay, head south on US 285 and drive just over a mile to CO 9. CO 9 will pick up Currant Creek by its side for approximately 10 miles to Yellow Soda Spring, where CR 59 cuts back northeast. Follow CR 59 to Eleven Mile Reservoir and follow the road along the southwest side to the Old Railroad Grade road. There are several dirt roads off of CR 59 that can get you to the water's edge, but Old Railroad Grade will bring you to the southeast boat ramp.

Browns, rainbows, cutthroats, and cuttbows all take flies-and-lures only— from the edges, from a kayak or float tube, or a boat. Pike are also present in the reservoir, but the regulations and a presence by the Colorado Division of Wildlife should keep the number and size of pike to a minimum, since they forage off of trout. There is no ice fishing here in winter, so the season is short.

The lake is only about 35 feet deep, which makes it easier to locate trout than in deeper lakes. Even with a floating flyfishing line, as long as you have a 9- to 12-foot leader and a beadhead on, you'll score. Start deep and work your way up till you find where the trout are suspending, which will often be where *callibaetis* are emerging. A fly called a Devil Bug seems to be a no-brainer choice for flies on Spinney when all other bug life seems extinct for the day. Twitch dries on top and create action when it slows, as well.

The CDOW reported that not only the number of trout are on the rise, but the size of fish are increasing, too—one reason why we highly suggest this reservoir. Apparently the protein-rich quality of scuds help fish grow fast and furiously, so take your scud box.

(See page 133 for Fly selection for Spinney Mountain, Antero, and Eleven Mile Reservoirs.)

Antero Reservoir is for those wanting a shot at splake (a hatchery hybrid of a female lake trout—a.k.a. Mackinaw—and a male brook trout). Splake, for most anglers, are difficult to distinguish. The fish are one unique point about Antero that the other two lakes don't have. But they do share rainbow, cutthroat, cuttbow, and browns, all growing to monstrous sizes.

As the first dam on the South Platte (hence the Spanish name *Antero*, which means first), this earth-filled dammed lake is believed to occupy the site of a former lake bed, Green Lake. So, while fishing here, you're actually fishing two lakes in one.

Antero, like Spinney Mountain Reservoir, is also reasonably shallow at 30 to 35 feet, which means easy-to-reach fish for almost any angler. And it's easy to get to from Fairplay. Just travel south on US 285 to CO 9 (about a mile or so out of town). Stay south on CO 9, turning right (west) on US 24, just before reaching Hartsel. The Antero Reservoir entrance will be on the right.

Like many waters, Antero suffered death from the Hayman Wildfire burn in 2002. The lake was hopelessly drained, yet not all hope was lost. In 2007 when the lake reopened, like an aqueous Phoenix arising from the ash Antero rebounded, and there were anglers landing huge fish right away.

Current regulations for keeping trout are stiff—two trout over 20 inches, and all trout under that must be returned. Bait fishing is allowed.

Eleven Mile Canyon Reservoir is absolutely gorgeous, with its round-rock edges and deep azure-blue water. At 100 feet deep, and even deeper in some places, Eleven Mile breeds some Godzilla-size beasts—trout in the double-digit weight range are landed every year. It's so deep, however, "trouting" can be tougher here than at the other two lakes, which isn't a problem for the angler with the proper timing, or the proper boating set up in the later part of the season when fish move back into the deeps.

When ice out occurs, most fish (the usual suspects, including rainbow, brown, cutthroat, cuttbow, pike, and kokanee salmon), even the gargantuans, will find themselves prone to flies around the edges, like midges and scuds when water temps reach 50 degrees F. Fishing from a kayak or a pontoon is perfect at this period of the season. Edge fishing is fun because the trout are often seen before spooked, and there will often be leviathan-size trout finning around the shores.

Eleven Mile. (I just love saying that—Eleven Mile—it just seems to roll off the tongue so pleasantly.) Anyway, Eleven Mile also supports a healthy supply of crayfish that dawdle around the pockety edges and grottos along the shore. Early season trout will cruise around the clearer, warmer edge waters for an easy and filling one-smash meal of crayfish, so find some of these patterns and toss them about here and there, too.

From Fairplay, head south on US 285 and drive just over a mile to CO 9. CO 9 will pick up Currant Creek by its side for approximately 10 miles to Yellow Soda Spring, where CR 59 cuts back northeast. Follow CR 59 to Eleven Mile Reservoir.

For several reasons, fish grow quickly in the South Park area. Burns, like the 2002 Hayman burn, tend to break down organic matter like grass and trees into a rich nutrient soup that trickles down and gets deposited in the earth and surrounding waters, which in turn feeds the insects. After burns, if moisture comes when needed, many areas, as South Park has, tend to see an explosion of bug life, which can produce huge fish, fast!

Patterns you will want for any three of these reservoirs will be tan, olive, or orange scuds like a Flashback CDC Scud from #12–20, with the mid-range sizes being the most crucial. But, also, midges like Garcia's Rojo Midge are killer candy to a trout, since midges are present the entire season. *Callibaetis* mayflies that imitate real bugs well are natural or olive Beadhead Flashback Pheasant-tail Nymphs #12–18. Damselflies also work here. Find an olive colored beadheaded imitation and this may be the only fly you need on certain days. Damselfly nymphs swim to shore to molt, so anglers on the bank should strip them in and wait for a smash.

For the Adventurer

Tarryall Creek (Wild Trout Waters—at least on this portion) will demand that you to have a Jeep like us, or at least a reasonable 4X4 or ATV. This creek has few public access points as it is, but the most brazen anglers will find themselves fishing the lower 2-mile portion of Tarryall, designated Wild Trout Waters. It's not easy to get to, but your story-telling will improve dramatically if you make it. You won't believe what you find.

FR 210 juts back eastward towards Tappan Mountain off of CO 77. The bumpy FR 210 winds around and eventually leads to footpath TR 619, where it goes directly over the peak and down to the infamous South Platte and Tarryall union. Fish upstream and bring a fistful of dries. If you don't catch something on the first cast, stomp twice really hard on the ground. Then continue.

South Platte (Cheesman Canyon below Cheesman Lake): As a flyfisher, or a fellow brethren thereof, our vernacular is often rather esoteric. No one outside of the flyfishing realm could possibly understand a thing we are saying when describing our gear or our experiences without the aid of a translator willing to put in the effort. Tippet, ferrules, Hare's Ear, backing, loops, amnesia, Stimulators, nippers, nymphs, mending—ask any layperson what they believe these things mean and you're sure to get a deep belly laugh with your buddies who "fly."

So no, Cheesman Canyon is not where the Nacho River drizzles through Wisconsin. Nor is the South Platte a new Creole seafood dish at Popeye's. The South Platte River and Cheesman Canyon are quite possibly two of the most recognizable words in the flyfishing vernacular. In the early part of the decade, drought, fire, ash, and flood all but destroyed this premier fishery. It seemed the Four Horsemen had their own respective appointments with the South Platte, all in successive years, starting with drought in 2002, the Hayman fire after that, then silt and ash spoiled the river for a spell, when finally, torrential floods squalled through the canyon and wiped away any trace of trout.

Good news, the river is finally working its way back to prime, and again it's time to make the trek down the Gill Trail (yes, as in a fish's gill) and slay some salmonids.

South Platte anglers will notice that South Platte bugs are tiny. In order to do well, you'll need to break out the itty-bitty fly box—size 18 and smaller, typically. And use the finest tippet possible. This is always a rule of thumb for me. I tend to use tippet two times lighter than most guys choose, and I rarely ever break off. Tippet is stronger than you'd think. It's the knots that lead to failure. So tie your knots like a sailor and test them before you cast your first fly after re-tying.

If you're gonna be nymphing around, which I would suggest, as nymphing is one of the most lethal of all flyfishing tactics, then try keeping as much line and tippet off the water as possible. When this doesn't work, and you're not landing any trout in places that are ultra-fishy, go through your nymph flies in smaller and smaller succession till something happens. If nothing happens, then go through your colors—tan, grey, olive, orange. Cheesman is difficult water to fish because the trout are so used to keying in on such a small array of tiny insects.

Something else that makes Cheesman tough at times is that the rocks are river-rubbed smooth, and straight chalky vertical lines running the length of the walls give evidence to the fluctuations of the dam release and past gully washers. Rock edges are slippery, so footing is key, and, although many manufacturers are moving away from felt soles due to the harmful parasites that can be transported from water to water through them, felt is definitely important here.

The pools here can run inky black. Not from soot or silt, but from depth. Deep pools translate into huge fish nearly 100 percent of the time. Swinging weighted beadheads or streamers through these "black lagoons" can dupe the older, bigger trout and might surprise an unsuspecting angler ill-prepared for a bout with a heavyweight. One hard-to-find fly that always seemed to trick every trout is something called a Buckskin, tan, #20. Also try running a Brassie below your dry fly in shaded afternoon waters.

Because the South Platte can be one of the most difficult endeavors in all Colorado flyfishing (the fish are so moody and picky), we have chosen to list for you the most functional South Platte flies for the summer months:

Royal Wulff #18, Parachute Adams #18, Renegade #18, Floating Nymph #18–24, Dark and Light Comparaduns #18–24 (tan, olive and brown), Emerger #18–24, Elk Hair Caddis (light tan, olive, black—sometimes anglers will cut the hackle off of these), Griffith's Gnat #22–28, Stillborn Midge #22–26, Red Ant #20, Orange Ant #20, Black Beetle #18, Hopper Patters #10–14, Pheasant Tail #18, Hare's Ear, #18, Tan Scuds, Trico Emergers #24, Brassie #20, orange Copper John #16–18.

Most importantly, the fish in Cheesman Canyon can tell when the clumsy anglers are around; they become very aware of your presence through the vibrations in the rock and from seeing those anglers who don't believe in low profile angling. Stay low, fish close, catch fish!

Kite Lake (via mountain bike): For a different sort of angling adventure, go to Bob Sheets' High Alpine Sports on the corner of 6th and Main in Fairplay and rent a mountain bike. Pack all of your fly gear for the day into one pack, including your rod. Be sure to bring a polar fleece and waterproof jacket, too. Then, from Fairplay, drive north on CO 9, and just before the town of Alma hang a Louie (turn left) and head west on FR 416 to Kite Lake. In the summer, this area is loaded with enthusiastic mountain bikers wanting to get away from it all, but in an energetic way. FR 416 fades to a dirt road that leads to the campground at Kite Lake, but you don't have to drive the whole way. Jump out and hop on the bikes and finish the ride to the campground. Kite Lake will have rainbows and small cutthroat trout, nothing major. Here, it won't be so much about the fish as it will be the setting and the situation. You will be at 12,000 feet elevation, and that's after you drop down to the lake edge! Trout will take an assortment of dries at the right time of day with ultra-thin tippet. But my favorite thing to do on high alpine lakes is drag Prince Nymphs, Brassies, or the varied colors of Copper Johns through them by stripping them in with twitchy series of pulls. Trout will nearly always hang around or circle the shallows, often just where the water turns darkest. They have a hard time resisting this technique.

13 Flat Tops/ Trappers Lake

When one has nothing left
make ceremonies out of the air and breathe upon them.
—CORMAC MCCARTHY (*The Road*)

The Hook

It's a long drive from Meeker to the Flat Tops. Doesn't look it on the map. Doesn't seem it as you drive up alongside the White River sitting pretty outside your window, flowing against your drive into this wilderness. You pass working ranches, nice resorts, cabins, agriculture, cows, and sheep. At one point, the asphalt road stops and turns into gravel and dirt; the last gas station is basically a guy's house in the one-house town of Buford.

We were loaded up and in the Jeep, kayak on top. A few miles after we turned off of CR 8, southeast on Trappers Lake Road 205, along the aspen stands and steep mountainsides, we ran into about two-hundred sheep on the

Trappers Lake

Our campsite at Flat Tops

road, give or take a hundred—we were immobilized. We looked over to see a Peruvian shepherd sitting on the side of the road calmly squatting, taking a dump, a carbine slung over his shoulder. Coyote deterrent. He was dark chocolate, a smile whiter than bleached bones. He waved sheepishly and we waved back and drove on, slowly, through the bleating sheep, the gurgle and rush of the North Fork of the White River background noise to this odd moment.

As an aside, the shepherd's one-finger confident wave (no, not that finger) reminds us of a Jeep thing, a club thing, something we run into in the mountains all the time. We've both driven Jeeps for years and there's this fraternity feel to owning one. We pass a Jeep coming the other way on the road and there's always a nod or a gesture of some sort from the other Jeep. Might be one finger slowly raised, an energetic two fingers up, a deadhand lift, the cool nod, a thumbs up, or a plain and simple howdy wave. Especially four-door Jeep Wranglers to our four-door Jeep Wrangler, and even more so on 4WD trails in the backcountry.

The closer we got to Trappers Lake, our home base, the more we saw the dead trees, blackened pointed shadows, weakly and sadly still erect. These green forests gave way to awkward stands of charcoal pencils, leaning this way and that, evidence of the devastating lightning fire, the Big Fish Fire, of July 2002, that burned thousands of acres. The pewter clouds that billowed over the mountains, dropped down on us and emptied their buckets of water. The temperature fell into the forties and the sun disappeared. We made camp in a steady cold rain.

The Facts

Trappers Lake (9,627 ft. elevation) is one of the most beautiful high-country lakes you will ever see. The picture-postcard lake is loaded with Colorado cut-throat trout, some of bragging size, too. The lake is isolated and loaded with insects, so the cutthroats grow bountiful and long.

Glaciers formed the beautiful and heavily photographed Trappers Lake in the Flat Tops Wilderness Area. This 300-acre, 180-foot-deep blue-ribbon fishery does receive relatively heavy fishing pressure, but special regulations, including the use of artificial flies and lures only, assist in maintaining the fishery's wild cutthroat trout population, the largest population of native Colorado cutthroat anywhere. The Flat Tops Wilderness Area has no road access, so reaching the streams and lakes is done only by hiking or by horse.

This beautiful cutthroat was brought to hand in what we call "God Creek."

The average cutt runs about 11 to 15 inches and doesn't vary much out of this range. You occasionally catch one 17 or 18 inches, but not much bigger. You know, the fishing is good, the insect hatches varied and prolific, the trout beautiful, but if you come here, come for the scenery. It's that good. I've missed fish more than once because I was just looking around, gazing at the big cliff-block of lava rock standing a thousand feet or more above the lake, imposing its will and sometimes its shadow. Or I was staring at the forests of fir, spruce, and pine reflected in the stillness of the water.

On this home base journey, we had plans to fish Trappers Lake as little as possible. Been there, done that. Our goal? Hike up wild streams, catch bunches of small wild trout, get a better feel for the plateau. We had three-hundred miles of trails to choose from. Wall Creek, Big Fish Creek, Marvine Creek, and a dozen others. So we fished them. We caught lots of wild trout, mostly on the small side, a few worth bragging about. But there's this one creek, this one day, the stuff of legends.

Everything is farther than you think. It's not easy to fish multiple waters in a day. Hiking and a road you can't speed on and distance.

The Story

We won't name the creek. We can give a number of the usual reasons: the fragility of the trout population, the small size of the creek, and so on. All true. But we also think that you'd probably be disappointed if you did fish this tiny creek because we hit the stream at the right time, the right day, the right weather, the right alignment of the stars.

Here's what happened:

We woke up to a gunmetal sky and saw the diffused light through the ashy forest. We scurried about camp to fill our packs and go fishing under this auspicious daybreak. At the outlet by the bridge and the no-fish zone, you can see some real whoppers. It's confusing figuring out where legally you CAN fish. We saw 5 big ones, one that was 3 or more pounds, and knew we were in for a great day. We met an old lady with a big dog. We saw a 10-pounder who disappeared under the bridge (or was a bridge, he was so large). The two families with fat kids swimming and dogs barking as we walked around the lake. Trying to figure out the trail and getting bassackwards. Canoes and boats sitting on the bank.

We saw the little creek and thought, yeah, whatever. I didn't even string up. The creek wasn't as wide as either rod was long. There was a bend pool that was the deepest water, but it was shallow. Mac caught one on the first cast, a brilliantly colored 13-inch trout. Dry fly smash.

Shock and awe.

Suddenly, we saw trout in every lie, stacked up, in every nook, every cranny. Cutthroats 13 to 19 inches glowing in the water, some with backs sticking out, and here's the rub: obviously in spawn or post-spawn. It was close. This was early to mid July. You can't fish close to the inlets and outlets of Trappers Lake for a reason—they want the cutts to survive and thrive.

But we were fishing legally and, in our minds, ethically. The lake is full of big fat long cutthroat. The population is beyond healthy. The fish we were seeing were two miles from the lake and plentiful, strikingly athletic. We got over our worries in a split second. So we fished.

We each caught 3 from this three-foot by three-foot pool, mostly from the other bank, where they held tight to the undercut as the water spun slowly to them.

Williams shows off a typical trout from a typical far area creek.

We moved upstream—Mac fished in the stream, cold rushing water, legs turning pink, three to four visible monsters holding in front of him, one probably 20 inches long but he only caught two lesser fish, one brook (orange crazy neon) and one cutt 12 inches long. The brush covered the banks and leaned out over the water so that the casting lane in places was six inches at best.

We walked and waded up, but still too many willows, too much brush, too small and fast. Then we struggled through vegetation and crested a hill, and what lay before us was like a Trout Unlimited calendar, one of those Val Atkinson type pics of a river and forest too good to be true. We were in a dream world.

We creeped through danger trees, Kenny sticks we called them. (Kenny, Mark's brother-in-law, stepped over a log like these and got impaled through his calf.) The fire had roared through here seven years ago, and trees fell like pickup stix. This deadfall had sharp short limbs sticking out such that, when you stepped over, you could slice open your calf or thigh if you didn't fully clear the horizontal logs or those 45-degree dead trees wedged into tree splits. Kenny sticks were laying everywhere, so just walking twenty feet might require stepping over ten to fifteen logs. We didn't dare step on the logs because they would crack and send you tumbling. We didn't jump over them because there were more wooden traps hidden beneath tall grass. The best route was in the stream.

So we scrambled down the hill and looked down on that one big pool and saw big fish. It was a huge risk to get there because the hill had no rocks, nothing to slow down our crawl or footsteps. We could slide right down into this big pool. Plus there was no way to set up to cast without spooking them. We did slide. We angled for this one wiry thick willow that protruded over the maelstrom, hitting it feet first then jumping into the riffles just above the pool. It was fairly risky, but oh so athletic.

The creek widened as we waded upstream. Shallower, too. The brush that suffocated the lower reaches had thinned out. The sun played hide and seek with the clouds that for two days had dropped rain and gray on our heads. The word *eerie* doesn't do justice to the surrealistic feeling we both had as we moved like Legolas through the strange forest. If you have never been in a forest decimated by fire, there's nothing like it. Light bounces around, shadows are long and thin, every sound is carried through the tall burned trees and reverberates. Looks like something out of *Lord of the Rings*. It's weird. *Wyrd*.

So we sight-fished, and every cast drew something (yes every cast), some kind of take. They slashed without taking. They opened their mouths gaping white wide. They tail-slapped the fly. Amazing. But these cutts were difficult to hook.

Mac's a damned good caster, and he was one-casting, back-sidearm casting, bow-and-arrow casting, throwing everything in the bag at them with a #14 Elk Hair Caddis, placing it right where he needed. We were switching up, letting each other fish while the other took photos and marveling at the Alaska-style, salmon-like happening. In a two-hour span, we each caught in the neighborhood of two dozen nice-sized, colorful trout. The largest was around 18, 19 inches, the smallest about 12. The cutts were feisty and so colorful they seemed hand-painted with glow-in-the-dark paints.

Then we came to the God Pool.

We call it the God Pool because if the Almighty were to construct a trout pool for himself, this would have been it. Because this morning had been building to a spiritual crescendo. A tangible shiver. Because we knew, absolutely knew, that when we were through fishing from tail to head, we'd have known one of the most thrilling fishing experiences of our lives.

Fishing on "God Creek"

Williams fights a splashing cutt.

So we sat down.

We studied the God Pool. We took out cigars and lit them and smoked silently, occasionally seeing an enormous trout break water, then glancing at each other with big smoky guilty smiles. We shooed away insects until we realized that we were in the middle of a caddis hatch. Bigger smiles.

From our haunches, we kept vigil on no fewer than 100 trout scattered up and down a pool-drop-pool system. These trout were the big boys, 16 to 22 inches and fat. They finned and fed side by side, sometimes on top of each other, oblivious to the rest of the world. One dark leviathan chased a skittering caddis across the pool like an alligator would attack a wounded wildebeest.

Mac had first dibs. He came in low and on the side, giving up a shallow run to position for the big pool. Casting was tricky because he couldn't make a normal cast. Overhanging trees to his left, trees behind him. He had to backcast across his body, flat planed, and then when the fly landed on the water, high-stick the offering over the open-mouth trout.

I made a miracle cast, from behind a tree. I couldn't repeat the cast if you gave me a million chances. Mac was the New Zealand–style guide directing my angle and length of cast because I couldn't see exactly where I was going to drop the fly. From his vantage point, he saw the big pig of the pool feasting on crazy caddis.

"Cast over the two pools in front of you, into that circle pool, and let it slide on down into the pool you can't see."

Uh, right.

Each pool was Tinkertoy designed, with Kenny-sticks creating little tubs of danger. We'd already each hung up several times on numerous dead trees and magnetic limbs. Even if I landed the fly over the two pools and into the target pool, the chances were nil that the fly could avoid the flotsam and jetsam and sticks to make it to the lower pool. I cast. It did. The trout complied.

Mac netted the aggressor. Nineteen inches and copper-colored. Brilliant neon pink slash on his jaw. A two-hander. I released him into a nearby pool and he confidently dashed back to his lair.

This kind of thing went on for hours, till midafternoon when we stopped for lunch.

We ate crackers and string cheese beside a narrow stretch way upstream, a deep narrow pool in front of us. Mac offered me a toast with his flask. Scotch.

"To today."

"Amen, brother."

Mac fished to this one massive trout who kept leaving his undercut bank and slowly rising then retreating. Mac deftly landed a #16 Goddard Caddis in the lane, and the beast rose like a submarine, then submerged. Pop. Gone like a spirit.

I took off my cap. This cap was twelve years old, my go-to fishing cap. The gray cap was once Dallas Cowboys blue. Threadbare. No fewer than a dozen holes. The thing sat funny on my head because it had lost its memory. I placed the talisman/pyre/sacrifice on a willow.

The site of the cap sacrifice

"You giving up the cap?"

"Yep."

"No better place."

"No better day. It's time."

We shook, tipped the flask. American poet Edwin Markham once said, "The crest and crowning of all good, life's final star, is Brotherhood." Either you get it, or you don't. We left the cap to the woods and the river and we fished our way back to the trail.

The Rest of the Story

Roads go every which way once on top at Flat Tops Wilderness (even though the Wilderness proper is roadless), and trailheads begin at every turn. The roads are alternately pretty good and pretty bad, and even though we had the Jeep and thought we wouldn't have gone back in there without 4WD, we saw lots of brave souls driving your basic passenger cars loaded with coolers and sleeping bags and children on these lumpy muddy roads. While you're on a mesa, the scenery is high country, loaded with aspen and spruce and pine, clear cool creeks and fecund lakes. Flat Tops Wilderness lies 40-plus miles to the east of the Meeker, the cleanest little town we've ever seen.

The centerpiece is Trappers Lake, a large natural lake holding Colorado cutthroats that average 16 inches. If you've never caught a cutt that size, you need to because the variations of colors and spots are kaleidoscopic.

The outlet at Trappers Lake

Streams criss-cross this wilderness, feeding lakes, leaving lakes to feed other bodies of water. They hold an amazing biomass of trout, sometimes Alaska-salmon-run-like, so don't overlook these. If you like flyfishing, hit the creeks. We lucked into one unnamed creek that fed a little lake, and in five hours we caught and released 20 trout each that ranged from 14 to 18 inches, with colors that would make Picasso jealous. The Flat Tops Wilderness is 235,000 of the wildest acres you'll ever see, the third largest wilderness in the state.

Favorite Places to Eat

Your campground. Your campsite is your home base; there are no towns nearby. You'll find overpriced gas, bread, and other sundries at the Buford store, but save money and time by being self-sufficient and stocking up beforehand.

Left: Dinner round the fire
Above: Trappers Lake Lodge

Favorite Places to Stay

Flat Tops Wilderness. Camp around Trappers Lake at any of five or six campgrounds. **The River Bend Resort** is right on the North Fork White River and has a great reputation; **Trappers Lake Lodge** (970-878-3336), **Sleepy Cat Guest Ranch** (970-878-4413). Lots of campgrounds—not just around Trappers Lake but along and just off the road—**Bear Lake, Bucks, Chapman, Cold Springs, Crosho, Cutthroat, East Marvine, Himes Peak, Horseshoe, Marvine, North Fork, North Fork Group Area, Shepherds Rim, Sheriff, South Fork, Trapline, Vaughn Lake.**

Fly Shops, Guides, and Tackle Stores

See Meeker, Glenwood Springs.

Fishing Places Solid Choices near Home Base

Trappers Lake: What you fish for: wild cutthroat and brook trout. You won't find: 1) a lake this postcard scenic that 2) is accessible by car, where 3) you can catch so many wild and large trout. Remote blue ribbon lake that you fish as much for the heavenly scenery as the colorful cutthroat. No motor boats allowed, so you'll have to wade or use a boat or personal watercraft (like a bellyboat or pontoon).

   In Trappers Lake lives a self-sustaining population of Colorado cutthroats that average nearly 15 inches long. Often, you will reel in a cutt that runs in the 18 to 22 inch range. Angling is restricted to artificial flies and lures, and any cutthroat over 10 inches must be returned to the water immediately. Up to 8 cutts 10 inches or less can be kept. Fishing is prohibited in all inlets and upstream for 1/2 mile, in the outlet and downstream to the falls, and within 100 feet of inlet and outlet streams.

   If families playing in and around the water are bothering you, or you feel like you just can't catch another 18-inch cutthroat, you can also shuttle-hike from Trappers Lake on the Stillwater and Bear River Trails to Little Trappers Lake,

Mosquito Lake, and Stillwater Reservoir past the Chinese Wall escarpment, then atop the Flat Tops plateau for some amazing views (and excellent angling). With the Big Fish Fire 2002, the scenery around Trappers Lake is haunting and brown, huge stands of pointy dead timber, evidence of the power of a forest fire.

We release another Flat Tops cutt.

   Big Fish Creek: Find the trail at Himes Creek Campground just a few miles northwest of Trappers Lake on FR 205. Typical stunningly beautiful narrow valley between heavy forests and screaming mountains. Quick water with riffles and runs, the occasional pool, but difficult to fish. What makes it tough fishing is that what should be a meadow stream is a stream canopied by trees and tall brush. The first half mile is private. Wildflowers galore. We fished it during a rainy week so the water was off-color and fast.

   Marvine Creek: What a scenic setting. Meadow—canyon configuration of a stream with awesome deep holes and wide pools, narrow runs along undercut banks. Weirdly, the hardest, steepest part of the trail is the first few hundred yards from the parking area, then it levels out. Campground near the trailhead. We caught brookies, cutts, cuttbows, and rainbows, and most were heavy-bodied but not very long. In these deep dark pools under shadowy canopies of trees, we found that a double beadhead nymph rig was a dead-on sure thing. Well worth your time and effort.

Lost Creek: Odd little creek that seems out of sorts with the other plateau streams. Lost Creek is silty and sandy, and the water is tan. The fish are small—the ones we caught, anyway, but the Forest Ranger shared with us that if you work your way up, through the tangle, you can land some nice browns. We didn't. You might. I wouldn't. Cottonwoods are the tree of choice around Lost Creek, and the cotton in the air in midsummer will drive anyone with allergies crazy.

Wall Creek: You won't find a series of beaver ponds any prettier than this. Below the beaver ponds, the creek is skinny water, narrow and shallow, winding back and forth through crumbling banks, difficult to fish because of the tall grass and thick brush. We saw trout and caught some small ones, but the larger ones were too cautious. Mac hooked a good-sized one, but in the shallow water

Above: Marvine Creek
Above right: Wall Creek
Right: Mac fishes Lost Creek.

the trout used tail and leverage to bust off. Our camp host loves Wall Creek and swears there are pools below the beaver ponds that hold whoppers. Good luck.

Wall Lake: Don't hike back into this wild country without a topo map and a GPS or compass. We're telling you, this is real wild scary hairy wilderness. We've hiked deep in on the trail on a foggy evening, after a rain and sleet storm, where the setting was right out of a bad slasher movie. This 45-acre lake is ideal for an overnight camping trip, but be warned, the trail is a steep one. Super fishery for cutthroats, some pretty decent-sized ones, too. The scenery is dramatic. Good campsites. If you're adventurous, you can find other small lakes (without names) in the vicinity that are worth fishing. This is high country, nearly 11,000 feet in elevation, so be prepared for cold wacky weather. To reach Wall Lake from Trappers Lake, walk south on TR 1818 for about five miles.

Coffin Lake: Not impressed. The lake looks like a coffin and, to our eye, acts like one, too. We talked to folks in camp who had splendid days at this narrow silty lake east of Trappers Lake (crazy talk of cutts over 3 pounds), but we had no luck over two days and didn't see much living in the waters. Six acres surrounded suffocatingly by tall empty trees. Lots of deadfall, long black skinny trout lies.

Coffin is just a short hike from Trappers, ten to fifteen minutes on an easy walk. Anecdotes from fellow anglers suggest (because you never know) that when the big lake is off, Coffin is on. Looks like a beetle pattern lake to us. To reach the lake, go to the Trappers Lake parking lot and walk around the east side of the lake to TR 1814. Take the trail east for approximately 1/2 mile to Coffin Lake.

South Fork White River: From the South Fork Campground on the western boundary of the Flat Tops, you can hike and fish 16 miles up the river. Brushy, with willows in spots to the point of insanity, canyon-y in spots, the trail follows the river. Get in and wade when you can. You'll mostly catch 12- to 14-inch cutts, but in the big pools and runs you can land some whoppers. Sightcasting to rising fat cutts on the South Fork is a real heartstopper. The North Fork begins at Trappers Lake, and the South Fork begins a few miles south. They meet up at Buford.

Main stem of the White River: More about this in the Meeker chapter.

North Fork White River: Below the lake, in the public sections, you can fish twisty, winding, deep-cut banks for cutts. You'll see guides with clients standing in one spot for hours sightcasting to rising cutts. Move on. You can find your own water, and much wilder, too.

OTHER FISHERIES WORTH INVESTIGATING: Too many to list. Crescent Lake, Mandall Lakes, Island Lakes, Lost Solar Lakes.

14 Glenwood Springs

Writing books is the closest men ever come to childbearing.
—NORMAN MAILER

We like Glenwood Springs. A lot. It's one of those trendy, new Main Street, magazine picks the top ten best small towns in America–kind of communities. In fact, *Field and Stream* recently voted Glenwood Springs as the number one flyfishing town in America. The town is clean, put together, a combination of crisp canyon-mountain vistas, resort town, turn-of-the-century history, and emerging western boomtown. This is a relocation spot, a retirement consideration, a definite home base from which to build a great trip, especially when you consider it's a much more affordable resort town than its sister mountain village, Aspen. In some ways, Glenwood Springs reminds us of Durango North, and that's a good thing.

Glenwood Springs' history is obviously built around its famous hot springs, which, if in town, you owe it to yourself to visit and relax. Everyone from Ute Indians who camped around the springs to outlaws to European dandies to movie stars frequented the springs over the years. The town sits at the confluence of the Roaring Fork and Colorado Rivers. Glenwood Canyon is east of town, and through it runs the Colorado, a real treat and must-do. A place to watch boaters galore, bicyclists on the bike trail, anglers floating the river. I-70 is pretty spectacular through the canyon, too, as it soars above the river and through the canyon, marvels both manmade and godmade.

Glenwood Springs welcomes the outdoorsy types.

From Glenwood Springs, anglers have more options in an hour to two hours' drive than perhaps anywhere in the upper half of the state. Flat Tops and Grand Mesa. Crystal and Roaring Fork. Frying Pan and Blue and Gore and Eagle. You have the I-70 Corridor to zip up and down. (Well, if you've seen the traffic on some days, you know that isn't true, but most of the time…) Regardless, Glenwood Springs is centrally located to reach all kinds of rivers and lakes in a short amount of time. The home base is ideal for families, romantic getaways, fishing buddy trips, any kind of excursion.

Parked along the Crystal River

We went through Glenwood Springs twice, but this last time was when we planned to get some real fishing done. We'd fished the lower Colorado near Dotsero a few days before and caught a few fish, but we weren't serious. Then the rains came. That means we usually move up higher, to the small streams, up to the headwaters where, even if it rains, the streams are clearer. We hit all the creeks we could find, and they were indeed clearer than the lower streams, but the trout just weren't striking. We caught a few, mostly by dredging deep with nymphs, hitting the edges. The rain drove us back to the trailer, but it was hard to pass up diners and bars. We owe the self-restraint to our amazing willpower, constitutions, and a budget strained by a summer of travel. Mostly the money.

Writing a book on a short deadline while on the road is a tricky thing. Glenwood Springs was the home base for us while we were in the middle of the aforementioned day-after-day downpours, real gullywashers. We were searching for our "story" for this chapter, and it wasn't easy. The recent heavy rains, timed by the fishing gods to coincide with our trip no doubt, had swollen the Colorado so that it was rusty and rolling, high as all git out, so that option, our main option, was out.

Writing is an odd process. Most writers I know are sportswriters and outdoorswriters. I know a couple of national names who write creative non-fiction, a couple of novelists who have had best-sellers. Every one of them is supremely confident and simultaneously childishly vulnerable. Mac and I are no different. Except that we've never had a best seller. My Harper Collins book, *So Many Fish So Little Time*, has been a good-seller for two years, and if they had a New York Times Fishing Book Good-Sellers list, it'd surely be near the top.

Here's an inside peek at the writing biz:

Writing outdoors for magazines and newspapers is one thing. Writing books is another. It's a long, drawn-out process that can take years from conception to finish. Writing books—it's a weird process. You start out with an idea, develop it into an abstract or an elevator pitch. *Hey, Editor, I've got this book about the best 1001 fishing spots in the world.* Next, you build an outline that somehow turns into a book proposal. If you have an agent—I've had three in twenty years—you send it to them to see what they think about the idea. You get to know what is selling, what your agent likes (and those can be two entirely different things, by the way), so by the time your proposal is in front of the literary agent, you have a pretty good idea that they'll like it enough to pitch it to a few publishers.

Take this book for instance. The book doesn't have the national appeal for a major publisher, so it has no interest to an agent either. They make 15 percent of whatever books you sell, and while a book like this might stay on the shelves a long time and do well for the author, it won't be a best-seller (or likely even a good-seller), so the agent will pass. In this case, dealing with a small to medium-sized publisher, we pitched the idea through an email, then sent a more detailed proposal. There was back and forth. (During which Mac and I were pretty sure the publisher wanted the book but just wanted to make sure the book they got was what they wanted. Get it?) Sometimes, without your agent, you get an advance on future books, sometimes you don't. That's why you want the agent involved because they likes them advances.

Shit. They sent a contract. We sign it and send it back. Due December 2009. Nothing to it. Let's go fishing.

So we are fishing the summer across Colorado. We are stuck in the Aliner in a campground near Glenwood Springs, each of us writing up our notes from the previous few days of crappy fishing in the rain. With no story.

I could write about the times in the last two decades when I've fished the Glenwood Springs area. One late June day, I caught more whitefish in the Crystal River than I ever want to catch the rest of my life. Boring. The Gypsum is loaded with small brookies and lots of brush, how about that? See what I mean? The story became the writing of the book.

When you fish a river, what do you remember at the end of the day? What details? Did you notice if those were willows by the stream? Any aspen stands? Granite-walled canyon? What insect hatches? Could you write down the exact directions to this stream? What other streams flow into this stream, what lakes are on its course, was there a footpath? If you didn't catch that many, can you tell what species were in the stream? You get the idea. Whenever we fish a river, cast in a lake, we are surveying (as second nature after twenty years of this) and collecting information. Because I turn fifty this year, I find that I better write it down in a notebook that night or some things slip away.

Mac and I had the idea for this book eight years ago, close to the time we first met. We were looking at my substantial fishing library at my house and it came to us, as we were in the tentative planning stages for a fishing trip, that most fishing guidebooks are put together by rivers and lakes, by drainages, sometimes by a region in a state. But not by home bases, which is what all of us anglers do. We make a home base. *We ought to fix that some day.* And here we are in the rain, in the Aliner trying to do just that.

As we sit here writing on our laptops, I notice that our legs are cut up like you wouldn't believe. We wet wade. Almost always except on big deep rivers. We wear neoprene socks (1 mm.) and lightweight wading boots and shorts. We walk and wade three to ten miles a day, easy, but we push right

through brambles and brush like it's nothing. Our legs are coldly numb from the 40-degree water, so we don't notice all the dings at the time. Sometimes we get back to the car or the trailer before one of us will mention, "Dude, you took a hunk outta your calf." Look down and there's a chunk of meat missing. Or a long deep slice from some errant sharp limb. Bruises. Nicks. Thorns. *Levon wears his war wounds like a crown.* We twist our knees, fall on our keisters, slip down steep banks, plunge over our heads from tricky unseen holes in the river, bang our shins on rocks, cut ourselves with knives while setting up camp, have limbs poke holes

Angler on the Colorado River near Granby

in our cheeks as we bushwhack. At the end of each phase of the trip, we are beat up by Nature. But we hardly even notice.

We are writing chapters after we collect our notes, finding the story for each home base, and we are in the story ourselves. Like I say, writing a book is odd. Writing a book with someone else is odder. I build books with lots of disparate chapters, not even saved together. I add a bit here and there, lines, facts, things to do. I call and email guides I know and don't know. I fish everywhere I can, am on the lookout for those things I don't see in other guidebooks. Now I had someone else with whom I could split all the work, another writer to do half the research. We will write our chapters, assemble them, re-write, re-assemble, write an introduction, send it all in to Johnson Books. Editor will suggest new assembly, re-writes, and additions. Back and forth for a month or two or three. A new title. What about the cover? How will the back page be laid out? Which name should come first? Galleys (the pre-press semi-final copy). Who can we send the galleys to for reviews? Approve the galleys, the cover. Finally, a finished copy of the book comes in the mail, and now the hard part begins. Sell, baby, sell.

Numerous small creeks feed the Colorado River.

The rain isn't letting up, so I write some emails. (Yeah, we have wireless somehow.) Amy and I are talking to one publisher about a series of books, *Top 30 Things To Do In* ____ fill in the blank. The first two they want are Durango and Telluride. These will be Amy's first books, too. Can I not write a damn book by myself anymore?

Mac and I are novelists. Neither of us has sold one yet, but we are novelists nonetheless. State of mind. I've only been writing sports and outdoors the last twenty years to support my novel writing. The teaching gig is for extra money, you know? One of these days, the novel will sell. If not, maybe the second one I just completed will rise to the top of the charts. The rain has stopped, the sun is out, and we are loading up the Jeep to run up and fish either Mitchell Creek or Elk Creek. We're out of here. Mac and I have a fishing book to write. Ciao.

Favorite Places to Eat

Like Durango, Glenwood Springs has a rep for good eating, and you have more good restaurants in this town than you can shake a stick at. We like **Sapphire Grille** (970-945-4771), **Juicy Lucy Steakhouse** (970-945-4619)—a bit pricey but worth it, **Florindos** (970-945-1245)—best Italian in town. We haven't tried **Sopris** (970-945-7771) or **Rivers** (970-928-8813), but friends recommend them.

Favorite Places to Stay

Hotel Colorado (970-945-6511), **Hotel Denver** (970-945-6565), and **Frontier Lodge** (970-945-5496). The Colorado and Denver are out of the ordinary and charming, so if you like historic over brand new modern, even though both have done remodeling, these are your ticket. The town has plenty of chain and clean mid-level Route 66–style motels and hotels.

Fly Shops, Guides and Tackle Stores

Roaring Fork Anglers (970-945-0180) in Glenwood Springs; **Alpine Angling** (970-963-9245) in Carbondale; **Frying Pan Anglers** (970-927-3441) and **Taylor Creek Fly Shop** (970-927-4374) in Basalt; **Crystal Fly Shop** (http://crystalflyshop.com/).

OTHER STUFF: Don't miss the hot springs or Glenwood Canyon—Hanging Lake. Other cool things include the Rio Grande Trail from town to Aspen, rafting the Colorado, day trips to Redstone and Marble, walking around historic downtown.

Fishing Places Solid Choices near Home Base

Colorado River: From state bridge to Dotsero, the river is a big mountain river, blue most of the time; CO 131 to I-70 is scenic, but mostly raftable. The Colorado below Dotsero is not pretty (in a typical trout river way) in these lower reaches, those along the highway, those sections that course mightily through steep canyons. The water color ranges from mocha to cappuccino to babyshit brown. The Colorado near Rocky Mountain National Park is blue and clear and calendar-worthy and small. In between, you get a solid blue ribbon fishery. In the lower stretches, especially below Dotsero, the fish on average are large and the chance for a trophy trout pretty darned good. The river is big.

Roadside access to the Colorado is common around Glenwood Springs.

Intimidating. Not much way to tell where to cast, so look for edges and breaks. The lower Colorado is a float river at its best. Hire a guide so you'll know how to fish it and where, ask where the best access points are located. An excellent spincasting river from the bank and a good start is from the bank at the No Name Rest Area a couple of miles east of Glenwood Springs.

The Colorado River is a Gold Medal stream that flows through both valleys and rocky canyons. Fishermen first have to get access to this interesting river, since much of it is private, and the reward will be a lot of trout 15 to 20 inches long, with chances at trout much larger.

Roaring Fork: Gold Medal trout stream 12 miles up from confluence with the Colorado. The Fork is a great freestone stream that holds some whoppers, rainbows and browns. The river is fully covered in Aspen and Basalt chapters.

Sylvan Lake State Park: Great choice for an all-day picnic and fish excursion or a secondary home base. Located in an alpine park in the West Brush Creek Valley, this 40-acre lake is stocked with rainbow trout and also holds wild cutts and brookies. I've heard there are browns, too. Some of the rainbows grow fat and large, but the brook trout are numerous and annoying. Non-motorized or electric trolling motors only. There are fifty campsites. Take I-70 East to Eagle, turn south at West Brush Creek Road, go 16 miles.

West Brush Creek: Would you believe it's brushy? It is. You can fish both forks, but since you might as well package in Sylvan Lake, stick with its beaver ponds and tight fishing. Most of the lower creek is open and, unfortunately, private. East Brush, Abrams, Hat Creek and a few others are solid small stream feeders to the Brush Creek system.

For the Adventurer

Four Mile Creek: Small fun stream that feeds Roaring Fork. Runs beside Sunlight Ski Area access road. Cutts and brooks.

Avalanche Creek and Lake: Here's your huckleberry, a real-live wilderness fishing experience with little angling pressure. Twelve miles up the Crystal River from Carbondale, this is your sleeper, hard-as-hell hike-in, worth-the-price-in-gold–views valley river. Backpack it. If you go in, you will not want to come out. Expect wild cutts and rainbows that fight like crazy.

Gypsum Creek: Feeder creek to the Eagle River near Minturn. The ponds can pay off sometimes, and the upper reaches are fun dry fly fishing. At the headwaters are several good lakes.

Grizzly Lake: Go south of Aspen like you're heading to Independence Pass; 9 miles off CO 82, turn southeast on Lincoln Creek Road and drive into the Collegiate Peaks Wilderness. On the far side of the reservoir, you'll find the trailhead. To reach the alpine lake, you'll endure a 4-hour hike. On this excursion, you get to fish Lincoln Creek, Grizzly Reservoir, and this little gem above treeline, Grizzly Lake. You better be in shape and be a good stalker. The payoff for your troubles getting to the high-country lake is a population of large, smart cutthroats.

Maroon Creek and Lake: Take CO 82 like you're going to Aspen, and turn south at Maroon Creek Road before you cross Castle Creek. The lower half of the creek is private, but you'll see postings when you hit the public water. West Maroon comes out of the lake, and to its east is East Maroon Creek, reached by trailhead near Silver Queen CG. Crater Lake is a short hike around the lake. Well worth your time—make sure you bring your camera.

OTHER FISHERIES WORTH INVESTIGATING: Thompson Creek, Thomas Lakes, upper Prince Creek, Canyon Creek, Crystal River.

Blue Ribbon Fisheries not far from Glenwood Springs

Flat Top Wilderness (focus on Heart Lake, Deep Creek, Deep Lake)
Flat Tops not all that far
Grand Mesa not far either
Homestake Creek
Deep Creek: good canyon stream that flows into the
    Colorado above Dotsero.
Rifle Gap Reservoir State Park
Frying Pan River
Eagle River

15 Granby

We are driving north to Kremmling, on our way to Granby. We've just been through a freakish windstorm that pelted us with red dirt and gravel, whooshed upon us by some curse of Greek-god happenstances just as we passed through a tight, ruddy-colored canyon with the terrifically scenic Green Mountain Reservoir to our left. We're fine now, but feel we've angered the trout gods once again. We had hoped to fish the Gold Medal Waters of

Gold Medal waters on the Colorado River below Byers Canyon

the Blue River, below Green Mountain (which is really above, since the river flows northerly out of the north end of the lake). But the storm pushed us on through. The "Gold" part of the Blue near Green Mountain is a trip in our not so far distance. On to Kremmling.

"If I was going to write and shoot a Western flick, Kremmling is where I'd do it," says Williams. "Look at that gray cliff in the backdrop there! It's perfect for filming an ambush scene! Stanley Marsh should have put his floating mesa thingy here, not Amarillo!"

Stanley Marsh is a well-known eclectic where we're from. He's world-famous for erecting the Cadillac Ranch outside of Amarillo. But he has many other bizarre projects under his belt that would probably befuddle the vast majority of us. Williams and I have always found him a fascinating character because, like us, he likes to stir things up. It can get quite boring and monotonous in the life. Mr. Marsh shares our sense of spirit and adventure, and we can appreciate the weird and wacky, so long as it has a point.

I gawk out the windshield at the most Western-looking backdrop ever. "Whoa! I swear I just saw a Ute Indian medicine man up there waving a spear at us." I point to fool Williams, and he looks briefly, but won't admit that he did.

My mind is still on Mr. Marsh at this point, so I continue. "Besides, Stanley Marsh is a wizard. He's probably a genius, like Stephen Hawking, only more mobile, and down to earth."

Mark shakes his head as if to say, *probably not*, at least about the down-to-earth part.

Lake Granby, from our campsite at the Arapaho National Recreation Area

"I love his ideas of floating mesas and Cadillac Ranches. Have you heard of his multi-acre pool table?"

Williams laughs in disbelief, but yet, he believes. One can't put anything past Marsh, and he knows this. I continue. "He also must have an enormous typewriter because I wrote him a letter once and he wrote me back and it was this huge envelope with a huge letter inside, with huge text! I can imagine him banging on this massive keyboard the size of a desk! Yup. A wizard, all right. Speaking of which, if I was a wizard, I'd turn you into a wizard. Then we could both be wizards."

"Uh oh. This isn't going to turn into that 'We are all just modern-day cavemen' conversation is it?" moans Mark. "You milked that theory of yours last trip. So we're all still basically cavemen looking for one thing. We only evolved to make getting it easier, huh? Are we really gonna go there again?"

"No, but if I was going to film a movie about cavemen, Kremmling is where I'd do it. Not only is it Western-looking, but it's prehistoric and primordial-looking as well. You could put Chakka or Geronimo up there and either would be happy to make it home."

Mark smiles. "Kremmling is the epitome of prehistoric meets Western. Except for that miniature Statue of Liberty right there. That's sorta weird," he laughs. "Why would that be here, of all places?"

"Fifty bucks says Stanley Marsh put that there," I declare. "He's a genius wizard."

Indeed, when we're on the road, the banter can go just about anywhere, and it often does.

We are stopping in Kremmling on our way to some someplace special. The cleanliness and unique setting coaxes us into shooting a u-turn to take some photos in town. The two of us look on the map to see what sort of fishing might lie around this place. Perhaps Kremmling could be a home base, we think. But the only liquid that seems to stand out at this point is the unmanageable Colorado River, and the place advertising a steamy cuppa joe. We didn't really care to sample either here in Kremmling, so on we strode to Granby. We didn't even bother to look for stickers.

Granby is clean, quaint, and close to some fantastic fishing.

Ian's Mountain Bakery is a unique treat.

Favorite Places to Eat

Brick House 40 on E. Agate Ave. is Granby's newest restaurant and makes nice New York–style sandwiches, hand-packed burgers, grilled checkered chicken breast sandwiches, soups, salads, gyros, pasta, and pizza. **Carrie's Corner Café** on E. Agate Ave. was formerly known as the Columbine Café. Now nicknamed the Triple C Café, it offers an assortment of affordable breakfasts, lunches and dinners, with breakfast all-day. **Ian's Mountain Bakery** on E. Agate Ave. is where you'll find Mark and Mac when they're in town. The place creates crazy-good pastries, sandwiches, and pizza—breakfast, lunch and dinner—and offers wifi for those who like to surf the web while drinking their cuppa joe. **Java Lava Cafe & Coffee Lounge** on W. Agate Ave. brews coffee and makes breakfast, lunch, and dessert in a great atmosphere, complete with wifi.

OTHER PLACES TO EAT: **La Guarecita** on E. Agate Ave. serves Mexican fare and ice cream. **Longbranch Restaurant** on Agate Ave. is a family haunt concocting American, German, and Mexican dishes. **Mad Munchies** on Agate Ave. whips up submarine-style "sammiches." **Maverick's Grille** on E. Agate Ave. provides outdoor entertainment area complete with two-level performance stage. **Pearl Dragon Restaurant** on W. Agate Ave. stirs up traditional Chinese food—great food and exceptional service. **Remington's Restaurant** on 4th St. is a family–owned and operated eatery making home-style grub, award-winning green chile, Mexican plates, and a special menu for the giblets (kiddos). **Seven Trails Grille** on Village Rd. serves great Mediterranean-style cuisine at the base of Sol Vista Ski Basin.

Favorite Places to Stay

Blue Spruce Motel is just a clean and affordable accommodation option. Granby, CO, 170 E. Agate Ave., 970-887-3300. **C Lazy U Ranch** is an Orvis-endorsed dude ranch, so you know it's posh. Granby, CO, 3610 US 40, 970-887-3344, http://www.clazyu.com/. **Frontier Motel** is one of those classic pull-up sort of old-school motels that has woodsy pine-paneled walls for a warm comfy-feeling stay. Granby, CO, 970-887-2544, http://www.frontier motelgranby.com/index2.html. **Home on the Range Bed and Breakfast** is a sweet getaway for the him-and-her outdoorsy type. Granby, CO, 62300 US 40, 970-887-2162.

In Kremmling, check out the **Elktrout Lodge.** 970-535-0881, 970-927-3850, http://www.elktrout.com/2009/.

OTHER PLACES TO STAY: Inn at Silver Creek, Granby, CO, 62927 US 40, 888-878-3077, 970-887-2131, http://www.silvercreekgranby.com/. **Littletree Inn,** Granby, CO, 62000 US 40, 970-887-2551, http://www.little treeluxuryinn.com/. **Spirit Mountain Ranch,** Granby, CO, 3863 CR 41, 970-887-3551, http://www.spiritmtnranch.com/. **Westerner Motel,** Granby, CO, 875 W. Agate Ave., 970-887-2093.

Fly Shops, Guides, and Tackle Stores

Mo Henry's Trout Shop (970-726-9754) in Fraser; **Blue River Anglers** (888-453-9171) in Frisco; **The Blue Quill Angler** (800-435-5353, 303-674-4700) in Evergreen; **Breckenridge Outfitters** (877-898-6104, 970-453-4135) in Breckenridge; **Cutthroat Anglers** (970-262-2878) in Silverthorne.

Fishing Places Solid Choices near Home Base

Williams Fork Reservoir: The former state record Northern Pike was raked out of the Williams Fork Reservoir in 1996. It was humongous. Had Tim Bone not scored a greater Northern, weighing in at 30 pounds, 11 ounces, and taping out at 46.5 inches, from Stagecoach Reservoir in 2006, Williams Fork Reservoir would still possess the record. (Google Bone's Northern Pike story. It's kinda funny.)

More leviathans of other species prosper in the Williams—rainbows, cutts, browns, Mackinaw (lake trout), and kokanee salmon. Apparently, the lake-bottom teems with an array of plant life that provides ample and rich enough habitat for all fish to dwell in segregated areas.

Non-motorized hand-launched watercrafts are allowed on the Williams Fork Reservoir, such as kayaks and float tubes, as well as motorboats. All ramps will be closed at night. Overnight beaching of watercrafts is prohibited. See the Lake's website for regulations and details. Ice fishing is allowed in winter, as well.

Colorado River (Gold Medal Waters): Driving on US 40 between Hot Sulphur Springs and Granby, we pull over on a turnout where Byers Canyon begins, overlooking the majestic Colorado River. After passing under a bridge, the river appears as barely a trickle compared to what it was just a few miles downstream in Kremmling, where by then the water is huge and featureless and must be floated. We know the Colorado is Gold Medal Water from the confluence with the Fraser (near Granby) to Troublesome Creek (a few miles east of Kremmling, where the Denver and Rio Grande Railroad has posted a sign that reads "Troublesome"). So, we just gotta

Gold Medal waters on the Colorado River just south of Granby

stop here and put in. We've passed far too much water. It's time.

Downstream of the deep crevasse-like fissure that is Byers Canyon, where the bridge crosses over and the water roars underneath like Godzilla, the Colorado shores up, and it's more easily waded and far more tranquil. Huge bows and browns are the Colorado's strongest denizens, even though this part of the river is often all but forgotten by rodsmen such as us. But we've read up on this piece, and we've found ourselves loving the looks of this broad, open expanse where the river widens, shrinks in depth, but never in character.

Williams wades in downstream of me, then flicks his characteristic laserbeam loop across the flow. The burgeoning sun peers into my camera lens, the line glistens like early morning webs spun by nighttime, and I capture a photo that sings of nature's rhythms. His mending seems effortless, a skill that has befuddled me until recent years. He hooks a trout almost on cue, of what species at this point I don't know. But it's a thing of beauty to see the rod arch, the line go taut, and to hear the reel sizzle from afar. Then, a telltale tailwalk, and a spray of mist bursts from the surface, and within moments my "breakwater brother" is netting his catch—a medium-sized Colorado River rainbow on this Gold Medal section. Yes, the day has begun well. The trout gods have blessed us once again.

But within moments of fortune, dark foreboding clouds slide over the canyon, blocking the slow-tracking sun, changing our boyish temperaments to growls and groans. We thought we had hit it! Here below a breathtaking Byers Canyon, where this epic stream is still small, a child itself, with a freestone bottom and legendary hatches, where the trout are rumored to reach 2 feet in length or more, especially up in the canyon where the river turns dark with depth, although being more dangerous to negotiate. It was already time to leave.

Our advice for jumping into the Colorado here is to fish where we did, below the bridge at the downstream side of Byers Canyon. Bring your 4 wt. or 5 wt. rod and plenty of dries like orange Stimulators, red or yellow Humpies, green drakes, caddis, and even patterns made for the legendary hatches of *pteronarcys*, known to most as the highly anticipated salmonfly. Yes, those hatches occur here, and when it does, it's insanity!

We pack up and head to the town of Granby, chased by rain. We're a little wet, and Williams is shivering.

He and I are standing in line at a popular local bakery joint in Granby called Ian's. This is where we've decided to sup a cup of lava java. Just about to order coffees and breakfast. The owner-man is a rather energetic chap, happily flitting back and forth from the kitchen to the counter, and he knows everyone in line by first name. Except us.

We are stretching, Mark is yawning, and I'm gnawing my jaw trying to work it out. It's a paralyzing pain that anesthesia wouldn't seem to ease at this point. I've lost sleep because of it. Lots of sleep. I'm grumpy. Hungry. In need of caffeine. And this jolly good baker-jockey guy is just amazing at what he does, and he loves his work to boot.

I belt out my order, "Tall Americano and a stuffed ham and cheese breakfast croissant," because it's kinda getting cold and wet out there and I want something substantial. Williams is eyeballing a strawberry cream cheese scone–sorta–looking thing. I know I will have trouble chewing but I don't care.

"If I knew how to hunt," Williams whispers, "I'd come here again. I love the vibe of this place. It's small hunting town charm meets sophisticated uptown cuisine. Did you see the restaurant next door? Wow. Very nice."

I nod yes. "But you don't even hunt. Do you even own a gun?" I mumble, barely moving my jaw.

"Yes." But then, he seems scared that I'll ask what kind of gun it is.

"What kind of gun?" I sound like Marlon Brando in the Godfather movies at this point.

"Hell, I dunno what it is. A 38 caliper yacht 6, or something like that. I think. I dunno. My dad left it to me. Never shot it."

The man in front of us turns around and shoots him a look that makes me feel like he's the Teflon Don of the Mafioso, and he may whack us any moment for not knowing the names of guns. All men should know guns. Because of the Guido-gangster's glare, I feel tiny, and I instinctively shake my head no, stepping away from Williams a wee bit so as not to seem associated with him and his firearm ignorance.

I'm silent now, thinking about this town we're in. It is awfully cute, after all. Granby appears as though a friendly tribe of Cheyenne may trot into town at any moment on horseback offering wacky tobacco and fresh fish from the river. The mountains and valleys on the outskirts are smoothed and quiet, non-dramatic, though verdant and gorgeous nonetheless. And it's evident that life here several hundred years ago for Native Americans would have been prosperous and comfortable, as it is now for the modern-day ranchers and storeowners like Ian.

Mark whispers now, to keep his ignorance under wraps. "It's drizzling. Where do you want to fish? There's Lake Granby down US 34. And then there's Lake Granby. And also, I think there's a place called Lake Granby near both of those, as well. This home base is all its own damn thing."

"Well, then why don't we hit all three?"

"Brilliant!"

(On our way out to the Jeep with our victuals...)

"How is it?" I probe about his strawberry upside down muffin cake thingy. Williams graciously breaks me off a chunk, insinuating simultaneously that, yes, it's incredible, and that, yes, he desires a proportional chunk of my delicious breakfast croissant in return.

"Dang that's tasty!" My voice muffled by pastry and pain—such sweet sorrow. "On to Lake Granby?" I whoop aloud.

"To Lake Granby!" he retorts, toasting with his coffee.

Lake Granby: The drive from Granby to the lake named after it is tranquil and serene, scenery included. We cross the Colorado River again on US 34 just before the lake entrance, and the tailwater looks amazing. Big, but manageable. Manageable, but big. *Surely there is a Frankenstein or two in there...*

(Moments later, in the Jeep...)

I'm reading up on the lake at this point, curious to know more about what to expect from this loch. An explosion of books, magazines, and maps inside the Jeep. It's so close to Rocky Mountain National Park that I feel I'd almost rather skip Lake Granby altogether. Keep moving on. Drive north. Ascend into Heaven. *Salmonidae* bliss. "The Park."

But reading up on Lake Granby proves vexing to the soul. It's massive—forty miles of shoreline. And deep—up to 221 feet in depth. Add all that H_2O together and you end up with a voluminous body of water, shores surrounded by "fishy" names, and a grand total surface area of 7,256 acres. Its capacity of nearly half a million acre-feet and its mythical setting on the outskirts of "The Park" forces us to stop. We knew passing it up would be a blunder. Plus, it's raining anyways. We might as well be in Hoboken, or Fargo, or Bangladesh for that matter. There will be no fishing here today. So what does it matter where we are?

We dock the Aliner in a pricey little spot called Arapaho Campground that costs us $25 for the night. It's right on the lake. We're both a little pissed about dropping a Jackson-Lincoln combo just to pop up the camper for a few hours. But I'm sidetracked with the map. And Williams seems as though he's preoccupied with rearranging his wallet from one back pocket to the other because it's so thick that his spine is tweaked and he's exaggerating about having a slipped disc. Whatever.

Particular place names on the lake edges focus me on why we stopped in the first place: Rainbow Bay, Kokanee Cove, Fish Bay, Cutthroat Trout Bay, and Lock Leven Bay. (Lock leven is another name for brown trout.) And hell yeah, you can catch all these in Lake Granby, as well as 30-pound Mackinaw, a.k.a. lake trout. (Why fish seem to need two names I'm not sure. Some say po-TAY-toe, some say po-TAH-toe. Some say Mackinaw, some say lake trout. Lock leven or browns? Sand bass or white bass? Black bass or largemouth? Go figure.)

"Twenty-five dollars? Really? A campsite is just kept-up dirt and rocks, and it costs $25 to park on it for a few spins of the hour hand?" I whine to Williams. Dastardly rates, but we need the rest, and the restroom is right next to us.

(Late afternoon...)

Rain. Cold and brutal. We wait, periodically glancing out the windows, checking for any change. No fishing is taking place, and we're huddled up with our notes on past voyages and highballs holding Early Times whiskey.

Darkness descends upon Lake Granby with more rain and heavy, ghostly clouds. Williams falls into a state of anxious slumber while my jaw prods me awake. I massage it, and toss a drink into the back of my throat. It's all I can do.

Williams wakes in the night with one of his fits of asthma. Deep wheezy gasps.

Crawling out of my nest early in the a.m., I make my routine route to the potty. A heavy unsettling veil of gray-silver velvet clouds blanket the area, and visibility is laughable—down to about twenty feet. The lake is eerily still, motionless as the dead. Not a breath of wind. Only a single crow, whose caw seems to mock me.

The Brady Bunch has apparently camped next to us. The sheer number of bicycles indicates many offspring, one of which, about five years old, is already up, tootling about on his tricycle. I thought I saw one of them juggling.

Another was riding a unicycle. One more hot babe was doing trapeze from a big pine tree.

As I make my paper barrier between my derriere and the plastic pot, the tot outside begins ramming the front wheel of his tricycle into the shithouse door while I'm trying to relax and go.

Bang! Bang! Bang!

Are you kidding me? I think aloud.

Bang! Bang! Bang!

Frustrated and unfinished, I burst out of the john at this kid (yes, my drawers were up), with my hand fashioned as a gun, and I clip off a few loud BANG! BANG! BANG!'s of my own right back on him as I stagger in agony back to the Aliner. The scary mafia-looking man standing in line before us the morning prior would have been proud, as I knew the name of my piece would have been a Loogie 9 millimeter. (Unlike the sleeping Curmudgeon, I know my guns.) Funny thing was, while this tot's "bangs" kept me from doing my business, I do believe he crapped his own pants at the sound of my "bangs."

I wake Williams with a grumble about the Brady Bunch debacle. I speak of going fishing in the kayak. Groggy and despondent, I rig up my 5 wt. and tell him that he should make us some coffee and cook breakfast burritos with the basil and tomato wraps we had left over. I trust deeply that he would not botch things up as I paddle my way out into the mist, trolling a large fly called a Zonker with some flash about it (a fly I use for catching carp back home) and dreaming of Rocky Mountain National Park in our near future.

Once I am literally out in the thick of things, the zip of my reel shakes me awake. I hook a big bow that puts up the weakest fight in history. Once I bag him, I reach for my camera to capture the thick-bodied brute, lazy as he is, only to realize I have left my camera in the trailer. "Ugh," I groan. "'Tis a strange morning indeed."

Four fish in all were caught on Lake Granby—all 4 were rainbows. I was hoping for something a little more, I dunno, unique. The creepiest part of the day was hearing a johnboat with three dudes inside puttering around for trout in the earliest of morning hours. I could hear them at daybreak, before I'd paddled out, having their conversations about their hometown of Granby, about their work, about their families, about their fish tales—I never saw them, only heard them. The mist was far too thick. They may as well have been Specters of the Loch.

For the Adventurer

Williams Fork River: If you possess an explorative spirit, the Williams Fork River is a well-known, yet infrequently visited top-shelf fishery. With sizable trout that will require a hike or a bike, the best fishing on Williams Fork is between Williams Fork Reservoir and US 40. From Kremmling, head east on US 40 and park near the tiny blip of a town called Parshall. Find your way to the stream and wade up the Williams Fork from its confluence with the Colorado. (Fishing just below the dam is not permitted.)

Another option for finding the stream is to turn south just east of Parshall on the road to Williams Fork Reservoir. You'll see the DOW parking area on the west side of the road. From here you'll have to find your way to the river as well, but others have ventured before you, so follow their footfalls.

A huge rainbow cruises in the shallows of Lake Granby.

Since this is a tail water that feeds the Colorado, the river fluctuates daily. When it's not too high, wading is possible nearly the 2 full miles of available public access from the Colorado confluence upstream to just below the dam. A variety of water winds through the grassy/ brushy area, with many paths along the bank. A light presentation is essential with dries, as the water is typically clear and it's easy to line these browns and rainbows. Practice catch and release below the dam to the Colorado River, and we suggest using a dry-dropper rig for those trout that won't rise to dries.

Fraser River: The Fraser is a forgotten piece. Not too big, not too small. The fact of the matter is, there are trout in the Fraser that will rival those found in most large rivers. Weirdly large trout for the size of water they're in, like that found in our secret "God Creek" or the Cochetopa. You just have to find them. (Google "Fraser trout motel" for more fun.)

There is no effective way for us to give written directions from Granby to the better stretches of the Fraser because the web of roads and trails leading to the stream off of US 40 south of Granby are unmarked or unnamed on most maps. You might as well ask Phil Spector for written directions on how he gets his hair to do that. All we can say is find "Elkdale" on your DeLorme topo map, and track yourself to it using common sense.

As for insects, *baetis* will hatch in April through May, midges from April to December, Pale Morning Dun from July to August, terrestrials from July to mid-September, Golden Stoneflies from June to September, stoneflies from June to August, green drakes from mid-June to August, and caddis from mid-June to mid September. So take your respective flies in a variety of sizes. Try a beadhead dropped off of a fat, puffy dry dressed with floatant when dries won't work.

16 Grand Lake

Williams and I stop in Grand Lake after leaving Rocky Mountain National Park one late August evening. We've just backpacked for three days. Lived off of nothing but couscous and treated water. Decided that backpacks are get-what-you-pay-for sorta items, and Mark is paying more than $59 for his next one. Decided that being without your woman for more than seven days is torture beyond all tortures. By then, even some of the crevices in passing rock formations seem provocative at this point. (Mark says he didn't feel the same way, but hey, he's old.) A man learns to ignore a lot in the wild.

"Man, I've lost weight. I aim to fix it in one meal," I dare. Something called a Dairy King appears outta the dark. Streetlamps illuminate the mist like the trail of a comet down the main street. A greasy spoon is just the sorta dive we're searching for.

Williams parks the Jeep, and I stand under a streetlight in the parking lot. I'm wiping my body down with a scented wetnap when I suddenly discover an intrigued couple watching from their car across the lot. I'm not naked, but I'm putting my hands in places they'd probably rather not have seen.

We're disheveled, unkempt, and we reek of moose ass and stale cigar smoke, and we appear to be in a beard-growing contest, as Williams looks like Walt Whitman and I am doing my best Hagrid impersonation. The town

Part of the boardwalks around Grand Lake

Windsailing is a favorite sport on Grand Lake after ice out.

seems to have gone quiet when we roll in as though two thirds of ZZ Top showed up for a free gig without informing Grand Lake of the appointment.

"Okay Williams," I say. "If Vale is Selma Hayek, Estes Park is Audrey Hepburn, and Aspen is... I dunno... Joan Rivers... (Williams grins)... then Grand Lake is *fill in the blank*?"

It's obvious this town's nothing like any other in Colorado, and Williams loves this game I'm playing. So before my voice is eaten by the Langoliers, the name Janis Joplin falls from his mug.

"Hm. Okay, I'm feelin' that. I was thinking more like Liz Taylor, but I know where you're coming from."

We stagger into the "King," order our dream burgers, plus some fried zucchini and tater tots. No one seems to even see us. Or smell us. We were ghosts. We blended. Faded. Unjudged we remained. It was nice not to have to worry about certain things, for once.

Grand Lake is comfortable in her own skin, pretending to be nothing other than who she is. Her clothes may be dated and out of style, but they are clean, and at one time they were the cat's pajamas. She's evidently had her heyday, but today isn't that day. Only signs of her era remain.

Even so, Grand Lake, well, she is full of unpretentious, hard-working people who love the mountains and don't need condos or European SUVs to enjoy life there. Though she is merely a stop-off sorta lover, she is the southwestern gateway into Rocky Mountain National Park.

Many miles of river fishing exist without going inside Rocky Mountain National Park, as well. However, we think "The Park" and all its protected glory offers the best water if home basing Grand Lake.

Favorite Places to Eat

Dairy King on Grand Avenue and Broadway will clog your arteries right up with a greasy burger, fries, and a thick vanilla malt. **Fat Cat Café** on Grand Avenue serves a delightful breakfast buffet and a lunch that keeps visitors coming back for dinner! Their croissants are insane! **Grand Pizza** on Grand Avenue makes this BBQ chicken pizza that you cannot put down! The service is always top notch.

OTHER PLACES TO EAT: **Pancho & Lefty's** Mexican restaurant, the **Sagebrush BBQ & Grill, El Pacifico,** and **Paul's Inferno Grill,** all on Grand Avenue, are positively tempting and will offer something for everyone.

Favorite Places to Stay

Our home base lodging suggestion for Grand Lake is to stay downtown in the historic boardwalk area at **The Inn at Grand Lake.** It's centrally located and the rooms are clean, reasonable and it's close to the water. 1103 Grand Ave., 800-722-2585, 970-627-9234, www.innatgrandlake.com. **The Daven Haven Lodge** offers many private cabins from which to choose. 604 Marina Dr., 970-627-8144, 970-627-5098, http://www. davenhavenlodge. com/DHL_cottages.htm.

OTHER PLACES TO STAY: **The Gateway Inn,** 200 W. Portal Rd., 877-627-1352, 970-627-2400, http://www.gatewayinn.com/ html/lodging.html. **Rapids Lodge and Restaurant,** 209 Rapids Ln., 970-627- 3707, http://www.rapidslodge. com/lodging.htm. **Spirit Lake Lodge,** 829 Grand Ave., 800-544-6593, http://www. spiritlakelodge.com/. **The Terrace Inn,** 813 Grand Ave., 888-627-3001, 970-627-3000, http://grandlaketerrace inn.com/room1. html. **Western Riviera Motel Cabins,** 419 Garfield St., 970-627-3580, http://www. westernriv.com/rooms.htm.

You'll find this sort of brook trout in North Inlet Creek above Grand Lake.

Fishing Places Solid Choices near Home Base

Grand Lake: There is some fine fishing in Grand Lake itself, the deepest natural lake in Colorado at 265 feet deep. Grand Lake is a mile and a half long and a mile wide, and it's filled to the top with rainbow, brook, Mackinaw, cutthroat trout, and some huge kokanee salmon (which are amazing to eat).

There are no restrictions on boats at Grand Lake, and it is known as the world's highest yacht anchorage, with the Grand Lake Yacht Club boasting 55 boats in its fleet. The boat ramp is located at the southeast side of the lake and can be accessed by traveling south on West Portal Road (CO 278). This is the best way to experience Grand Lake. Consider hiring a guide service to tootle you around in their watercraft.

Trolling, jigging, bait, lure, and flyfishing all are worthwhile ways to land fish, even through the winter ice. But since pumping through the canal continues, fish activity in the channel and around the West Portal remain good; these areas remain open for fishing most of the winter season.

Shadow Mountain Lake: Connected to Grand Lake is Shadow Mountain Lake, home to brown, rainbow, and salmon. Like Grand Lake, the best way to fish it is to charter a guide trip and let them do all the work. It's what they do. Otherwise, bring your boat and enjoy the amazingly stunning scenery.

Mac trolls a #14 beadhead Prince Nymph behind his kayak.

For the Adventurer

Tonahutu Creek: The trailhead for reaching this headwater to the Colorado River is just outside Grand Lake, and it's called the Tonahutu/North Inlet Trailheads. This stream is full of small but frisky brookies and brown trout and is a blast to fish as you hike along the Tonahutu Creek Trail. Take 1 wt. to 3 wt. rods and small dry flies like Irresistibles and Parachute Adams.

Lake Nanita: The North Inlet Trailhead is located just north of Grand Lake. Stay on CO 278 and bypass the main road through Grand Lake by bearing left. Continue to a marked turn left (north) about 0.8 miles from US 34. Follow this narrow, unpaved road to the North Inlet Trailhead.

Here you will traverse the North Inlet Trail to Lake Nanita, which is approximately 22 miles round trip—a two-day hike for most adventurers. The North Inlet Creek along the trail will be full of brown, brook, and cutthroat trout, so we recommend camping at least a night, or three, in the backcountry. You will need a back country permit, so connect with the rangers in the area.

Once at Lake Nanita, you will most likely be alone, with the exception of bears, elk, and moose—and of course, the wild trout.

It is critical to be prepared for backcountry commitments such as the North Inlet and Lake Nanita trails. Do not attempt this trip unless you are experienced in hiking, backpacking, camping, and surviving the elements posed by the harshest of outdoor environments. Visiting with the rangers is mandatory, and the rental of specific gear will be, as well.

> **Best Colorado Waters for Kayak Fishing**
> • White River near Meeker
> • Williams Reservoir north of Pagosa Springs
> • Trappers Lake
> • Yampa River above Steamboat
> • San Juan in Pagosa Springs
> • Lake Granby
> • Spinney Mountain Reservoir
> • The Arkansas between Buena Vista and Salida
> • The Animas in Durango
> • La Jara Reservoir

Mac landed this hefty rainbow from his kayak on Grand Lake.

17 Grand Mesa

Grand Mesa is a strangely foreign sort of place. Almost like it's an entirely different country within the country, as though the mesa cliff edges are its fortress borders, and all things inside them have been hidden away from us for all time. There is simply too much to fish—too many lakes, too many ponds, too many streams, too many beaver ponds—and too many fish, too many roads, too many trails... It's an amazing cut-out of Colorado that has to be experienced in order to be appreciated, to reveal what all it has hidden. Therefore, this chapter is our homage to such a beautifully huge, overwhelmingly beautiful wilderness. It is written in screenplay script form because when we were there we felt unimportant, insignificant, miniscule—chess pieces upon the board of life. We are but pawns within a game.

> *All the world's a stage,*
> *And all the men and women merely players;*
> *They have their exits and their entrances,*
> *And one man in his time plays many parts...*
> —WILLIAM SHAKESPEARE (*As You Like It*)

Ext. Co 92 Near Delta, Colorado—10:14 a.m.

The flats of the Gunnison River Valley. It's July 6th. The pomp and circumstance of fireworks and light parades are now fading into a nebulous patchwork of nameless streams, creeks, alpine lakes, dirt roads, highways, forests, pine trees, even more Subaru Outbacks, and endless granola bars as fast as pages can be torn away from a calendar. Two round characters, Mark D. Williams and W. Chad McPhail, are exploring northwestern Colorado. Both writers. Both teachers. Both in love with trout. Williams is gnawing on beef jerky, pondering the proper discourse for the next ten days of journeying, and wrestling with the cord that charges his iPhone, all simultaneously. McPhail is simply wondering how Williams is still alive at his age.

Williams: Dude, check out Grand Mesa from here. It's like K2 with its legs cut off.

McPhail: Yeah. It's Ozymandias. Or no. It's the trunk of the tree Paul Bunyan chopped down.

Williams: No. Even better. It's Mauna Loa, but only the part you can see underwater.

McPhail: It's like Ayers Rock times a million times infinity.

Williams: It reminds me of Golan Heights, near Galilee.
McPhail: You killed it.
Williams: I did, didn't I?
McPhail: We're driving up that, huh? (McPhail appears daunted. He genuflects.)
Williams: I know, right! Giddy-up! (Williams appears deranged.)

Atop Grand Mesa, the cap is as expected. As with any other mesa, it's flat, only on a grander scale. It's the largest mesa in the world, after all. Some print references say there are over one hundred bodies of water. Others say over three hundred. The two characters are not sure how many there are. They do not pretend to be experts in this area. Either way, the two characters realize immediately by the map that it would take an entire summer to fish the entire mesa. After all, Grand Mesa IS the largest flat top mountain on earth.

Williams: Pick a few lakes, and we'll go fish them.
McPhail: Okay. Hmm. Where should we start? I mean, Damn. So many...There are three main areas to go to: Land O' Lakes area, Mesa Lakes area, and Plateau Valley area.
Williams: Let's start with the obvious. Any lakes called Fish Lake? Trout Lake? State Record Lake? Anything good like that?
McPhail: Uh, I don't see a Fish Lake. But here, I'll name some off and you can pick. How's that?
Williams: Okay.
McPhail: Holy Terror Reservoir....
Williams: ? ? ? (Question marks literally appear floating above Williams' head.)
McPhail: Okay, I take that as a 'no.' How 'bout Dogfish Reservoir?
Williams: (doggedly) Isn't a dogfish a shark? I mean, how would a dogfish get up here? I'd rather not. No Catfish Reservoirs, either. A catfish is like the opposite of a shark.
McPhail: Okay. Here's one! Goodenough Reservoir...
(McPhail highlights this one with Williams' hot pink highlighter in hopes that he'll like this one.)
Williams: Nope. Not good enough.
McPhail: (dejected) Okay then. Well how 'bout Neversweat Reservoir?
Williams: Huh? What is this, an antiperspirant commercial? Just find us a regular-named lake with some fish in it!
McPhail: How does Sunset Lake sound?
Williams: Sounds like something you fish at sunset, Mac. It's not even noon. We can go there later. Someplace else! Is there a Nooner Lake?
McPhail: ? ? ? (Question marks literally appear floating above McPhail's head.)
This word volley goes on for approximately 27 minutes.

McPhail: This website I printed off says the rivers cutting through this mesa have an incision rate of 0.18 meters per one thousand years. That's about how long it takes you to make up your mind to fish a place, you know that!

Williams: We need to find a campsite. The shadows are getting long.

McPhail: Yes! There is a god! A reprieve from the pressure of finding a lake. There's only 18 campgrounds to choose from. There's Little Bear Campground, Jumbo Campground, Cobbett Lake Campground...

Williams: Wait a minute. Eighteen?

McPhail: There are 260 campsites.

Williams: Jeez! Is there one called Club Med Campground? Just find us a good place. You're taking longer than the rivers do at .18 meters per 1,000 years.

McPhail: Dude, the maps don't have photos printed on them. There's just a bunch of squiggly lines and teepee icons. How do I know what's good and what isn't? No. There's no Club Med Campground. But there's an Island Lake Campground! Is that close enough?

Williams: Hell no. Alcatraz was an island. Would you want to camp there?

McPhail: ? ? ?

Cobbett Lake is one of the prettiest atop Grand Mesa.

With the Aliner bouncing around behind the Jeep like a lowrider, the two characters course a web of poorly kept dirt roads and apparent ATV trails for hours, passing lake after lake, each encircled by towering pines, all seemingly carbon copies of the lakes prior, though with a different shape, size, and name.

McPhail: These lakes all seem the same, just with different names.
Williams: Yeah. Sorta like women…
McPhail: (smiles with a smirk and a nod)
Williams: (nods with a smirk and a smile)
McPhail: How many miles have we driven up here today?
Williams: All of them.
McPhail: ? ? ?

Some of the lakes and reservoirs are within earshot of one another. Others are alone in the woods. Trout rises speckle the surface of nearly all of them, and many are connected by thin, transparent creeks that hold three, sometimes four species of trout—brook, rainbow, cutthroat, and a few browns scattered here and there. Most of the campgrounds are full to capacity this time of summer. Stratified layers of campfire smoke rest in the forest among the denseness of trees and gooseneck trailers and smells of yesteryear. A deer rests in the shaded foliage, hiding from all Mankind, while chipmunks nibble at the bootlaces of unsuspecting grandfathers eating steamy breakfasts with anxious grandsons. Amid the beauty of this ancient fortress, there is one looming impediment, though neither is aware.

After more hours of driving and photographing a string of relentlessly reminiscent lakes, our two characters have yet to find an open campsite. Swear words and cigar fumes waft from the Jeep windows.

Williams: There's a spot. Let's take it.
McPhail: That's not even a campsite. It's just an opening next to the road.
Williams: So?
McPhail: Okay.

The sun, by now, is setting, and the hum of mosquitoes is thickening. A dozen bites at once. Williams swipes and kills six on his arm. (50 percent ain't bad.) McPhail makes attempts at building a fire with wet wood, to no avail. Thick smoke billows from the logs like London skies during the Industrial Revolution, but not even Armageddon could stop the onslaught of the winged pesky insects.

McPhail: We're going to die.
Williams: Yes, we are.
McPhail: Let's get in the Aliner and fish tomorrow.
Williams: Okay.

Int. Inside the Aliner—April 7, 1:14 a.m.

Williams is snoring and swatting at phantom mosquitoes in his sleep. He also dreams that he tells McPhail Ward Creek Reservoir is one of the first easily fishable lakes when arriving from the south on CO 65 from Cedaredge and sustains a healthy strain of cutthroat. Rainbow trout are stocked regularly. McPhail is dreaming of fancifully dressed women from Aspen adorned in Spandex and sports bras.

Ext. the Banks of Ward Creek Reservoir—10:46 a.m.

Fog rests upon the glass surface of Ward Creek Reservoir like weary ghosts as the sun breaks through the pines. McPhail quickly gears up and heads down the grassy slope, 3 wt. in hand, to the inlet where trout feed on insects trapped in the current filter into the mouth of the lake. Rises are everywhere, more numerous than Williams' polar fleeces, and the lake seems like a long, deep scar upon the surface of the plateau. On the first cast, a trout rises and nips at the fly, but misses. Moments later, McPhail catches a rainbow trout in the same tailout. Williams seems undaunted, unaffected, complacent, and walks across the paved road to the feeder creek. He is in another place, another time. McPhail continues to sightcast to 15 to 20 trout in the opening of the feeder, but nothing works.

Ext. Ward Creek (Feeder Creek to Ward Creek Reservoir)

Williams: (whispering loudly, waving McPhail to come thither)
Mac. You won't believe this. Come see! But be stealthy.

Trout packed in close in Ward Creek

McPhail sashays across the road. Williams points to the stream with a smoldering cigar in hand. He's decided to take photos instead of fishing.

Williams: Look at all those trout!
McPhail: Holy Schmoly!

Williams: Ward Creek, if that's what it's called, it's an anomaly!

McPhail: So are these mosquitoes. They're back. And they're pissed. And they've brought friends. I didn't realize skeetas woke up so early.

Williams: Quit being a wuss. Go catch a trout down there in that inlet creek. And don't come back till ya have.

McPhail: Okay. Ten trout. Then we leave? Agreed? Pinkie swear or I'm not going down there. I'll let the mosquitoes suck my soul out! Right here. Right now!

Williams: Ten trout, and we're gone. I swear.

McPhail, our protagonist at this point, descends quickly to the banks of this shallow creek. Clear as warm vodka…only colder. On three successive casts, McPhail connects with 3 trout. First, another rainbow, a twin of the one in Ward Reservoir. Then a brown. Next, a cutthroat.

Williams: (backlit by the sun, from the road above, with smoke billowing around him like Cheech and/or Chong, only it's NOT marijuana smoke, but Maduro smoke) Nice, Mac! Seven more! Just like that!

McPhail: Wait. That will make eleven total, counting the one in Ward Reservoir!

Williams: Nope. We agreed. Ten trout, AFTER the one in the lake.

McPhail: (in a minstrel show-type voice) Ugh. Whatever you say bossman!

Williams: Only seven more now!

McPhail: (to himself) No pressure…

McPhail eyeballs a turn in the river where trout are holding nose to tail, pectoral to pectoral, as though trained by Hitler's regime to do so. Dewdrops glisten in the shin-deep grass. Pine trees are thirty feet from the river's far edge, where the mountain top seems to scrape the clouds. From this point, McPhail, not taking a single step from where he was in the stream, nets 6 consecutive brook trout without losing his fly, nor his wits.

Williams: How come all those were so small? You know how I like big fish.

McPhail: Because your glasses are so thick. They just looked tiny from there.

Williams: Catch a big one! C'mon! Stop sandbagging!

McPhail: (in a put out tone) Fine. So be it. Let's walk up and find a pool. There will be big fish in here coming up from Ward Reservoir. Big pools equal big trout.

Williams: (magnanimously) Agreed!

The two characters walk less than thirty yards and creep up on a deep pool behind a spill. It appears as a boiling cauldron—a cold witch's brew of rainbow, brook, and cutthroat trout, no doubt.

Williams: If you land a big fish in that pool on the first cast, I swear on all things sacred to me, I will buy you a steak dinner.

Deus ex Machina (Look it up if you don't know what this means.) Williams is in a self-induced pickle of a predicament. He wants to see a big fish. But he doesn't want to buy a steak dinner. Unfortunately for him, the "Giant Rainbow Trout in the Sky" takes the fly on the first cast and pulls McPhail and Williams off-stage, saving them from assured death by means of mosquito bites. They are saved, and all conflicts are resolved simultaneously in one fell swoop. But the story is not over...

Mac lands a rainbow at the inlet to Ward Creek Reservoir.

Int. the Ghost Ranch Saloon in Steamboat Springs—
Approximately Three Hours Later

McPhail: Damn. How come BBQ purchased by your buddy always tastes SO MUCH better? (He grins and smears dribbling BBQ sauce across his face with a swipe of his sleeve.)

Williams: Kiss it, Mac. (He pauses momentarily while chewing his locally grown cheeseburger.) But nice fish. That Ward Creek was teeming with trout swimming up from Ward Creek Reservoir—rainbows, cutts, and white suckers too. Colorado River cutt fingerlings are stocked periodically from what I've read.

Favorite Places to Eat

Other than the restaurant in Mesa Lakes Resort and Thunder Mountain Lodge, you won't find much food plated atop the Mesa. Grand Mesa is really camper's paradise, so most bring food of their own.

Thunder Mountain Lodge (formerly Spruce Lodge) boasts a restaurant and a bar. Cedaredge, CO, 20658 Baron Lake Dr., 877-470-6548, 970-856-6240, http://www.sprucelodgecolorado.com/. **Mesa Lakes Resort** will put food in your tummy, put a few groceries in your bag, AND put you up for a spell. The Stiers Family owns and operates the entire place and welcomes you to stay a few. Located 50 minutes east of Grand Junction on CO 65, near milepost 36, 12 miles south of the town of Mesa. Exit 49 from I-70 and go south 26 miles. 970-268-5467, http://www.coloradodirectory.com/mesalakesresort/.

The Mesa Lakes Country Store

Grand Mesa 17

Favorite Places to Stay

You'll find **Aspen Trails Campground, Store and Cabins** 3 miles north of Cedaredge. The Merceps welcome you to join them for your stay. Cedaredge, CO, 19991 CO 65, 970-856-6321. **The Cedaredge Lodge** is an extremely well kept motel- style accommodation right on the edge of a stream. Very clean and comfortable place with a nostalgic feel. Cedaredge, CO, 810 N. Grand Mesa Dr., 970-856-3727, 970-856-3728, http://www.thecedaredge lodge.com/. Carol and Terry Jarbo are adorable and would love to have you stay at the **Creek Side Bed & Breakfast** right next to the stream. Cedaredge, CO, 790 N. Grand Mesa Dr. (CO 65), 970-856-7696, 970-485-2496, http://www.creeksidebed-breakfast.com/index.html.

Grand Mesa Lodge is located 16 miles north of the town of Cedaredge and has it all, horses, fishing, cabins, you name it. Cedaredge, CO, 2825 CO 65, 800-551-6372, 970-856-3250, http://www.coloradodirectory.com/grand mesalodge/. **Thunder Mountain Lodge** (formerly Spruce Lodge) has cabins, a restaurant, a bar, wifi, a hot tub, and plenty more to brag about. See previous page. **Mesa Lakes Resort** will put food in your tummy, put a few groceries in your bag, AND put you up for a spell. See previous page.

OTHER PLACES TO STAY: Lovett House Bed & Breakfast, Cedaredge, CO, 210 N. Grand Mesa Dr., 970-856-4375, http://www.lovetthousebandb. com/. **Tri R Motel,** Cedaredge, CO, 885 S. Grand Mesa Dr., 970-856-3222.

Mac casts to rising trout on Ward Creek Reservoir.

Battlement Mesa Outfitters offers camps, as well as guided fishing trips, half-day and full-day trips from the ranch. They can also pack you in for a few days up on Battlement or Grand Mesa. 970-487-9918.

Campsites
Grand Mesa Campgrounds: Visit the website (http://www.forestcamping. com/dow/rockymtn/gmsa.htm) and call ahead to reserve your site at any of these campgrounds if you plan a stay during the busy season. Don't let the number of sites on this list make you complacent. They fill quickly, and like what happened with us, if you don't have a site on the mesa you'll spend valuable fishing time searching for what may not exist!

Cedaredge Area Sites: Cobbett Lake (18 sites), **Island Lake** (41 sites), **Little Bear** (35 sites), **Ward Lake** (40 sites).

Collbran Area Sites: Big Creek (26 sites), **Cottonwood** (36 sites), **Crag Crest** (11 sites), **Weir & Johnson** (12 sites).

Mesa Area Sites: Jumbo (26 sites), **Spruce Grove** (15 sites).

Fly Shops, Guides, and Tackle Shops
Battlement Mesa Outfitters (970-487-9918) offers guided fishing trips, half-day and full-day trips from the ranch. They can also pack you in for a few days up on Battlement or Grand Mesas. They provide a very comfortable tent camp set at 10,000 feet.

Fishing Places Solid Choices near Home Base
Ward Creek Reservoir Area
Cobbett Lake sits right off CO 65, so our two characters couldn't miss it. However, at 10:30 a.m., there was a group of rowdy gypsies on the bank throwing rocks in the water. Trout were rising everywhere, and Williams photographed some edge-cruising rainbow trout dodging the flying stones before they decided to move back down to Ward Creek. Both lakes were rippled with round rises, but Ward was absolutely abandoned.

Eggleston Lake Area
Eggleston Lake is about 2.5 miles east on FR 121 once we turned off of CO 65 before reaching Carp Lake. Eggleston has regularly stocked rainbow trout,

and they will bounce off the water in the mornings and evenings. There are numerous campsites around Eggleston Lake. Fishing pressure is often heavy, but trout will always be present since it's stocked all the time.

Young's Creek Reservoir #2 will allow anglers to fish brook trout and rainbows. White suckers are present as well, but we weren't about to fish for those. Follow the unpaved road (121) to the left around the north shore of Eggleston Lake about 2 miles farther until you reach FR 124. Turn right and go 0.6 miles to Young's Creek Res. #2. You will not regret this trip if you hit YCR#2 at the right time of day.

Small, wet streams and big dry flies

Young's Creek is easily accessible and holds brook trout and Colorado cutthroat trout, which we love to fish for. In the upper stretches between Young Lakes and Kiser Lake, the stream held trout passing from still water to still water, and the few miles of stream below Kiser Lake that are public hold smallish wild brookies and cutts as well, and fishing pressure is almost non-existent. Just do it!

Crag Crest Trail Area

Upper ("Little") Eggleston Lake is easily reached by remaining on the left fork of FR 121 that moves around the north shore of Eggleston Lake and ends at the Crag Crest Campground. There, the Crag Crest National Recreation Trail was visibly marked, and taking that footpath about 0.4 miles led us to Upper Eggleston, where brookies and rainbow literally leapt from the water for "buggage."

Butts Lake is farther down the left fork of the Crag Crest National Recreation Trail once passing Upper Eggleston. Here, fingerling Snake River cutthroat trout are stocked annually or semi-annually, so some of the trout we saw were of the 12-inch size, since fishing pressure is light and some trout survived the ice.

Trickle Park Area

Park Lake is easy to find, but seems way back in there. From the north shore of Eggleston on FR 121, remain heading east-northeast until FR 125 allows you to turn southeast. FR 125 will skirt Park Reservoir rather quickly. The reservoir is home to rainbow and cutthroat trout, and has a few less anglers on it.

Fishing the tiny streams that connect the Grand Mesa lakes pays off.

Military Park Reservoir is not as heavily fished since it is a little more out of the way, so definitely bring the war toys here. It's shallow, so go before it gets too low. It's directly northwest of Park Reservoir, so you will see it off to your left before reaching the right-hand turn onto FR 125.

Cottonwood Lakes Area

Silver Lake: Traveling farther on FR 121 past FR 125 about 5 more miles north of Park Lake will bring us to FR 257, which turns back abruptly to the left (southwest) and past Bonham Reservoir. A ¼-mile foot trail leading up to Silver Lake (off to the left side of the road) will be almost 2 miles down FR 257. Colorado cutts live in there. And if you get lucky, maybe you can figure out why they named it Silver Lake.

Neversweat Reservoir: Drive in 3.3 miles down FR 257, and there will be a fork in the road. Turn right onto FR 258 and proceed down to Neversweat, where the lake will be off to the right. A weak boat ramp is there, but don't try it. Just fish from the bank for rainbows and brooks in the shallows.

One of Mac's rainbow trout on Grand Mesa

18 Gunnison

At the end of the movie *Whale Rider*, the old grandpa says to the granddaughter as she lies in the hospital bed, wise leader, *forgive me for I am new to flight* or something like that—that was my dad at the end—he was wise and should have known, but he could not see. Then in *Whale Rider*, in the last scene, the two are riding on the whale boat, she is a whale rider and her lineage goes back to such and such and he has his arm around her, and with their people, on the water, they ride, they row, they move across the water. That is the way it should have ended with my bear of a Dad and me. But he lay in that bed and struggled for breath and succumbed. Water haunts me.

I have a lifetime in a day some days on the water, wishing my ursine father could have seen fit to join me, wading and casting and catching trout. We didn't get along, not until the last year when he lay in bed while the cancer took over his body. I didn't understand him, he didn't understand me, and respect for each other was hit or miss. I wonder sometimes if Dad wasn't imitating the

The Gunnison River

heroes we watched on the screen, Gary Cooper, John Wayne, Clint Eastwood. Gritting his teeth, not saying much and when he did he said a lot in a very few words—Dad bought into the hero thing. I wish he'd have bought into the father-son thing, seen what I find so important, visited the place, the San Juan Mountains, that I find so meaningful. Gunnison. Lake City. Powderhorn. But he didn't, and that's just the way it is.

I have a bear encounter story. This is not my first, and as much time as I spend in the wilderness, it won't be my last. At least I hope that any future bear encounter story is not my last, but that's another matter altogether. The Gunnison area is where I've had the most bear encounters, even if you added up all the other bear meetings I've had elsewhere combined.

I go fishing with my brothers-in-law Kenny and David every summer when we all get together for our family vacation in Lake City, Colorado. Seems like at least one fishing trip with Dave each of the last few summers has resulted in meeting up with a bear. One summer, Dave and I met up with a big black bear as he ambled along the game trail and poked his head out of the willows by one of the tributaries to the Gunnison. The furry beast studied us (much like a hungry trucker might study the 72-ounce steak at the Big Texan) as he stood no further away than the length of our rods. We intrepid anglers held our ground (and our breath) as the bear considered the menu. Finally, he snorted and barked in annoyance, then he turned away and went back home. Not enough meat. Too sinewy.

None of the three of us is scared of bears, not black bears anyway. We have a healthy awareness for certain, but when out in the middle of the woods, we stay focused and pay them the proper respect. If you respect and understand bears, all is well. If you don't, one can sneak up on you, and there's hell to pay.

We took my Jeep Wrangler on a drive on what some might call a road but Mother Nature is in the process of taking back and turning into a rock field. Our destination? The best unknown creek in the state of Colorado. On the map, it's a tiny blue trickle. At its confluence with a bigger river, it rushes in like another of those tumbling, fishless creeks. But our special creek, one we nicknamed Cutthroat Creek so no others (save those who had passed a blood-brother ceremony) could figure out the location, is not fishless.

Cutthroat Creek is a clear, cold creek, bigger than it ought to be this high up, and it holds umpteen-inch cutthroats in every bend pool. Perhaps there is something special about the insects these fish eat. Whatever it is, these are the most dramatically colorful cutts we have ever seen. There are more cutthroats here than in a Washington, D.C., law firm. And not a human soul in sight.

From the minute we jumped out of the jeep and into the thick of things (no hiking trails except for the game trails), we saw evidence of how wild it could be. Mountain lion tracks, moose tracks, and, yep, bear tracks. There's not a soul in sight because this place is in the middle of nowhere. This is not easy fishing. Thick alders line the river, making casting difficult except from the middle of the stream. Once in the stream, you are locked in until the next clearing and can't see anything but the clear drop-pools in front of you.

We always want to see a bear when we go out fishing. I know, crazy, right, but what's the use of being in nature if you run from it?

From the git go, we caught fish, working our way upstream. At first, we were downstream enough where all we caught were brook trout, so colorful it looked as though Walt Disney himself had painted them. As we moved upstream, we got into the cutthroats. At each pool, a successful cast of a Royal Wulff or Goddard Caddis would result in a hookup with a fat 15- to 18-inch cutthroat.

The cutt would go airborne, unusual for a cutthroat, then bend our 3 wt. rods into the butt and zip three pools below before we could land them. This was a two-man operation at times because the fish were so heavy and athletic.

All along the way, we kept seeing signs of deer, elk, bear, moose, and cougar. David and I lost Kenny at one point, leaving him in a canyon while we went up and over it. He was down in this inaccessible canyon he always finds, and he was catching them left and right. He likes the tough spots, the crazy

One of three reservoirs on the Gunnison

sections where, if you can scramble in, you can be pretty much assured no one else was stupid enough to fish that season or for several seasons. So we left him and hollered that we'd meet him upstream later in the afternoon. No specific time. None of us wear a watch when we're fishing.

We guessed we were two hours and thirty fish ahead of him by late afternoon. When it started hailing and raining, and looked like it was going to snow, we got out of the river and considered doubling back and finding him. David suggested, "It's 4:30, so maybe we ought to go back at 5:00 and look for Kenny." About that time we saw a cutthroat rise in the pool in front of us.

"How about 5:30?" I countered. We laughed. Then we heard the animal in the woods about twenty yards upstream. It was big and headed our way.

David has a Pied Piper way about him. Kenny and I once followed him on the ill-fated Alpine Loop biking adventure, in which a predicted three-hour tour turned worse than *Gilligan's Island*. Kenny and I also followed him on a grueling five-hour trek up a steep mountain peak, intelligently avoiding the easy switchbacking trail two miles to the east ("That's for sissies," he told us at the base). He just has that 'follow me into the fire' sort of way about him. Plus, two minds can conjure ghosts and bears and monsters.

Angling in a Gunnison-area stream

You've seen the horror movies. 'Didja hear that?' they say to each other, responding to what might otherwise be thought of as the house creaking or a benign noise like trees swaying. But get two folks together and alertness meets ingenuity, and in the end paranoia can run rampant. So when he and I heard the big animal crashing through the woods, coming our way, rightly or wrongly I looked to Dave to confirm what I was thinking.

"Son of a gun. That sounds pretty big," I offered.

"That is big. Moose or bear," Dave said. "Bear would be much better than moose, trust me."

Then we heard another limb breaking, and then another, each time bigger and closer. I have been face to face with both bear and moose, and I will take the bear any day. Moose are big and ugly and ill-tempered. Then the woods filled with the biggest crash yet, the limbs on the willows shook, and I looked at Dave.

"You think that's a bear or moose?" I asked.

"I don't know. I just know it's big," Dave answered.

"Think we ought to stick around?" I asked.

"All I know is that it's @#$% big!" he muttered and turned.

I took the turning as the sign to high-tail it out of there, so I flew across the river, up the embankment, dashed through the willows—and then all hell broke loose.

My foot landed in a hole, my knee twisted, I fell hard, my knee hit a pointed rock, my wife's new Nikon camera went splat into the mud, and the bushes were still shaking with the coming of the creature. I lay moaning at my hurt knee and muddied camera, waiting for whatever judgment came my way.

I now turn to Kenny to tell his part of this adventure:

Kenny: My two partners in crime left me in the canyon fishing what I believe is the best fifteen yards of river in Colorado. If I could, I would buy it, but they haven't even seen it, choosing instead to be-bop along the ridge and out of harm's way. I kept fishing fairly quickly, quicker than normal, skipping this hole and that one, in the hopes I might catch up with Mark and David. I ended up catching and releasing countless fish, but never could catch up with those two clowns.

There are those times in life where you come upon an opportunity too good to pass up, but too morally ambiguous to rush into. I gave up fishing around 4:00 p.m. and started up the side of the canyon, hiking along the game trail on the slopes, hoping to overtake Dave and Mark. Bingo.

The two scrambled out of the willows and started talking (not surprising if you know Mark). I imagined they were figuring out how to go back and find me. Yeah right. These two turn back to go into the river and start fishing again, even though it's hailing and I could be far upstream being eaten by a bear. Of course I would do the same for them. Our family rule is that if you're catching fish, family be damned.

And that's when it hit me. I thought about the prank for, oh, maybe two seconds, then went ahead with it. They never saw me. I sneaked up close enough to them where I could hear the murmur of their voices. They stopped at the edge of the willows when they heard the first rock I tossed in the woods upstream. I picked up a larger rock the second time. That got their attention.

The third rock was a wanna-be boulder and as I swung it overhead and heaved it, I lost my footing and slid, busting through the willows as the rock landed with a crash. I got up in time to see Mark walk across water and jump the bank and crash and burn.

I ran over to them, busting through brush and willow. When Dave saw me poke through the alders his voice was excited, and he cautioned me to hurry and watch out for bears. I kept thinking that 'boy am I going to get in trouble for this.' I felt like a first grader going to the principal's office, and I know how that feels.

David: Contrary to Mark's remembrance of the facts, I did not run first! I hadn't seen anything in the bushes, I just saw the "oh shit" look on Mark's face as he wheeled around, flew over the creek and through the thick alders on the opposite bank with unexpected swiftness and athleticism. I followed fast, thinking he must have seen clear and present danger because I'd never seen him move like that before. When I finally broke through the bushes to a clearing, I found Mark down and hurt. I knew this was not going to be good since none of us would show pain unless absolutely necessary. As I started to help him up, the situation worsened. Next to Mark's writhing body, the back of the brand new Nikon camera was sticking up from the mud. I love Nikon cameras. Having my priorities adjusted, I quickly began administering CPR (camera-priority repair). God would heal Mark in time, but only I could help the poor camera. As I revived the Nikon, I heard Kenny holler at us from the cliff above us.

"You guys okay? What's going on down there?"

"Hey, Kenny. Keep an eye out to your right. Mark fell and he's hurt. There's some kind of big animal in there, not far away."

Kenny: I sure didn't want Mark to get hurt. You should have seen the look on those guys' faces. They were convinced something was about to come barreling through the brush and eat 'em up. They're normally not scaredy-cats, so this reaction kind of surprised me. And here Mark is down and injured, David looking after him, and they're taking the time to be telling me to be careful. I rushed over to them, hoping Mark was okay so this practical joke wouldn't backfire. When I got there, Mark and Dave were standing, each with peculiar smiles on their faces. I wondered if I had been duped.

Mark: My knee was hurt, I knew that much. Whether it was from the twisting or the impact on the rock, I didn't know, but the bear was secondary in my mind, maybe even third once I saw how muddy Amy's new camera was.

David: In case I was not clear the first time, I never would have run if Mark hadn't run. I saw his eyes, then saw him take off, so I figured he must have seen something. I told Kenny again to check for the animal as he started down the steep slope to help us but he shrugged me off and made a motion indicating he had thrown rocks. Rocks, big ones, in the alders across the steam where we had heard the big game. Son of a gun, we'd been had.

Kenny: It was bittersweet. Funny that they were fooled. Not so funny that one of them was hurting. Well, kinda funny. At least the Nikon was okay and no rods were broken. I know the guys weren't totally scared—I've been with them too many times in tight spots. But I do know I will have to watch my back from now on.

We fished all the way back up to the Jeep, in the snow and rain and hail, Mark hobbling but catching fish, yakking all the way about how good a prank that was, but in the same breath plotting his revenge. David stayed silent, smiling, his quietness somewhat unnerving as he no doubt planned his payback as well. On the rugged drive back, David re-nicknamed the secret stream, Wounded Knee Creek.

Mark: We had fun telling the tale back at the cabins that night. My knee was all banged up, bruised and cut, but I wasn't going to let them think me a baby. Kenny's wife Betsy chastised Kenny for his actions.

"Kenny, I can't believe you pulled a stunt like that where someone could get hurt. Mark has a right to be mad at you for hurting his knee." Then she paused and thought about me and my goofiness and what I'm all about, then continued with a sly grin, "but he probably deserved it anyway." And then she hugged her bear of a husband. Sometimes what you think is a bear, isn't a bear at all.

It's days like those when I wish my father could have, would have fished with me. I'd have hugged that ol' bear of a father.

Mac and I hit Gunnison several times this year, usually on our way through to other home bases. We stop to grab ice, stock up on food, eat a good meal, catch a pale ale. We ate at the Gunnisack on the main drag twice, and each time we ordered pale ales and cheese fries.

We went to Gene Taylor's Sporting Goods three times—a decent outdoors shop, complete with ornery young clerk/guides. They knew much more about trout fishing than us. Just ask them. We bought bumper stickers and maps and

Downtown Gunnison

books and, of course, some flies, but passed on their overly confident, just-for-the-newbie-angler advice.

Two customers mad-dogged Mac one time in the store. The younger, heavier Mac would have already been up in their ass, but this version is wiser, slower, and meaner in a patient mature way. Both Macs are fun, but this one keeps us out of trouble more.

Gunnison is a blue-collar town, a working man's town. This is not a resort community. The population is 15,000-plus and has a real college (like Durango). Unlike Durango, it doesn't have the same charm. Gunnison is spread out, with lots of grocery stores and liquor stores and Wal-Mart and other bigger city amenities. I've been through and shopped in Gunnison for two decades, but haven't stayed in Gunnison proper. I've stayed and fished a lot around Gunnison—Lake City, Crested Butte, Almont, Powderhorn, and so on. Because Gunnison has all the right stuff, I have considered looking into teaching opportunities at Western State College. But neither Amy nor Mac nor I really think enough of Gunnison to want to do that. Besides, have you ever seen Gunnison on the weather report in winter? Brutal.

We like to:

Shop in Gunnison.

Eat in Gunnison.

Gas up in Gunnison.

Buy flies and gear in Gunnison.

Eat BBQ in Gunnison.

Hit the bars in Gunnison.

Fish around Gunnison.

We don't get the impression we want to make it our home base for

Almont

a fishing trip. You might. A lot of folks do. We like nearby Crested Butte and Almont and Taylor better. Gunnison is great as a home base (for you) because you might sleep elsewhere but you can run into town for groceries, gas, and dinner and get back out to your camp or lodge or cabin easily. The scenery in Gunnison proper is marginal, pedestrian at best, but two minutes out of town, west or east or north or south, is stunning. If you stay in Gunnison, get out, explore, be rewarded. If all you need is a cheap motel and trout fishing choices, then Gunnison is your kind of home base.

What's great about Gunnison as a home base for some (even though it's just too much like a town for me): Gunnison is an amazingly centralized locale. You have so many outdoor opportunities—blue ribbon waters, national forests, wilderness, ghost towns, alpine lakes, campgrounds, big reservoirs, high-country lakes. And the drive to any of them is short.

If you want big water, Gold Medal water, here you go. If you want medium canyon streams, meadow streams, high-country rushing cold clear creeks, remote alpine lakes, big reservoirs with big trout, it's Gunnison, baby. The Upper Gunnison River is underrated for its beauty and quality angling. The main stem of the Gunnison is a major tributary to the Colorado (second biggest), and it has great hatches, big trout. Powderhorn, Cebolla, Taylor, Cimarron, and Lake Fork Gunnison are all quality drainages close to Gunnison, river systems that we've frequented a lot over the years.

Favorite Places to Eat

We always stop and have a pulled pork sandwich at the **5BS** (970-641-7360). We also like **Garlic Mike's Italian** (970-641-2493) and **Sugah's Café** (970-641-4990).

Favorite Places to Stay

Your choices range from the 1950s-style ranch motels to chains like Holiday Express and Rodeway. My cousins stayed at the **Water Wheel Inn** (970-641-1650), and it's pretty and all, so it's up there on our list. Cabins are all over the place, but it'd be best to contact the chamber to get a complete updated list. http://www.gunnison-co.com/.

Fly Shops, Guides, and Tackle Stores

Gunnison Fish & Raft (www.floatfish.com) and **High Mountain Outdoors** and **High Mountain Drifters Guide Service**—in Gene Taylor's shop (970-641-1845, www.highmtndrifter.com) in Gunnison; **Almont Anglers** (970-641-7404, www.almontanglers.com) and **Three Rivers Resort** (970-641-1303, www.3riv-

ersresort.com) in Almont; **Black Canyon Anglers** (970-835-5050, www.gunni son-riverfarms.com) in Austin; **Dragonfly Anglers** (970-349-1228, www.dragonfly-anglers. com) and **Troutfitter** (970-349-1323, www.trout-fitter.com) in Crested Butte; **Gunnison River Expeditions** (970-249-4441) in Montrose.

Almont Anglers

Willowfly Anglers in Almont

Fishing Places Solid Choices near Home Base:

Gunnison River: The result of the marriage of the Taylor and East Rivers, once free-flowing, now dammed by three reservoirs (Blue Mesa, Morrow Point, and Crystal Reservoir). We like the inlet at Blue Mesa Reservoir, on the Gunnison, because of the large trout. We favor streamers at the inlet, but in the Upper Gunnison go for hatch matchers, attractors and beadheads—it all depends. The Cooper/Neversink public access downstream from Gunnison is choppy and hard to figure out, but we have hooked into and seen others hook into some nice browns. From Almont to Blue Mesa Reservoir, the Gunnison is known as the upper Gunnison and should be a must fish if you stay in this area. Pools so deep you could drive a VW van into them and it'd disappear. Long deep runs that are inviting, but if you step in them you'll be swimming. You'll fish with cottonwoods and willows in this flat valley. Great insect hatches,

The Gunnison River

Preparing to float the East River

thick long rainbows and browns and Snake River cutts. It appears the river's rainbows are doing well after whirling disease hit the river hard a decade ago. We like the Gunnison stretch that flows from Almont, North Bridge, Ohio Creek. Perfect for a float trip. Do it right and hire a guide.

Black Canyon Gunnison River: Below the impoundments, near Montrose, you get the Black Canyon, you get all public land, but you can't access the big river very well. You'll be in Black Canyon National Park. Bust out the checkbook and hire a guide—don't risk the trails to the river. Too hairy. The Gunnison River rainbows are among the feistiest and most colorful I've ever caught. They pull like gangbusters and have spirit. But where we used to catch more rainbows than browns, it's about even or close enough, and the browns are getting bigger on average. The Black Canyon, except in times of big stone hatches, is not a dry fly river. You nymph with a variety of subsurface offerings, including weighted stonefly nymphs, or you crash big streamers.

Remoteness, solitude, spectacular gorge, abundant wildlife, including eagles. The Gunnison in the canyon is difficult to fish. Nevertheless, these finicky fish have been what has kept fishing pressure low. Catches of brown trout regularly exceed 5 pounds and 25 inches. Fourteen miles of river takes two to three days. Access is so limited on this river, at least the Black Canyon of the Gunnison section, that once an angler completes the difficult 8-hour descent into the canyon, the next takeout point is two to three days away as one floats the river. Because the river is so tough to reach, it is a highly productive fishery. At one time, rainbows and browns over 4 or 5 pounds were common.

Watch for both golden and bald eagles, and peregrine falcons. Fishing the Black Canyon is a true wilderness adventure. The Gunnison River from Almont to Austin covers over 75 miles of water, but that part of the river not in the canyon pales in comparison. Erosion and other factors have contributed to the demise of a once-fine trout stream. BBU. Ask a guide what that means.

East River: Wild trout stream that begins at Emerald Lake, picks up flow through Gothic, and thirty-some-odd miles later joins the Taylor River at Almont to form the Gunnison River. The East is a typical western stream—small, clear in the upper reaches, alternating between canyon and meadow character, then building into a wider persona in the lower stretches. Major sections are private but well marked. We especially like the upper reaches, where we always see snow on the mountains in mid-July. The Wild Trout section of the East River begins at the bridge near Roaring Judy Fish Hatchery and moves down for a mile. From Gunnison, travel north on CO 135, stay left at the fork (which is still CO 135) and you'll see the hatchery.

Ohio Creek: This drainage to the northeast has several fun creeks including Coal, Carbon, and Mill Creek. Ohio Creek is a solid choice, too. It's also almost entirely private. Drive up CO 135 and turn northwest on CR 730, which follows Ohio Creek. Amazing scenery, but awfully primitive, so be prepared.

Try Mill and Carbon Creeks. They're smaller and farther back (Mill is off CR 727 and Carbon off CR 737) but wild and great dry fly choices. You won't find much prettier scenery, either.

Lake Fork Gunnison: This feeder river to the Gunnison is one of the under-sung rivers in Colorado. The river is medium-sized, runs through a magnificent canyon, and features magical green pools deep enough to submerge a two-story log cabin. Large fish lurk in the Lake Fork: browns and rainbows, brooks, and some cutts. Personal best, now 24 inches, big and round as a loaf of peasant bread. The lower Lake Fork Gunnison runs beside CO 149 as the river flows north to its confluence with Blue Mesa Reservoir and the

Mark's nephew Chase Medling with a rainbow trout from the Lake Fork of the Gunnison River

Gunnison River. At Gateview, CO 149 turns east, so take 64 RD to follow the river into Sapinero Canyon or CR 25 northwest to reach Gateview and Red Bridge sections.

The river is a patchwork of clearly marked public and private land north of Lake City, easily accessible from CO 149. This is the lower Lake Fork Gunnison. The river flows from steep mountains above Lake San Cristobal, wide and clean and cold. The upper Lake Fork enters the deep cold lake, exits, and runs through the hamlet of Lake City and courses north to enter the Gunnison River system.

Kenny Medling on Cebolla Creek

Blue Mesa Reservoir: This massive reservoir 26 miles west of Gunnison was dammed up out of the Gunnison River back in 1965. You'll find rainbow and lake trout, with some browns and kokanee salmon. The kokanees are good eating, and they do quite well in this lake. Tough to catch them at times. Tan moonscape surroundings set against a cobalt blue lake. Most folks troll with cow bells or spinfish. Hundreds of campgrounds around the lake, marinas, boat rentals, the works. Take US 50 west out of Gunnison.

For the Adventurer

Big Blue Wilderness (a.k.a. Uncompahgre Wilderness): A great day trip from Gunnison, ideal to teach beginning flyfishers or take the family for a picnic. Big Blue Creek, and two feeder streams, Soldier Creek and Fall Creek, run through the eastern section of the Uncompahgre Wilderness, past groves of colorful, singing aspens, past forests of spruce and fir. These creeks are three of the prettiest small trout streams in Colorado, perfect for fishing dry flies. If you'll drive the 12 miles of dirt road back to Big Blue CG, you'll see the best scenery in the Gunnison Area and reach a great high mountain stream, perfect for flyfishing. Be sure to check out the beaver ponds near the campground for some challenging light-leader fishing. The Big Blue has good beaver ponds, nice pools, and undercut banks, and it offers anglers a chance to catch brookies.

Powderhorn River: Three forks, open casting, no other anglers. Beat

We landed this cutt on North Clear Creek, equidistant from Gunnison and Creede.

Blue Mesa Reservoir

Camping on Lake San Cristobal south of Gunnison

that. Plenty of public access, especially along CR 27 as it leaves CO 149 at Powderhorn. The Powderhorn feeds the Cebolla, and its three forks have superb flyfishing for brook trout (and some cutts and browns). There are not big trout for the most part, but we've landed plenty of 14- to 16-inchers over the years.

Henson Creek: This canyon creek joins the Lake Fork of the Gunnison River right in the heart of Lake City and offers wonderful flyfishing, considering its close proximity to town. A fast, tumbling creek, Henson's chilly waters (with some big pools) hold good numbers of rainbows, browns, cutthroats, and brookies averaging 8 to 14 inches, with many larger. The creek is flanked by tall pink and gray canyon walls, meaning that the creek will have some shade on the water most of the day.

OTHER FISHERIES WORTH INVESTIGATING: Taylor Reservoir, Taylor River, Spring Creek (see Crested Butte chapter).

Blue Ribbon Fisheries not far from Gunnison

Cimarron   Saguache
Cochetopa   Rio Grande
Los Pinos   Lake Fork Gunnison

19 La Jara Reservoir

Against the Capitol I met a lion,
Who glared upon me, and went surly by,
Without annoying me: and there were drawn
Upon a heap a hundred ghastly women,
Transformed with their fear; who swore they saw
Men all in fire walk up and down the streets.
And yesterday the bird of night did sit
Even at noon-day upon the market-place,
Hooting and shrieking. When these prodigies
Do so conjointly meet, let not men say
'These are their reasons; they are natural;'
For, I believe, they are portentous things
Unto the climate that they point upon.
—SHAKESPEARE (Casca, from *Julius Caesar*)

We are pulling the Aliner south. The San Luis Valley is a lonely stretch of earth. Miles string for days. Terribly flat. Hazy when it's crystal clear. Lonesome as hell.

We are always looking for signs. Not road signs, mind you. *Signs.* Real signs. As in, *from the gods* kind of signs. Not just today, but all days. To let us know things. Where to go…which rods to fish…how the fishing will be.

Our favorite campsite of the summer was on the south side of La Jara Reservoir.

Signs we've witnessed before that bade well:

The leg of a dead deer on the bank of the Sevier River in Utah—we mopped up on browns there.

A dead mouse on the road near a feeder stream to a lake we knew nothing about—the number of fish in that stream were unbelievable.

One sign was literally a sign. It read *Fish Creek Rd*. We took it. We found Fish Creek. And inside Fish Creek, we found...FISH!

A dead rabbit on the bank of the Conejos River (which means "Rabbits" in Spanish)—we both hooked up on huge browns the following morning, despite what the "sign" should have provoked.

This day, we were looking for any kind of sign, as the La Jara area is a mystery to us both—unknown as the dark side of the moon, mysterious as the purpose of ear hair, enigmatic as the quadratic equation to two English majors. Virtually no one writes about this place—as far as we know. So we know nothing of where we are going or what to expect.

Signs we hope to see might be two dead crows. Water parting on its own. Unplanned solar eclipses. Literally anything. Just to break up the monotony of Subaru Outbacks on the road, and the redundant semolina wheat crops flanking us on both sides, if nothing else.

But the San Luis is offering nothing, although the glow from the Great Sand Dunes to the east seemed ominous enough to pray to. As far as "signs" go, however, nothing is surfacing.

Continuing on. South. CO 15. Looking for our turnoff to head west into the Rio Grande National Forest. The road's name seemed curiously suggestive—*Road X*. But Williams remained steady. Unmoved by the omen. *Means nothing till it proves itself,* he dares.

Finally we see it. An "X." *Of all things for our turn off.* "Really," I pondered. "X Road? Honestly?"

For two well-rounded storytellers, the letter "X" portends no less than treasure, loot, and, yes, even booty. Images of Robert Louis Stevenson's *Treasure Island* danced in our minds. Neither of us could deny the road name's significance. *Could this be the gateway to Trout Heaven?* Or the spiral path to the River Styx?

We saw this augury as we pulled onto X Road heading to La Jara Reservoir.

La Jara Reservoir

Either way, we turn, and we take it. It's too late in the day to do anything else. The pavement ends and dust rolls up behind, clouding our past.

Discovery awaits.

It is here, next to the lake, where we find what we believe is the greatest campsite on earth—a grassy bowl protected from wind on three sides, the open side offers views to the north where the reservoir murmurs to us. The Aliner never had it so good. Bedazzled by a raging campfire and a full bottle of Early Times whiskey, we ponder the

Feisty Rio Grande cutthroats are predominant in Jim and Torsido Creeks.

mysteries of the world as men have for millennia when sitting around the warmth of flames, and life seemed somehow suspended in the air behind us, as though we were not actually living, as though these days did not count against us as part of our tallied, running lives. Somehow we were lost within time, caught somewhere between the earth's troubles and the stars' eternal wistfulness.

Clay lies still, but blood's a rover
Breath's aware that will not keep.
Up, lad: when the journey's over there'll be time enough to sleep.
—A. E. HOUSMAN

Favorite Places to Eat

Driving back to Antonito for a meal probably isn't feasible since home basing in La Jara is such a long, slow drive. However, if you choose to do so, drive to **Dos Hermanas Restaurant** on 435 Main St. These ladies serve authentic Mexican dishes that warm the tummy.

OTHER PLACES TO EAT: In the wee town of La Jara there are several small joints, all either on Main St. or US 285: **The Wagon Wheel, Ann's Café,** and **El Vallecito.** We never tried any of them because we were always in a hurry to be somewhere else. We did buy beer there once. That beer was good. I can tell you that.

Favorite Places to Stay

La Jara Reservoir: Again, La Jara is best suited as a home base if you camp at one of the many sites available at La Jara Reservoir. Chances are you will be alone, or perhaps you will only see a visitor or two, even in summer. But there is a gratifying peace about being out there all alone. When I was there, alone, I found myself referring back to the works of Eugene O'Neill. He once wrote, "Life is a solitary cell whose walls are mirrors." I don't think I ever understood what he meant by that till we spent a long, dark night by the glow of a nice conical fire, deep hours of night, when the sky mirrored back to me my past and future. "There is no present or future, only the past, happening over and over again, now," he also wrote.

There is no time like the present to make plans to visit La Jara Reservoir and her babies, Jim and Torsido. Our past proves that your future will be lucrative there.

However, there may be a couple of feasible places to stay nearby.

Best Western Movie Manor in Monte Vista has kept rooms with big windows that face the giant outdoor movie screen. Kinda cool, huh? 2830 US 160 W., 800-771-9468, 719-852-5921, http://book.bestwestern.com/best western/productInfo.do?propertyCode=06029.

OTHER PLACES TO STAY: Monte Villa Historic Inn, Monte Vista, CO, 925 1st Ave., 719-852-5166. **Rio Grande Motel,** Monte Vista, CO, 25 N. Broadway, 800-998-7129, http://www.rio grandemotel.net/.

There's no overhanging vegetation to foil a cast on these La Jara Reservoir–area streams.

Fly Shops, Guides, and Tackle Stores

Conejos River Anglers, full guide service and fly shop (719-376-5660, http://conejosriveranglers.com/) and **Fox Creek Store** (719-376-5881, http://www.foxcreekstore.com) in Antonito.

OTHER STUFF: The upper La Jara Creek above the reservoir does not sustain trout. Just below the dam, the stream seems to have very few if any trout in it until a mile or so downriver below a series of small falls, where springs and feeders add more substance. To get there requires a Jeep and a hairy climb down a canyon slope. But reports of big browns make this a quest for only the brave and diligent. The guides at Conejos River Anglers can provide essential maps, directions, and tactics for this section.

Fishing Places Solid Choices near Home Base

La Jara Reservoir: At daybreak, La Jara Reservoir is a sight to behold. Flat and beautiful, it lays out like an old weathered map on a pickup hood, seeming to drape over on the ends it's so big. Containing mostly brook trout and

splake, this lake is particularly serene, with very light fishing pressure, probably because of the long, bumpy ride in down Rd. 232.

A kayak is one hell of a fine piece of equipment to have on La Jara Reservoir, as are the float tubes the only two other anglers on the lake are in. Although we don't speak, I know what they're searching for: big fish.

Use a low profile on Jim Creek to dupe the native Rio Grande cutthroats.

While Williams sleeps in a bit, I spend a few lonely hours sliding through the unbroken waters of La Jara Reservoir, pulling out five brook trout that would easily go a pound and half, seemingly hand-painted by Georgia O'Keeffe. The Sage that Dave Rittenberry has loaned us for our summer journeys allows for long, direct casts even while sitting on the surface.

Like most lakes, the edges of La Jara fish well most of the day, with larger, smarter fish lurking in the depths. Landing those lunkers may require traditional spinning gear or a sinking line with weighted flies such as Woolly Buggers, beadheaded Prince Nymphs, chironomids like Snow Cones or Black Ice, assortments of Copper Johns, or common colors of damselfly nymphs.

Jim Creek: Feeding into the reservoir are Torsido and Jim Creeks. They flow in at different points, Jim from the west and Torsido a bit north of there. Both hold plenty of those amazing native cutthroat, as well as brook trout and possibly some splake, if you know how to tell the difference. A few browns exist in Torsido. But the Curmudgeon and I love our cutthroats, so Jim Creek was a blessed gift that we just happened to stumble upon. It's always those surprises that end up being our favorites.

A flat grassy valley with hidden braids of water merging and diverting, sometimes only eighteen inches wide, while other places Jim Creek is four feet ore more. Ultralight gear is perfect for a day full of rare trout on Jim Creek, and expect to catch 40 to 60 wild trout here.

For the Adventurer

Torsido is no more a substantial water than Jim volume wise, only it's a single rivulet and not a web of intricate waterways weaving to and fro. Plus, it's very well secluded. We put in near a culvert. I landed a 12-inch cutt on the first cast. (Williams owes me a steak every time I do that. By now, I own forty head of cattle in unpaid debt.) Then I caught 8 more in the hour, plus a few brookies.

Williams is determined to match me. He's landing two trout to my one, but simply never lands a cutt. I feel sorry for him, even though he's got me beat in numbers, so I give him the famous culvert back upon on our return trip. I had quit fishing thirty yards below it in order to allow him to catch a cutt. I let him have it all. He lands 3 brookies in that time, with several misses and lots of spooked fish. But no cutt.

Befuddled, I recall Bro Code Article # 68, which states, "If a Bro be on a hot streak, another Bro will do everything possible to ensure its longevity, even if that includes jeopardizing his own personal records, the missing of work, or, if necessary, generating a realistic fear that the end of the world is imminent."

I feel I have done my job as a true Bro gifting him these stretches. But his confidence teeters when no native fish take his flies. Disappointed as hell, I got his final goat by sweeping up behind him and catching a Rio Grande cutthroat exactly where he'd decided to throw in the towel!

Lazily, I finish the day by soaking my bare feet in the coolness of the stream and watching the Curmudgeon mumble obscenities toward me while changing out of his wet boots.

20 Meeker

Williams and I are gassing up at a convenience store. It's called Kum & Go. No, it's not a house of ill repute, but it does take us a few moments to make sure. Our discussion for the past hour—creating a *Saturday Night Live*-style skit for an invention we have decided would make us a fortune. "The Shmitten."

When we ride side by side for thousands of miles, we become inventors and entrepreneurs. Williams expounds upon this in greater detail. But the fact is, this particular idea seems doable.

Our invention: a mitten-shaped roll of toilet paper for campers. Two-sided, complete with a dry side and a damp anti-bacterial flip side with peel-away wipies. Ingenious, right? Yeah, we know you want one. An extra upshot to the Shmitten is we figure they might double as potholders for us in the Aliner.

Anyways, the catch phrase at the end of our prospective commercial: *"I'm smitten with my Shmitten!"* Williams smiles and waves in a circular swiping motion to the camera with one of our makeshift prototypes on his hand. Clean and white, of course. (Or maybe not!) We have work to do on the Shmitten, but for now, we leave it be.

We concur at this point that it feels awkward pulling into a place named Kum & Go. And we also agree that, whatever it is they sell inside, we probably don't need it.

Williams points to a vehicle in the parking lot and chuckles. It's a lowrider sorta SUV *slash* hybrid thing. Strange indeed. It's obnoxiously gold in color, and

Meeker keeps true to its historical roots and vintage appeal.

across the brow of the windshield, the owner of said vehicle has paid an exorbitant amount of money to have "Ack in' a Fool" stenciled in gold. Needless to say, "Ack in' a Fool" becomes our catch phrase for a fortnight and some odd days.

Moments later, we're pulling into the cleanest town you've ever seen. More strange irony! (Hell, we'd just left a store on the outskirts called Kum & Go!) The first business we spot is an orange and white striped hamburger joint called Clark's. We order, but the town of Meeker is not any in hurry to do anything, except maybe clean. Waiting for our orders is like watching sap drip from a tree...in December. Take your time while you're here and enjoy their relaxing slower-paced lifestyle.

Meeker is so clean...(How clean is it?) Meeker is so clean, I envision a small band of meter maid–like scooter-riding cleaning crews whizzing around town in a vespine manner plucking up spent cigarette butts before they've even expired, sucking up empty styrofoam cups and dirty Shmittens at a moment's notice. Twenty-four seven.

The chamber of commerce works hard in squeaky-clean Meeker.

Favorite Places to Eat

Clark's is an orange roof burger joint on Market St. that gets the juices flowing the second you walk in. With very crispy fries and a rich vanilla shake, don't pass this up unless you're looking for finer, uppity cuisine. **Meeker Café,** inside the historic Meeker Hotel on Main St., will take you back in time to an era when you might-a got shot for smacking too loud on your vittles. Since 1883, the Meeker Café has been serving food to folks like Billy the Kid, Teddy and Franklin Roosevelt, Gary Cooper, as well as simpletons like Williams and me. Order the spare ribs, and enjoy a fine cup of espresso after. Also, they have a very clean restroom, as we both found out. **Gary's Steakhouse** seemed to be the only place in Meeker for a fine cut of red meat. We didn't eat here, but locals told us it is well worth what you pay. Gary's is on Market St. as well.

Favorite Places to Stay

Blue Spruce is a new two-story hotel on Market St. 488 Market St., 970-878-0777. **Buford Lodge** will allow for private water fishing on the North and South Forks of the White. 20474 CR 8, 970-878-4745, http://www.bufordstoreandlodge.com/Cabins.php. **The Meeker Hotel** will make you feel like a king. Very historic, very clean, very sleek. 560 Main St., 970-878-5255, http://www.themeekerhotel.com/. **River Camp RV Park** is a full hook up campground with riverfront fishing and an extremely helpful owner/host, Walt Brown. 38723 CO 13, 970-878-5677, 970-942-8345.

OTHER PLACES TO STAY: JML Outfitters (Cabins), 300 CR 75, 970-878-4749, http://www.jmloutfitters.com/cabins.html. **The Valley Motel,** 723 Market St.,970-878-3656. **Pop's Place** is a cash-only dry camp for anglers/adventurers home basing in Meeker. No hookups, but water and porta-johns are available for $15 a night. Only 5 campsites available on solid level grass skirting the White River. Guests are welcome to fish if they practice catch-and-release tactics. 2 miles west of town on Hwy 13, 903-241-5010.

Fly Shops, Guides, and Tackle Stores

You will want to come prepared with gear and know-how to home base in Meeker. There are no fly shops or tackle stores per se in town, but the small stop of Buford about half way to Trappers Lake will offer some fishing supplies, as well as lodging and guide services.

Buford Guide Service (970-878-4745, http://www.bufordguideservice.com/), **JML Outfitters** (970-878-4749, http://www.jmloutfitters.com/fishing. html), and **Welder Outfitting Services** (970-878-9869, 970-314-5923,

Above: The White River, east of Meeker
Right: Use beadheads like this red Copper John to fool brookies in Marvine Creek.

970-878-4559, http://www.welderoutfitters.com/) in Meeker. **Winterhawk Outfitters** (970-487-3011, http://winterhawk.com/fishing/index.htm) in Collbran; **Sable Mountain Outfitters** (970-878-4765, http://www.sable mountainoutfitters.com/)

OTHER STUFF: As of this publication there is a pending lawsuit which may determine the amount of rafting allowed on the White River near Meeker. Rafting is definitely one of the most enjoyable ways to fish the White, since it's so large. None of the guide services we spoke with offer float trips down the White near Meeker, but if you have a kayak or drift boat, bring it. The lawsuit may actually open up more floating on this spectacular piece of water.

Hunting is the main sporting event in Meeker, with guides and lodges supporting bear, deer, elk, and some reports of snipe. Meeker's economy is stimulated by the vast number of hunters visiting this undiscovered area of Colorado. Be safe while angling, and it might be a wise choice to wear something brighter than you might normally wear on the river. Outdoorsmen are shot accidentally every year, being mistaken for big game animals in the wild. Take no chances while home basing in Meeker. Crosshairs are everywhere.

You may see people horseback on the Marvine Creek Trail.

Fishing Places Solid Choices near Home Base

The North Fork and the South Fork of the White River combined allows for over 50 miles of public access trout fishing. Besides the river, there are numerous small creeks for fishing, such as **Marvine, Ute, Papoose,** and **Fawn.** There are more than a hundred backcountry lakes and ponds, such as **Mirror Lake** off of Rd 8 heading south on TR 1821, **Swede Lake** on TR 2248 south of Rd 8, and the spectacular **Marvine Lakes** at the end of TR 1823. Most all of these waters will hold plenty of brooks, cutts, and some rainbows and browns. Stop in the Buford Lodge store for directions and open water areas, or just general information about any of these locations. But don't "Ack a Fool" when you go in there, or you will get shot the look from the owner man.

The White River: The infamous White River flows directly through the town of Meeker. At forty feet wide and more, the White is a crushing monster in early to mid-July. Unfishable for flyfishers until late July to early August.

We're distraught about the muddy conditions and decide to move along to Marvine Creek, but know this river is a blast when it's lower and slower. Huge fish are uncannily camouflaged in the dark pools but can be caught "Ackin' a Fool" along the edges with hoppers, and in the currents with dries and nymphs. (Okay, I'll stop with the Ackin' a Fool stuff now.) More solid choices when home basing out of Meeker to fish are as follows:

River Camp RV Park on the White: Campground patrons can fish 3/4 mile of the White surrounding the three sides of the park located 2.5 miles west of Meeker. Artificial flies and lures only for rainbows, browns, cutthroat, and gigantic whitefish.

Meeker City Park section of the White: Within the Meeker city limits, anglers fish for rainbows, browns, native cutthroat, and whitefish. The White here is open to public from the Circle Park Bridge at 4th and Water St. downstream to the 10th St. bridge.

The Green Cabins to the Nelson-Prather Trout Unlimited Access on the White: Head upstream on the Flat Tops Scenic Byway (CR 8) east of Meeker. Set your odometer as soon as you pass the "Begin Scenic Byway" sign shortly after turning onto CR 8 from CO13. After traveling exactly 1.0 mile, look across the river to the small, green cabins on your right. Starting at the bridge going to the cabins, the general public may fish upstream, 2.2 miles to the Nelson-Prather Trout Unlimited Access. Fish only on the side of the river closest to the road, and do not cross the bridge, fish from the bridge, climb fences, or cross to the other side of the river.

Marvine Creek, east of Meeker in the Flat Tops Wilderness Area

Sleepy Cat Access on the White: Upstream 14.4 miles rests the Sleepy Cat ponds. Two miles of fishable river upstream of the ponds is accessible to the public. At the upper end of this public access stretch, a path will lead you back to the road.

Rio Blanco County Access of the White: At 24 miles upstream, CR 8 intersects with CR 14. Turn right on CR 14 and drive the mile to the campground. The river is open to fishing downstream through the county picnic area. We suggest walking to the picnic area and fishing your way back to the vehicle if the White is your kind of river.

Lake Avery: You will find Lake Avery secretly tucked away off to the north of CR 8, east of Meeker. Just over 18 miles upstream from the Scenic Byway signage on the north side of CR 8—if you see the spillway, you've passed the turnoff to Avery. Since you cannot see the lake from the road, be watchful of the odometer and look for Rd. 82 cutting north just west of the one-shop town of Buford.

Rainbows like this are common in Meeker-area fisheries.

There are a few cutthroat and brook trout in Lake Avery, but the main species you will find here is rainbow, which can be stolen from the bank or by boat. Since Trappers Lake and all of its magnanimous companion waters are in such close proximity, Lake Avery is not considered a stellar fishery, but it is fun.

For the Adventurer

Fawn Creek: For the angler who wishes to fish for wild, native trout, Fawn Creek (according to a local ranger) apparently has plenty of cutthroats, and they're fairly easy to get to. FR 236 heading north off of CR 8, just west of the Marvine Creek turnoff, follows Fawn Creek for approximately 2.5 miles. Light rods and the usual array of small stream dries will be all you need.

Lost Solar Lakes: This backcountry trek is possibly the most isolated in the Flat Tops Wilderness. It's an easy but long hike, where fishing along both the South Fork and Lost Solar Creek will slow your pace dramatically. There are three Lost Solar Lakes (#1 is 4 acres, #2 is about 1 acre, and #3, the largest, is around 15 acres), and all support cutthroat trout fishing. Recommended flies are Hare's Ear nymphs, Beadhead Prince nymphs,

Pheasant Tail nymphs, Caddis, Stimulators, Irresistible Adams, Griffith's Gnats, mosquito patterns, ant patterns, and beetles. To get to the Lost Solar Lakes, travel southeast off of CR 8 on Rd 10. The trail heading towards the South Fork Campground is what you're looking for. Hike east on TR 1827 for 4 miles to TR 1828, where Lost Solar Creek comes in from the north. You will hike about another 6 miles to the lakes. We highly recommend the use of a topographic map when traveling in this section of the backcountry. (USGS Buford, Oyster Lake, and Blair Mountain Quads)

Marvine Creek: Because we love a challenge, Williams and I go straight for Marvine Creek, where our drive, turning from CR 8 onto CR 12 to the Marvine Creek trailhead takes on a life all its own, becoming yet another briefly bizarre adventure entirely.

We nearly hit a whitetail buck as it bounds across the road just in front of us. But when we stop to photograph the stag, it's gone, as though it was only a deer spirit, which are creepier than regular deer, but don't eat rose bushes. Then Williams believes he spots a red baby wolverine (which Savannah would have called a baby "wooferine," and so that's what we decide to call it).

Williams fishes a deep bend in Marvine Creek.

To me, it looks more like someone dragging an orange shag rug across the road with a string. (Williams wears thick glasses, so I'll let the readers decide.)

Next, after parking, we're gearing up for the hike up TR 1823, which skirts the creek all the way up to Slide and Marvine Lakes. As we're snacking on yet another of countless versions of high-tech granola bars we've smuggled into the wilderness, a psychotic bird divebombs us multiple times for no apparent reason other than perhaps it has rabies, or we smell of putrid rotting meat and it wants us gone. Or maybe it was both.

Due to recent rains, this trail is nothing shy of a nightmare at this point—mud mixed with horseshit, and the consistency of it reminds me of these endless fields of "gumbo" through which I surveyed petroleum pipelines in Mississippi during the wet season. And although it sucks to be muddy, there are not many canyons prettier than this one.

Williams takes the first run and within two casts discovers Marvine fishes easily for these chubby brook trout that look almost goofy they're so thick. These trout are finicky at times, but proper fly selection and placement will help get them to hand. The river's edge is grassy and drops off in cutbank fashion the length of Marvine, so edge fishing is key.

The valley soon opens up into a wondrous meadow where views of the Flat Tops Wilderness take our breath away. There are more wildflowers here than the eye can behold. Friendly families riding horseback amble by every so often and tip their hats politely at us while our trout just keep bringing smiles.

Williams and I both catch tons of athletic brook trout, some rainbow trout, and a handful of cuttbows. Marvine has plenty of trout and diversity to satisfy even whiners like him and me.

Our time is limited on Marvine, though. We've heard of this mystic place up the road from us, and the weather is turning grim. Towing the Aliner requires we find specific characteristics where campgrounds and sites are concerned. We back out of yet another heaven in the wilderness and head for Trappers Lake.

Top 10 Powerbars:
- Luna Lemon Zest (yes, we know they're for women)
- Clif Bar Oatmeal Raisin Walnut
- Luna Chocolate Pecan Pie
- Kashi GOLEAN Chewy Peanut Butter & Chocolate
- Special K snack bars Strawberry
- Clif Bar Chocolate Brownie
- Kind Walnut & Date
- Kind Macadamia and Apricot
- Special K Vanilla Crisp snack bars
- Quaker Oats Chewy Granola Chocolate Chip

21 Pagosa Springs

It had gotten to be a pain in the ass with the kayak. It wasn't the kayak's fault. We just didn't have a good way to carry the damned thing that didn't involve a major rebuild every time we stopped to camp. Through misadventure, we discovered the kayak rode best atop the Aliner camper. The kayak did us well when not on top of either the Jeep or trailer because both had their downside. We lugged that thing from pillar to post, and in the water the sleek craft handled wind, shallow water, expansive water. The red brightness against the blue fluidity is a photographer's dream. Transporting it was another story.

Mac fishes from the kayak on Williams Creek Reservoir.

We had to be careful that the kayak didn't slide forward and bust open one of the skylights. We had to watch out that we didn't let the kayak slide side to side, or it could torque in the wind and tear something up. Mac had to strap it down in the front, strap it down in the back, then we had to tie it off from the handles on each side, attaching each to not much of anything because there's not much there to attach to. The handles on the kayak were fraying by the third week and were withered down to half. It took ten to fifteen minutes to load, five minutes to unload.

Did I mention that the first day out of Amarillo, driving 65 mph west on I-40, the kayak that we had painstakingly strapped to the top of the Jeep was flying alongside us right out the driver's window? We looked at each other, then at the kayak, at each other, the kayak. The straps that had only moments before held down the kayak were flapping against the Jeep, making an awful racket. The skinny red boat was skidding along the interstate, in the passing lane, four-feet off the asphalt, doing 65 miles per hour. I'm willing to bet not many other kayaks have gone that fast. We pulled over, ran to the kayak and lifted it up, carrying it to the safety of the shoulder while two semis were bearing down on us. Five seconds later, and this could have been a real disaster. As it was, the kayak barely had a scratch. Nice way to start the trip.

The Pagosa area was our first destination of the summer for the kayak. Some folks might not like Pagosa Springs. It's sort of a smelly place. Hot springs sulphur fumes waft through town.

The numerous pedestrians will cross the street right in front of unsuspecting drivers, without even looking. Parking isn't easy to find. Plus, it's like the longest town in southwest Colorado—one drawn-out strip of a town that sneaks right along the San Juan River, with just a few little side streets and lots of little shops and eateries. That's all it really is.

But if you look closely, like we writers might, the town has a class and style all its own.

For instance, River Pointe Coffee Cafe. Nice tables and chairs, couches, outdoor seating with wonderful views, and ambiance. And the espresso is rich and frothy like a vanilla malt. They serve their coffees in absurdly big cups, something out of Alice in Wonderland. We hang out here every time, and on one article deadline where we were feverishly typing while sitting in comfy chairs, an Amazon beauty wearing perfume that lingered in our minds for several weeks served us memorable cappuccinos. The retail shops are a mere one hundred yards from the San Juan River. The hot springs are the tops in the Southwest. The range of lodging is wide and comparatively inexpensive. The people are friendly, the town receptive to tourists and anglers, national forests ring the quaint town, and the scenery is unparalleled.

The San Juan River in Pagosa Springs

But what about the fishing? This land of the hot springs is ideal for a home base to fish all the surrounding quality trout waters that include the main stem of the San Juan River, the East and West Forks of the San Juan River, Four Mile Creek, Turkey Creek, and numerous high-country streams and lakes.

Imagine if you will five old farts sitting around in a fly shop in southern Colorado, for instance, at Let It Fly fly shop in Pagosa Springs. These good ol' boys talk about the good ol' days when the fish in every local river was long, fat, and wild. These veteran anglers, including the owner of a fly shop, and a guide or two, reminisce about how we five were the only ones who ever fished these streams. Ah, the good old days, made sweeter by passing time and gauzy memories. I interviewed these old farts one summer day, and they knew more about this region than anyone else I'd met. Still, there's a pervasive attitude, not unusual in western towns, that the waters should not be fished except by locals. Save the best waters for those who earn the right. Don't write about them. Don't encourage others to fish them. Kinda sad, but understandable. Sometimes, a river receives more attention than it can handle and the quality of the angling declines. Truth is, the fisheries around Pagosa Springs are doing better than this water cooler talk would have you think. This growing town sees more and more anglers on area waters each season, and for long-time locals this influx of pressure is the quintessential dilemma of those who both fish often and sell fishing goods. You need the business, you fear the added anglers on your precious waters. Conundrum.

Because the fishing is so good in this area, the sulphur smell of Pagosa is a smell we particularly like. After a bit, you don't even notice the smell.

So anyway, we fish the Pagosa Springs area a lot, and we'd already hit it up four times during our research summer (twice there and twice back on our way to other places). The first time, we were two weeks in and we'd already seen two wolves in the wild (Mac's daughter Savvy calls them woofs), fifteen to twenty antelopes (one baby/calf suckling her mother twenty yards away from us), elk by the dozens (four bathing in La Jara Reservoir), multiple bear tracks and scat, and a wolverine; we'd had our kayak fly off the Jeep, our battery fly off the trailer while motoring, had a pit bull chase Mark into the river complete with splash and noise. One night, it got so bitterly cold at 11,000 feet that overnight our Aliner had ice inside and our olive oil froze solid. Our goal for the summer was no longer fifty days of fishing but coming back home to Amarillo alive and in one piece.

We know the East Fork and West Fort of the San Juan. And we've fished in town on the main stem several times in all seasons. We like Turkey and Four-Mile Creeks, but we needed a new scene. We asked Paul Nogueira at Wolf Creek Anglers Fly Shop (where we of course, bought flies), who mentioned that Williams Creek north of town was fishing well. Twenty-two miles in, the

Above: Williams Creek Reservoir
Right: This big rainbow was landed on the San
Juan, right in the middle of Pagosa Springs.

man's words rang true. Not only is the area a family camping paradise, but Williams Creek is a tail water that's fishable for rainbows and browns nine months out of the year. Williams Creek Reservoir could possibly be the most beautiful setting we've encountered on our trip. It's surrounded by three major peaks, and the craggy summits seem to scrape their way out of the earth before your very eyes.

At an elevation of 8,241 and with 508 acres at pool, the kokanee salmon, rainbows, and brook trout are in heaven here. A bald eagle circled overhead in dizzying search patterns for the same take as I was as I fished the inlet in the kayak. Three fat trout later, we hit the river and snagged more than 20 between us in an hour below the spillway. I'd been up Williams Creek twice before, once to fish the upper Piedra and once on a quick one-day fact-finding fishing tour under a heavy rain with my niece Megan and her fiancé Michael, so I know we didn't do all that well.

We parked Mac's Jeep at the Piedra River trailhead parking lot because we would be on a long tour once we left the area. We stopped to fish the Piedra at the bridge and upstream to the private water. Lots of 8- to 12-inch browns and one in the mid-teens. We made camp at Bridge Campground and fished Williams Creek outside our door—we fished from the campground up to the canyon, probably about 2 miles. Mac and I normally don't separate on the water, but this part of the creek is smallish and brushy and twisting so somehow we lost each other for five to six hours. The fishing was tough. These fish in Williams Creek are used to small insects, predictable hatches, stealthy approaches. This 2-mile stretch gets hammered by campers. I used a low-approach, upstream, high-sticking to keep the line off the water, striking the water right against the bank. I had one strike per pool, per run, per riffle and not many hookups. Six fish in six hours. None of size. Missed twice that many, and I wasn't certain if it was early summer rust or rusty hooks or genius trout.

I ran into no fewer than eight anglers during the six hours, which doesn't seem like a lot, but it is. The river is typically about as wide as Mac is tall (which means, it's not a wide river), so while the river is loaded with habitat and fish, it's still a small river by any measurements. All eight anglers were fishing downstream, which means as I was carefully working my way upstream, they were meeting me headlong, tossing ultralight spinners, covering lots of water.

A dog attacked me as I clamored out of the river. It was a medium-sized dog. A pit bull. He attacked in this sense: I was in the water, shuffling out

Upper Williams Creek

clumsily, when the dog saw me from about fifty yards and sprinted toward me growling. I jumped back in the water and waded to the deepest part. I met up with Mac, me holding a big-ass stick in hand because the damned dog cornered me in the river and I needed protection. I had to wait until the owners whistled for the dog and he ran to the truck and the inconsiderate folks left. Leave the pit bulls at home when fishing, or at least don't let them run free.

We drove up the next day to Williams Lake, where Mac unloaded the kayak in a cold breeze, under a cloudy sky. Mac paddled across the lake and toward the inlet. I fished around the shore, near the spillway, and caught a couple of nice brook trout. I took pics of birds, especially orioles, at the faux

lake behind the big lake because Mac on a lake is one slow-moving angler. He caught 3 keepers, something we seldom do but Mac had a hankering for fried trout and there was no shortage of trout in this big lake. I got bored after a while, cold as well, so I bundled up and sat in a blue chair and watched the world stand still while my cigar smoke curled and looped and vanished against the backdrop of green mountains and gray skies.

We put the fish on ice, hiked in to the

Williams Creek Reservoir

dam, crossed, fished below where the spillway rushes into where the river created a big wide pool and islands of pocket water. I was fishing an Adams when a mayfly hatch came off, so I caught 15 in an hour— half of them around 10 to 12 inches and the other half 7 to 10 inches. Mac was

rocking a Stimulator for a long time till he changed over and caught 7, lost 4. We hiked out, picking up firewood. We started a nice big fire, traded flies, drank three whiskeys each, ate dinner, sat in our camp chairs by the orange fire. In our first night of downloading a thousand photos from the digital cameras, we screwed up (I screwed up) and lost the pics after transfer, somehow deleting them off both the card and the computer. Go figure.

In the morning, the Jeep wouldn't start. We stupidly left the plug hooked up to the Jeep, and, because we couldn't move the Jeep or the trailer, there was no way to even unhook. It was the fridge, the first of several problems with the fridge. We love the Aliner, but the fridge draws too much

The fridge was the cause of this dead battery.

battery and doesn't keep things that cold anyhow. So we unplugged it. For the summer. Mac has this humongous thick-walled cooler that could survive nuclear winter or a Mercury summer, so we were okay on our cold goods.

We left Pagosa in mid-June and a few weeks later picked up our buddy Jorgen Wouters in Durango. Wouters is my former editor at an outdoors web magazine and a writer in his own right. He is also bearded, Norwegian, and a better caster than either of us. All three of these things factor into to our story. Mac and Jorgen had never met, but they hit it off immediately. For one, they had an easy two-on-one situation against me (bring it on). Two, Mac and Jorgen are anal-retentive meets obsessive compulsive disorder about everything, from clothing to folding towels to cutting veggies, but especially about camp, predominantly about campfires.

Hey, I'm pretty good at building campfires. My fires light, burn a long time, I put it out before I go to bed. My fires keep me company in the cold dark night, they dance for me while I drink. But with Mac, with Jorgen, it's downright Felix Unger meets the guy on *Flipping Out*. The logs have to be the right logs, the right wood, the right length. They spend inordinate

Another near-accident woodcutting

hours searching for the correct kind of wood, then sawing it, cutting it, nipping off limbs, stacking it. They admire their handiwork as though they just painted a masterpiece. It's pretty darned amusing. And annoying.

I took Jorgen to Williams Creek while Mac prepped dinner. Jorgen is a long caster, used to wide open eastern waters and match-the-hatch small fly fishing. There's no room to do that on Williams Creek. You've got to short cast, high-stick, pick and mend when the fly hits the water. Guerilla tactics. Jorgen was a good listener but it took him a while to warm up to this choppy pocket water and smaller pools. He caught a few brookies and rainbows, and we got back to see Mac chopping wood.

"Mac, you ought not be chopping that log so close to your feet." I said it sarcastically because Mac is big on camp safety, plus he had told me that a year ago. The ax slipped out of his hands on the downswing and he nearly sheared off his ankle. We laughed that nervous laughter when you know you just had a crazy close shave. Bit of skin gone but other wise okay, so we drank IPAs and then went to wine, and when we ran out we switched to Early

Times. When we saw nine cars drive in late and start setting up tents, we let out a collective "oh crap." Boy Scout Troop. Must've been a hundred of those khaki-clothed pimplefaces running around like rabid chipmunks. We could hear them shouting (think Goodnight John Boy times a hundred) into the night as we all turned in.

Apparently, Boy Scouts still blow Reveille to wake up the troops. Mac and Jorgen are early risers, but 5:00 a.m. is ridiculous. There are forty sites in this campground, some with small children, and these idiots are blowing the trumpet over and over. One Reveille was not enough.

Camping out doesn't mean you can't enjoy the finer things in life.

Favorite Places to Eat

I am not and have never been impressed with the restaurants in Pagosa. I used to like the hamburger joint by the river in the faux western town front shopping center, but not in the last few years. The taco joint, **Kips Grill and Cantina** (970-264-3663), is pretty good, and **Farrago Market Café** (970-264- 4600) is always crowded. Your wife will like the décor and atmosphere of **Victoria's Parlor Café** (970-264-0204). The men will love wearing the hats. Keep the pinky out while you hold the cup.

The Malt Shoppe (970-264-2784), which is right on the river, has a great greasy burger and crispy waffle fries, and fantastic malts. It's where we celebrated Mark's 49th birthday (I know, he looks A LOT older doesn't he?).

The Malt Shoppe is best for lunch or if you're looking to feed the family on the cheap. Expensive: **JJ's Riverwalk Restaurant and Pub** (970-264-9100); Moderate: **Plaza Grille** (970-731-2737). For bakery goods, go to **Pagosa Baking Company** (970-264-9348). For coffee, sit down at **River Pointe Coffee Café** (970-264-3216).

Favorite Places to Stay

The Springs Resort and Spa (970-264-4168)—come on guys, pamper the little lady, the **Metropolitan Hotel** (970-264-4237), **Cool Pines RV Park.**

Of course, like South Fork and Creede, you can stay like most do, renting cabins for a week or two. Check with the chamber for options: www.pagosasprings chamber.com/.

A deer watches us at our campsite at Williams Creek

Fly Shops, Guides, and Tackle Stores

Let It Fly Shop (970-264-3189); **Bow and Arrow** (970-264-2370, www. ski andbowrack.com); **Wolf Creek Anglers** (970-264-1415, www.wolfcreek anglers.com/); **High Country Fishing Charters** (970-946-5229, http://www. highcountrycharters.com).

Fishing Places Solid Choices near Home Base

San Juan River in town: One Pagosa Springs area fishery that has gotten better with time (and management) is the San Juan River. The roughly 2-mile stretch runs right smack-dab through town. Pops Miller owns and runs Let It Fly and sees several advantages to taking the time to fish the San Juan in town: 1) proximity to town. You're *in* town; 2) while the family/wife are at play, perhaps at the springs or shopping, you can break away for a few hours fishing; 3) easy access from the walking trail; 4) fishable from the bank, but still offers wadeable water; and 5) the quality of the angling and the river habitat has continually improved over the years. Add to this the fact that the river in town is fishable all-year long, and you have a nice adjunct fishery to your trip to Pagosa Springs.

These 2 miles of the San Juan have seen ongoing instream improvement, and especially notable are the big rocks that form pockets and chutes and deep pools. Fishing in town is odd. Plain and simple. Car noise. Pedestrians

The East Fork of the San Juan River

on the riverwalk. Rafters and kayakers and tubers (tubists?). Houses and businesses overlooking your shoulder. Kids splashing in the water, jumping in that pool where you just saw a trout flash. It's worth it. The fish they stock are healthy and colorful and big.

Echo Canyon Reservoir: This 118-acre reservoir is also called Echo Lake (7,100 ft. elevation). The species range from rainbow trout to largemouth bass, including yellow perch, green sunfish, crappie, and channel cat. The lake is very accessible, sitting just off the main highway (US 84). Travel south of Pagosa Springs about 4 miles, turn right on Echo Reservoir Road from the highway.

East Fork of the San Juan River: The East Fork hasn't really been fishable the last couple of years, not since part of the road slid and tumbled off the mountain, cutting off all access into the canyon. That means the fish will be bigger, right? Here's one of the gems of the West. East Fork is off the beaten path but close Pagosa. East Fork is a medium-sized dry fly water that's hard to get to in spots (think steep canyon), but if you're not feeling chipper, the road follows the river. You get pocket water with fat fish. Beat that. East Fork holds lots of fish. Beat that. And you get scenery Ansel Adams would love.

West Fork San Juan River: Twenty minutes north of Pagosa Springs flows one of the prettiest mountain streams in all of southern Colorado. The lower 4 miles, those beautiful meandering meadow sections you can see from US 160, are guardedly private. You'll need to drive to the campground and hike 3 miles into the public water to see this idyllic trout water.

According to one of Mac's friends, there's some hot springs somewhere along the river where an angler can sit in the springs and fish in the river. We aimed to do such a thing, but we never found the hot springs. We weren't looking too hard because the fishing was so good. The West Fork rushes through narrow canyons on its confluence with the San Juan River. For the most part, the West Fork is a canyon stream with bottomless pools, hard-to-reach deep runs, and a wilderness setting. The West Fork holds both rainbow and cutthroat trout, 10 to 12 inches on average, but we have caught several 14- to 16-inchers (and friends have caught bigger) plumbing the blue-green runs and dropping big dries on the slick pocket water. Drive US 160 from Pagosa Springs to West Fork Road (FR 648), turning north. Follow to the West Fork Campground. Continue to the end of the road to the trailhead. This can be a rough road at times. Hike upstream from the trailhead at end of road.

Turkey Creek

For the Adventurer

Buckles and Harris Lakes: You almost always see these two listed together, and since they are both scenic and hold nice-sized rainbow trout, as well as only being a half mile from each other, why not? You drive 20 miles south of Pagosa Springs on US 84 (like you're going to Blanco and Chromo). Turn east on Buckles Lake Road (you'll see the sign). Follow the road until you think you've missed something and set up at the parking area and V-Rock trailhead. The trail has a steep section at the beginning

Fishing the Piedra for feisty browns

followed by some switchbacks, but it's a short trail (about a mile). When you reach the mesa, your views are stunning. Buckles and Harris are the headwaters of the Big Branch of Río Blanco. These two popular lakes (Buckles is 30 acres at 9,520 feet and Harris is 49 acres at 9,460 feet) are off the beaten path but worth the time. At one time, we used to catch brown trout out of both lakes, but recently just rainbows.

Turkey Creek: This San Juan feeder creek is a must-fish for those who love backcountry dry fly fishing for wild trout. The creek lies north of town 8-or-so miles on US 160 (the road to Wolf Creek Pass) just south a couple of miles from the East and West Forks of the San Juan. You'll see Jackson Mountain Road, and that will mean you'll turn left (north) and drive for 5 miles until you find a parking lot and a trail. Hike in for 3 miles (nothing to it) and you'll access the creek. You can fish for another 6 miles up to the headwaters at Turkey Creek Lake. Ten to twenty feet wide, chockfull of brook, rainbow and cutthroat, ideal for dry fly fishing. An adjunct trip, because who could pass up fishing their way up this beautiful trout stream, is a 9 mile hike into Turkey Creek Lake. The payoff? Colorful and sometimes big brook trout, rugged timberline scenery.

Opal Lake: Good for rainbow trout. We like the creek below the lake. Eight miles south of Pagosa on US 84. Turn on Blanco Basin Road.

Blanco River: Small gentle freestone stream good for something different, especially if you like small stream fishing. From Pagosa Springs, travel south on US 84 to FR 656 then turn east (left). This accesses most of the lower section. To access the upper sections, turn east on FR 326 and travel on Blanco Basin Road.

Big Meadow Reservoir: Good for camping or a day trip. Ideal for families and picnicking. Located north of Pagosa Springs, over Wolf Creek Pass and 6 miles to the turnoff. We like the small creek below the lake for some surprisingly nice trout. Big Meadow Reservoir holds brook trout 8 to 12 inches and rainbows from pan-size to 12 inches.

Wolf Creek

Wolf Creek: Little feeder stream to the West Fork of the San Juan River originating near Wolf Creek Pass. Amy loves this little creek that flows through Middle Earth kind of scenery. The four to eight foot–wide creek is paralleled by US 160 from its headwaters to its confluence with the West Fork.

Quartz Creek and Lake: Small but productive high-country lake of 7 acres at the headwaters of Quartz Creek in the South San Juan Wilderness. Quartz Creek is a feeder to East Fork San Juan. A remote perfect canyon creek with heavy trout (including cutts). Hike TR 571 south from FR 667.

Four Mile Creek and Lakes: Flyfish for cutthroat trout in a scenic alpine locale. The hike to the lakes passes through fir and spruce forests, meanders through open meadows, and runs past impressive waterfalls. The creek is crazy good, but if I wrote that as the lead, everyone might go there. Moderate hike of 6 miles. Travel north on CR 400 for about 9 miles, then stay right to get onto FR 645 (Four Mile Road). Stay on FR 645 traveling north until the road ends about 5 miles later. From the trailhead, hike 6 miles from the end of the road to the lower lake, Lower Four Mile Lake.

Shaw Lake: Two miles past Big Meadow Reservoir, good for cutthroats.

OTHER FISHERIES WORTH INVESTIGATING:
Williams Creek Reservoir
Williams Creek Fork of the Piedra River

Blue Ribbon Fisheries Close to Pagosa Springs
Animas River
South Fork Rio Grande
Rio Grande

"Traveling is a brutality. It forces you to trust strangers and to lose sight of all that familiar comfort of home and friends. You are constantly off balance. Nothing is yours except the essential things— air, sleep, dreams, the sea, the sky—all things tending towards the eternal or what we imagine of it."

—CESARE PAVESE

Williams is driving. My map is open. Traveling again, the two of us. Brothers of the road and river, not necessarily of siblings of blood, but of something. Maybe not as evident or traceable as lineage. But travel is the stuff of men. And he and I have often left port, metaphorically, where no matter how high we climb the mast, home is nothing short of a memory. A mirage. The recent past.

Off in the distance, out in front of us, a tornado scrapes across a rolling northern New Mexico horizon. Like the Devil's tail, it probes the ground from a temperamental cloud. We're on our way to a new place for me, Platoro, a Spanish combination word for the "gold" and "silver" mined in the area. He forces me to acknowledge and analyze yet another dark omen. Like black cats or broken mirrors, tornados and black clouds rarely bode well.

Rio de los Pinos below the Cascade Creek train bridge

I pretend not to notice all this. But Williams tends to instill horror in the minds of companion anglers in order to jockey for the edge once upon the river. He tortures me with macabre lore and myth—La Llorona, man-eating grizzly bears, threats of an impossible-to-reach fourth meadow on Elk Creek. I swoon in fear. But the twister passes, and we're soon back in southern Colorado ready to terrorize the trout.

Platoro is definitely a be-all and end-all destination. The season is short here, too. You won't pass Platoro on your way to anywhere. Like going to Key West. Once you're there, you're there. And there's no place else to go but back from whence you came, which usually means home. But there is possibly more quality water to fish from this home base than any other in this book. Fishing it all would require a lifetime, and since Williams and I are already old, we know there are areas of Platoro we may never see.

Off of CO 17, FR 250 heading north for the 23 miles to Platoro is pure hell. Imagine skating over gravelly corrugated metal with rusty vintage metal skates with loose wheels and missing bearings just after dental surgery with no anesthesia. Agony, my friend. Perhaps it seems longer than it is (like a typical Catholic wedding), but he and I are travel-ninjas, prepared for anything. The lengthy stretches of magnificent scenery are our only repose, despite washboard-induced migraines. This road, FR 250, is epic.

Wildflowers paint the landscape—tie-dyed arrays of color and pattern where the sky seems tiled with lapis lazuli. And suddenly a UPS truck appears. Dust billows behind, and for a moment we feel robbed of our solitude and of nature, that all of this is all somehow phony. But only momentarily.

The village of Platoro is a helluva heavenly sight after a drive down FR 250. Barely a town, some fine cabins stand like reminiscent monuments to a ghostly past that won't seem to leave this place. I'm wanting to price one so I don't have to return down this road.

Earlier, we'd visited Jon Harp at his shop near Antonito, Conejos River Anglers. He professes, "Most anglers from the Front Range know nothing

You can float-tube Trujillo Meadows Reservoir to get at the bigger fish.

about this area." And according to the Curmudgeon with whom I am riding, "This area was the last place a grizzly bear was ever seen in Colorado."

Indeed, it's mysterious. These mountains are different. Big-scenery stuff. Majestic, lengthy, drawn-out structures protect this forgotten canyon where the Conejos serves as a drain for Platoro Reservoir.

Favorite Places to Eat

The Skyline Restaurant of the Skyline Lodge will be one of the ONLY places to grab a true meal near Platoro Reservoir. Therefore, we recommend you eat there if based near the lake.

OTHER PLACES TO EAT: **The Canyon Café** of the Conejos Ranch is open to the public and serves breakfast and dinner year-round. Chef Shawn Ramsay, who lives on the ranch, creates delectable meals for a great price.

Favorite Places to Stay

The Skyline Lodge rents 13 cabins and 6 lodge rooms in Platoro. Their clean and rustic cabins rent for $100 to $425 per night, and, believe us, every penny is worth flipping to them. Their lodge rooms go for $60 to $100 a night. Close to the lake but the farthest to reach. Platoro, CO, 23040 FR 250, 719-376- 6040, http://www.skylineranchreserve.com/. **The Conejos Ranch,** 14 miles west of Antonito, has fully equipped streamside cabins and quaint bed and breakfast rooms available for anglers and couples alike, with happy clients returning for over fifty years. The Ranch is impeccably manicured and is as peaceful a retreat as one could ask for on the Conejos. Antonito, CO, 25390 CO 17, 719-376-2464, http://www.conejosranch.com/. **Conejos River Anglers** has clean, affordable fully furnished cabins on the downstream end of the Conejos River, close to Antonito. Cabins house four adults with satellite television, free wireless internet, living rooms, 2 bedrooms, private bath, and large grassy areas outside for unwinding. Full-size kitchen appliances, outdoor grills and a large fire pit makes staying here fun and easy. Antonito, CO, 34591 CO 17, 719-376-5660, http://conejosriveranglers.com/.

OTHER PLACES TO STAY: **Platoro Valley Lodge and Cabins,** 877-752-8676, http://www.platorovalleycabins.com/.

Campgrounds: There is a plethora of available campsites in the area. Lake Fork Campground, Mix Lake Campground, Conejos Campground, Spectacle Lake Campground, Elk Creek Campground, Trujillo Meadows Campground, Aspen Glade Campground, and Mogote Campground.

Fly Shops, Guides, and Tackle Stores

Fox Creek Store (719-376-5881, http://www.foxcreekstore.com/) in Fox Creek; **Conejos River Anglers,** fly shop and guides (800-877-2133, http://www.conejosriveranglers.com/) in Mogote Meadows; **Conejos River Outfitters** (719-376- 6040, http://www.conejosriveroutfitters.com/) and **Platoro Valley Lodge and Cabins Store** (877-752-8676, http://www.pla-torovalley cabins.com/) in Platoro.

OTHER STUFF: SIDE NOTES ON PLATORO

- Williams brings along his single pal, Jorgen, which does not violate Bro Code Article # 71, which states, "As a courtesy to Bros the world over, a Bro never brings more than two Bros to a party.
- Mac nearly chopped his leg off with a hatchet by missing the log on a downswing. Yes, he had been drinking.
- Tree-elves dropped a pine branch on Mac as he was attempting to chop wood and gashed his face open above the lip—mystery-creature #4. (#1. Mountain Chickens. #2. Snow Elves. #3. Musky-smelling creatures of the backwoods Conejos.)
- We may have set the record for the coldest outdoor BBQ in US history... 12 degrees and flurries.
- Mac caught a rainbow with his hands below the Trujillo Meadows Reservoir dam in the Rio de los Pinos.
- Fresh bear tracks in the road petrify Williams and the Nightcrawler and force them to drinking Early Times Whiskey far deeper into the night than normal.

A bank fisherman lands a rainbow on Platoro Reservoir.

Fishing Places Solid Choices near Home Base

Platoro Reservoir: The namesake reservoir is the highest manmade lake in
the U.S. at 9,993 feet. Neither Williams nor I love still waters, but peering
over I can see cruisers swimming around the banks. Big fish rise then, dart
away. I dream of hooking one with my 5 wt. as Williams mocks a Talking
Heads video with, *"How did I get here?"*

   The regularly stocked rainbows and kokanee salmon, browns, brooks,
and an occasional Rio Grande cutthroat take an array of flies and lures in
this lake. Boaters have a distinct advantage on Platoro, as they can easily fish
the "Narrows" section, a portion of the lake distinguished by a brusque point
jutting out from the eastern bank. Silver or gray Rapala minnows (floating
divers work best) work fantastically
for apprehending big browns and
rainbows. Trolling using Christmas
tree-type rigs works well for fat kokanee salmon, too. Flyfishers can be
just as lucky with a moderate sinking line and burly lake flies.

Above: Mac releases a heavy brown on the
Conejos River near Platoro.
Right: Jorgen Wouters fishes the inlet to
Trujillo Meadows Reservoir.

   Bank anglers with spin gear fare best on the north bank near the dam
using Panther Martin spinners, salmon eggs, and or nightcrawlers. Fish near
the creek inlets, too, where streams supply the lake with oxygen and insects,
especially the turnout on the map marked "No. 4." Shimmy down the steep
slope to the waters edge for a shot at solitary fishing.

Conejos River: The magical thing about the Conejos? It can be whatever you want it to be—easy wading, frothy rapids, deep pools, thin riffles, narrow canyon, open meadows, pocket water, still pools, etc. Depending upon what an angler wants to fish, there is a section of this river tailor made for it. While driving into Platoro, keep notes on where your favorite type of water is. You will probably be traveling FR 250 quite a bit, so feel free to flag tape a few areas. Just don't overdo it and be sure to remove it when you're done.

Below the dam churns the Conejos River, which holds trout worthy of epic campfire tales based on honest truth. It is scary-big water in places, like "The Pinnacles" section recommended by Mr. Harp of Conejos River Anglers. It's challenging. Huge browns dawdle in the flow. Most, hard to catch. We figure it out with ad hoc oversized San Juan worms we'd heard gossip about. Word has somehow trickled all the way from Colorado to Texas, and back. Williams and I both land two 18-inchers that bring loud "whoops" echoing off the rocks from one another, and glares from lesser anglers. Trout are everywhere, finicky and irreverent. As if they were in high school, these trout turn on us for no reason. We can see grand-sized fish, smarter than us, refusing even our makeshift worms. So on to the next trick.

A favorite water-type of ours to fish here is these sandy-bottomed, slow-moving pools in which lazier, unsuspecting trout hang out and feed. Approach them from behind and you can see how clueless trout can be. Neither of us mind creeping, stalking, crawling up to water, even prone on our bellies if need be to corral a nice fish. There will be plenty of offshoots of the main stem of the Conejos where this type of stealthy approach is possible, and even necessary. Keep a lookout for posted water.

Many sections of the Conejos along CO 17 are open to public angling, with the Wild Trout Waters section about 3 miles west of Aspen Glade Campground being one of the more popular pullouts.

Best access points for the Conejos include:
- The headwaters of the Conejos, which originate above Platoro Reservoir. There is little road access above the reservoir, so to get to the headwater creeks you will need to hike into the South San Juan Wilderness heading west.
- The Lake Fork of the Conejos from its headwaters to the main stem on FR 250.
- Saddle Creek to the South Fork of the Conejos, with flyfishing only, which includes some of the Pinnacles area in the canyon.
- South Fork to Menkhaven Ranch has some access on U.S. Forest Service property, so respect posted private property in between.

- The Conejos River SWA (fishing easement) from Aspen Glade campground upstream to Menkhaven Ranch (about 4 miles) and some portions downstream from Aspen Glade. This easement is flyfishing only with no camping.

Mix Lake: This is a sweet little pond on the other side of the road from Platoro Reservoir with tons of trout that the young-uns will find fun and easy to fish. (Not as easy as throwing a chunk of dynamite in the water, but still pretty easy!) Mostly holding rainbows, Mix Lake may not be challenging enough for the Gung-Ho angler (unless you've promised the family a fish dinner and you've been skunked everywhere else).

Trujillo Meadows Reservoir: About halfway between La Mangas Pass and Cumbres Pass, on CO 17, the turn off for Trujillo Meadows Reservoir cuts back into the South San Juan Wilderness. This lake at one time was a remarkable fishery for rainbow, brook, brown, and sporadic Rio Grande cutthroat. However, as of our summer 2009 visit, the lake was having problems and biologists were actually staying in the campground trying to decipher the culprit. There were literally no rises on the lake at the time of our visit. I kayaked the entire lake, trolling several sure-bet patterns, and nothing happened. If home based in Platoro, call any of the fly shops or guide services listed for this base for information on Trujillo Meadows Reservoir. Hopefully this fishery was simply experiencing a lull. My gut instinct says that something catastrophic occurred in the stream above the lake.

For the Adventurer

Kerr Lake: North of Platoro on FR 250, turn east on FR 257 (more or less a Jeep trail that may require 4-wheel drive, a high clearance vehicle, or even hiking). Kerr Lake is out of the way and about 1/5 the size of Platoro Reservoir. Rio Grande cutthroat trout are the key species here. For a true adventure, pack all your junk, lunch, and your small rod into a pack and mountain bike your way there. It's faster than hiking, and more fun than bumping around in the car on those bad roads.

Lake Fork of the Conejos (Wild Trout Waters): The Lake Fork of the Conejos River is designated Wild Trout Waters from its headwaters through and including Big Lake and Rock Lake. The Lake Fork is accessed by trails off of FR 250 near the Lake Fork Campground, where we saw another Aliner crew set up and relaxing. Hiking this stretch for wily wild trout is an experience like few others in the area, with Rio Grande cutts and browns in the 8- to 12-inch range.

Elk Creek: To make the Elk worthwhile, we hike an hour in. First, a vertical climb that sucks the wind right out of my lungs. Next, a steep scree slope with a danger factor of about nine, followed up by dark patches of mosquitoes floating in the air with an annoyance factor of about eleven.

I've never "Elk-ed it" before, but I crave unknown waters. The Elk is moderately difficult, lonely, eerily quiet, but with huge payoffs. Steep, V-shaped canyon fishing, a magnificent waterfall view, perfectly dreamy meadows above, sight casting to browns, brooks, and rainbows alike.

Williams outfishes me due to the fact that his body possesses not a single nerve ending and seems unaffected by the hordes of mosquitoes about to lift me away. Escaping the swarm meant jogging out. Two miles. Quickly.

The Elk is a special place, and traffic has picked up in recent years due to more and more writer/anglers divulging its secret stashes of fish. For more lonely fishing, try another creek.

Upper Rio de los Pinos: My favorite river in southern Colorado has always been Rio de los Pinos above Trujillo Meadows. Rainbows, browns, Rio Grande cutts, and brook trout all dwell in this medium-sized canyon stream. These trout used to feast on nearly any pattern if it was the right size and tossed in properly. I was always partial to Yellow Humpies and Lime Trudes here, as well as Royal Wulffs and Elk Hair Caddis.

However, recently it seems something sinister has occurred to my baby. It uncharacteristically offered us not a single fish the last time out. The water was tainted a faint copper hue, and although we didn't see any evidence of foul play, there were tons of log trucks in the area, and quite a bit of clearing was happening up there. We can only pray there wasn't a spill of some kind.

If you go, you'd better know how to read a topo map, because getting lost is a serious possibility. Follow FR 118 to a small campsite-looking place. The river will require a hike down, so mark a tree along the bank with flagging tape where you put in, or you may never find your vehicle on the way out. We found out the hard way that coming back downstream looks nothing like it did when we were fishing upstream.

Studying our topo map, we discover a stretch below the reservoir dam we want to pillage. But misfortune would prevail.

We find access off of a dirt road just where the river crosses CO 17. We scurry down a huge slope, across a mosquito-infested slough, and over several unmarked fences. Feeling we've reached the public section, our rods begin to "do what they do."

One of the most impressive hatches of mayflies we've ever witnessed together fills the sky. Trout are leaping and Williams has perma-grin. The bugs were huge, so we were imitating them with #14 dries. It was the time of our lives...for a minute.

However. After 4 huge fish caught and released, I feel a tap on my shoulder as I'm sitting on a high cutbank tying on a different bug. A new twist.

Initially, I believe this "tap" to be an insect. The hatch is amazing and seems like a summertime snowstorm. But when a gun appears and dirty words sprinkle the side of my face, Williams cowers and dashes away.

Even a smooth-talking devil like me with a vipercated tongue can't negotiate out this deal, so I decide to bolt for the trees where the Curmudgeon has vanished.

Williams high-sticks on the Rio de los Pinos below the Trujillo Meadows Reservoir dam.

Anglers beware. Stay between the dam and the canyon opening on Los Pinos. Even though the river between CO 17 and the dam is accessible by the dirt road and remains unposted along it, it's apparently private! Trust us.

We move back upstream to the part of the Pinos we know is public, just below the dam. Jorgen Wouters, Williams' former editor at Gorp, convenes with us at about this point. Because of our yarns of the ghosts of Los Pinos past, Jorgen (who Williams nicknamed the "Norwegian Nightcrawer") expects to see no less than four species of trout between us on the Pinos—Rio Grande cutts, brooks, browns, and rainbows.

Sadly, below the dam, 2 trout find their way to my hand, but nothing from Trujillo Meadows Reservoir. Rumors of the worried biologists pass through the campground. Needless to say, the Pinos and the reservoir are all but dead, and as of this publication the source remains yet another mystery.

Osier Creek (Wild Trout Waters): Jorgen and Williams wake up late with hangovers from too much Early Times whiskey (such a sweetly ironic name). I take it upon myself to griddle up some blueberry pancakes so beautiful that they could rival anything on the cover of *Bon Apétit* magazine.

The fellas wake and try to shake off the cobwebs with the strong coffee I made and hand-rolled cigarettes from Nightcrawler. I'm trying to chop a little wood for our morning fire when all of a sudden the dull son-of-a-bitch hatchet Williams has brought glances off this chunk of wood on my downswing and glances my shin. The sots—er—I mean, the fellas nearly fell back in their camp chairs, knowing that it could have been much worse. I still have a deep scar, if you ever wanna see it. I don't mind showing it at all. Chicks dig scars. It gives them a sense of your rugged past.

With tummies settled, it was time for the Wild Trout Waters of Osier Creek, from its headwaters to the Rio de los Pinos confluence. We're in awe of this breathtaking drive. Yes, it may require a full tank of gas, but it's well worth it. The historic Osier Train Station is worthy of a stop for lunch and pictures.

Osier Creek is tiny. Really tiny. Did I mention Osier Creek was tiny yet? However diminutive, it's considered a fine stream. A fish is stamped over it in most maps, but you'd better have a machete to hack down the alders on the lower section between the "Pinos" and the rail tracks. Above the tracks, Osier is private for about a mile, then more prolific public waters ensue.

We were skeptical of Osier Creek. In fact, I still am. I did catch a 16-inch brown dapping in a micro-pool, one of those browns with the huge, gaping jaws! Shit, it barely fit in the pool. We likened it to Falstaff in a kitchen sink. I set the timer on my SLR and took a hero pic with this fish as we both said "cheese" just before the flash.

23 Ridgway

> "There is no there there."
> —GERTRUDE STEIN

In the early '90s I spent time in Ridgway while fishing the Uncompahgre and the Big Blue Wilderness. There wasn't much there, there. But sometimes, intuition tells you that there will be there, there, it's just when. At that time, Amy and I talked about buying land so we could build a cabin one day. I could see that while Telluride was the big deal, and since Ouray was locked up in a box canyon, Ridgway was the natural growth bridge between the two of these mountain villages. It had to grow. We liked the rawness of the town—a couple of gas stations and a café. How could one not love the drama of the land-scape—big dramatic valley surrounded by snow-capped rugged peaks. Amy and I decided to pass—what if it didn't grow, no airport close, all kinds of excuses. Boy, were we wrong.

This is *True Grit* country. Most of that John Wayne movie was in fact filmed in and around Ridgway. The famous scene in the meadow where Rooster Cogburn takes on Lucky Ned and the other three outlaws, reins in teeth, fill your hands you son of a bitch, took place at Owl Creek.

This bit of Ridgway was in the movie *True Grit*.

I've visited Ridgway annually for ten years, but I was always bypassing it, heading elsewhere, reaching Telluride through Dolores and Rico. So I have missed the amazing growth. The last time I visited Ridgway was five years ago with Mac as we came back from Utah by way of Telluride. Camped and fished at Pa-Co-Chu-Puk.

So speed ahead five years. Mac and I enter Ridgway from the south, from Ouray, the winding Million Dollar Highway. Ridgway has grown. Immensely. You can tell Ridgway is going moneyed, but this big valley town surrounded by big dramatic mountains still has enough Wild Woolly West about it that you won't mind all the new construction and big homes.

We were hungry and discovered that now in town we had all kinds of eating choices. We hadn't had a burger in a while, so we chose a brand new burger joint, the Union Café, that had great vittles but more flies buzzing about than packs of sugar on the table. We had a hankering for French fries, but a hand-scrawled sign at the register said that while they might be on the menu, they weren't available that day. Great. I loves me some fries.

Mac invented sugarmomma.com while we ate burgers. Actually, I ate a Cuban sandwich. (Which I learned to love in Puerto Rico, thanks to Hall of Famer Tony Perez and his wife. A long story, I know. But if you haven't ever had a juicy heavy Cuban sandwich, do it.) Mac got divorced a couple of years ago, and he's a handsome guy, the girls tell me, so he has had no shortage of suitors. I'm 49 and happily married for 21 years, and I got the better deal in my marriage because Amy is so beautiful and puts up with me. I'd hate to have to get out in the dating life, and so that, because it was new to him and mysterious to me, became a staple of our summer conversation.

On the road, we are entrepreneurial geniuses. We come up with all sorts of ways to get out of teaching. We thought up the Taos House (a.k.a. the Taos Haus), a New Mexican-fusion restaurant that mixes folksy comfort native food with new exciting techniques and ingredients. Amarilloans love Santa Fe and Taos restaurants, but there's nothing in town like it. We invented the Shmitten (Mac wrote about this in the Meeker section). We wrote business plans for fly shops, international guide tours, internet retail shops, consulting firms, and so on.

He was talking to one ol' gal who had short-term memory loss and would forget important details from one conversation to the next. He was chatting with another whose last two (maybe three) boyfriends had died. He found that most thirty-plus-year-old women came with what most would term "baggage." We don't normally go sexist, but on the road, all macho and that, it's easy to do. Trust that we are normally not like this.

Sugarmomma.com. There might be a website out there like it already but we didn't know it at the time. Here's the gist:

Downtown Ridgway

Mac and I were talking about how some women he dated had just been looking for a sugar daddy. We're both internet and digital savvy, so it was natural that he said, "Sugarmomma.com." I knew what he meant immediately.

"An internet dating clearinghouse for lonely rich women and single men who need special love."

"Match.com meets Courtney Cox's Cougar."

"Would you really want a sugar momma?"

"You mean, a handsome but slightly older lady who paid for all my toys and rent and loved me up all the time?"

"Yeah. That."

"Not in reality, but theoretically there are days when that sounds mighty good."

"Would she have to fish?"

Mac hesitated. "I could always teach her."

We were kidding of course. I think. You never know on these trips. Surely we were.

Ridgway is a town on the rise, booming it appears, made perfect for both hunters and yuppies who can't afford Telluride. Lots of solid eating joints. A burgeoning artist community or at least art galleries. The local fly shop is RIGS and it's a great fly shop—friendly, they don't expect you to buy a million bucks worth of stuff. Amy interviewed them for an article for an outdoors magazine and they were forthcoming, friendly, informative, and fun. We didn't tell them we were writers or writing a book about their area or any of that. We bought flies (of course) and tippet and exchanged friendlies. Then we went and fished the Uncompahgre before we got bored and drove over to the Cimarron drainage and stayed two extra days, fishing up and down the river and its forks. And talked about new businesses we could start.

Our friends and readers have asked us: so how do you guys figure out a home base?

Six steps:

- We get out our maps. We get out our books and articles. We search on-line. We talk/email to friends and guides and fly shops.
- We look for wildness.
- We look for fisheries we haven't fished or haven't fished in a while.
- We look for small to medium river options. That also means we look for lakes close by that will entertain anybody we bring along who doesn't fish all the time, and lakes a good hike away that will entertain us.
- We look for lots of fisheries close to the home base (and diversity of said fisheries).
- We look for things we can do, other than fishing.

Leadville made the list initially, and then later we kicked it off. Leadville is growing, is improving, but if you've been there, Leadville has no immediate fisheries and is still recovering from a hundred years of scarring and progress. We had others that rattled around in the gray area but ultimately didn't make the cut.

The Uncompahgre River below the reservoir

Then we plan, read, talk, and plan some more. We have fished Colorado for decades (fifty years between us, which is a scary number), so we know the state and its waters pretty well. Then when we figure out where we'll be camping and what we'll be fishing, we drive there. When we get there, we only have a loose plan—choices. We drive upstream, usually past the main river, get out, look, watch for insects and rises and water quality and character. We are looking for that one place that is harder to get to, that has larger fish than it ought to have.

Our style has changed a little over the years—when I was younger, I was a trophy trout hunter—go to Ridgway and fish Uncompahgre for the huge brood trout. Been there done that now. We like wild, isolated, natural places. Nothing like a wild trout. Size of water doesn't matter. We are guerillas, trout terrorists, hit and run, moving moving, up the river, pass the risky spots unless we see a big one, get to the headwaters, get to where the water begins. We wear lightweight wading boots that are soft and broken in, neoprene socks (or just plain socks) and shorts. No vests any more. Chest packs and fanny packs. Three to four pack rods. Only occasionally a 5 or 6 wt.—big brawling river. We like the simplification of it all. Even getting skunked.

Some days, we each catch dozens. Some days, the other guy catches dozens. Some days, we get into big ones or the other guy does. We revel in that. If he catches it, I do, and vice versa. We might hike and wade ten miles in a day, easy. We are flexible. We might be fishing a medium-sized creek and locate a smaller feeder creek, and we spend the rest of the day exploring. We might spend three days fishing up one stream instead of what we had originally planned. We might see that one fishery is off, like Trujillo Meadows Reservoir or Rio de los Pinos (so we fished the Osier Creek and lower Rio de los Pinos). Happy accidents.

Favorite Places to Eat

You must go to the **True Grit Café** (970-626-5739). It's hokey but sincere. An homage to John Wayne and the cowboy heritage of this region. The **Galloping Goose Bakery** (970-626-5531) is solid for breakfast (maybe not so much for lunch), and a weird one we didn't understand but we did like was **Drake's Restaurant** (970-626-3113). **Union Café** (970- 626-4466) was going through growing pains, but their burgers were the best in the San Juans, so says Mac. The **White Horse Saloon** (970-626-4484) is fun and rowdy for after dinner.

Favorite Places to Stay

Chipeta Sun Lodge (970-626-3737), featured in the *New York Times* article March 2, 2007. (Which just shows that Ridgway is already doomed to boomtown problems, right?) http://chipeta.com. **Ridgway-Telluride Lodge,** http://www.ridgewaylodgeandsuites.com/. Many folks stay a few minutes away in Ouray or 45 minutes away in Telluride.

RIGS Fly Shop

Fly Shops, Guides, and Tackle Stores

RIGS Fly Shop (http://fishrigs.com/). You can find outfitters that fish Uncompahgre out of Telluride and other nearby towns but RIGS is the only local.

Fishing Places

Solid Choices near Home Base

Uncompahgre River: The Uncompahgre River runs past brown hillsides dotted with juniper and pinyon, sparse but beautiful country. I am often stunned to watch anglers catch (and release) trout measuring over 20 inches, many weighing over 5 pounds, from this oddly configured water. The river is only thirty-feet wide in the park and is barely hip-deep even in the pools created by the rock weirs and submerged logs. Seeing these jaw-dropping monsters caught in this small water was at first surprising. Upon return trips, I am disappointed when I land a mere 15-incher. Talk about spoiled. Did I mention the time Amy and I were fishing and (she was) catching 22-inchers on a stonefly pattern? You'll want to go in at the Pa-Co-Chu-Puk Recreation Site (a Ute Indian word for Cow Creek pronounced Pak-o-chew-puh). It looks fishable on your own, but these trout are finicky so hire a guide and learn the tricks before you go solo.

The Uncompahgre River fishes well downstream from the reservoir to Billy Creek a few miles north of the state park, but mineralization has damaged the fishery as it courses northward. Travel 5 miles north of Ridgway on US 550.

Canyon Creek: One of the few good streams in the Ouray area for fly fishers. Both brook and rainbow trout are found here.

Ptarmigan Lake: Stocked 5-acre lake situated at 12,939 feet elevation below Imogene Pass. Reachable by trail (TR 869) from Imogene Creek.

Dallas Creek: This large feeder creek flows into Ridgway State Park Reservoir, but access is limited. Dallas Creek is wide-open with cloudy blue water, but don't be fooled—the stream holds some nice brown trout. In its upper reaches, the East and West Forks of Dallas Creek have decent fishing for cutts, rainbow, and brook trout. West Dallas Road (CR 9) takes you upstream on the West Fork of Dallas Creek; East Dallas Road (CR 7) follows East Fork of Dallas Creek. Both roads run south off of CO 62 west out of Ridgway. You can also access Dallas Creek from within Ridgway Recreation Area (Dallas Creek).

Ridgway Reservoir: Might be showing its age, but the camping areas around the lake are some of the best in the state—over 280 campsites with hookups, marina, laundry, picnic tables, trails, dump station, restroom, the works. Gives you perfect proximity to the Uncompahgre River. Call 800-678-2267 for reservations. Big browns of 2 to 6 pounds are not all that rare, and some catch a 10 pounder or two every summer. Lots of stocked rainbows and even splake and kokanee salmon. Drive out of Ridgway 5 miles north.

For the Adventurer

Cimarron River: I think this drainage might be the most unknown trout fishery in the state. You can find a few miles of fishable water from the confluence with the Gunnison, but I like the water just below Silver Jack Lake and above. Rainbows and browns mostly, but in the upper reaches brook and cutthroat trout. No lunkers but pure wild fishing for wild trout in remote rugged mountain terrain. From Ridgway, take the scenic route over Owl Creek Pass. I think the Owl Creek drive is the prettiest in the state.

Much of the lower Cimarron is private and off limits to the public, but 3 miles of water above where it enters the Gunnison are open to fishing. The water to concentrate on is the water below Silver Jack Reservoir beside the campgrounds on FR 858.

Silver Jack Reservoir: This reservoir is primarily used for irrigation and attractive as a camping home base. There are excellent campsites located below the dam.

Crystal Lake: Located just a few miles from Ouray, up Red Mountain Pass to Ironton Park, and on your left is a crystal clear spring-fed pond that has some nice dry fly fishing.

Silver Lake: Long, steep, moderately difficult hike that covers nearly 6 miles and takes about four hours round trip means you won't find many other anglers at this scenic high-country 6-acre lake. Start your hike from Bridal Veil Falls.

An angler on the Uncompahgre River

Blue Lakes: These three lakes can be reached by way of a fairly easy and very scenic 4-mile trail (TR 201) into the Mt. Sneffels Wilderness Area at the headwaters of East Fork Dallas Creek. They can also be accessed by trail at the headwaters of Sneffels Creek. Great as an adjunct fishing excursion if you're heading to Yankee Boy Basin. Can be crowded on weekends.

East Dallas Lake: Small lake located at the Willow Swamps Campground, 4 miles west of Ridgway, 7 miles south on East Dallas Divide Road.

Blue Ribbon Fisheries not far from Ridgway

San Miguel River
Gunnison River

Gear We Love
- Simms wading shoes
- Fishpond San Juan Chest Pack
- Li'l Streamer 7-1/2 foot 3 wt. fly rod, by Global Dorber
- Sage Flight 8 foot 4 wt. fly rod
- Monic "Riser" Leaders
- Aliner Classic Pop-up Camper
- CFO Fly Reel
- Ross Evolution Fly Reel
- Payette Floatant, by Loon
- Simms Pursuit Wading Shoe

24 Rocky Mountain National Park

Oncorhynchus clarki stomias. The greenback cutthroat trout.

We looked forward to the Rocky Mountain National Park swing of the summer tour more than any other. Back in February, we ran across some videos on YouTube of a guy who videotapes his trips to the high country in or around the park. His videos show him at various high-country lakes at or above treeline catching greenback cutthroats that ranged from 14 inches to several pounds. A couple must've gone 6 to 8 pounds, fat as my Uncle Bob. I've caught greenbacks in the park and in the upper Arkansas River drainage, and 14 inches was about the biggest I'd caught.

We did our due diligence and called around, scoured maps, read articles and books and forums. Mac and I were in search of a sure thing, a lake we could hike into, a long way if necessary, that almost guaranteed us we'd have a chance at some of the larger greenback cutthroat. We didn't think the lakes this YouTube angler was hiking to were in the park, only near it, but since

Working a small beaver pond

we needed to update the park as a home base, we kept our short list short. Lawn Lake and the Roaring River seemed to us to be the safest bet given time constraints and some other considerations. Arrowhead and a couple of others didn't make the cut (no pun intended).

I've traipsed all over the park the last two decades and don't feel like I've made a dent in seeing it all. For the longest time, I fished where the books and articles told me to fish and rarely got off the trail. (Kirk's Fly Shop knows exactly where I mean, but it's not time to write about that cutthroat fishery

Roaring River

just yet.) I began with the touristy spots first, like Big Thompson River in Moraine Park, Big Thompson in the fateful canyon, Fall River in Horseshoe Park, Lily Lake, Cache la Poudre. Then it was fun to search out spots like the upper North St. Vrain in Wild Basin and West Creek.

This was August. This summer had been unusually cold, more like what we knew of Colorado summers twenty years ago than the heat waves we had seen in recent years. This was August, but when we left Steamboat to visit the park, the weather turned sour. The day we entered the park might have been the foggiest day God ever saw. Two anglers in search of the elusive, rare, and once nearly extinct greenback cutthroat trout. The weather you ask? Inclement and cold and wet and gray. Early to mid-August. Highs in the 40s. Great backpacking weather.

We were lucky to find a campsite. One campground had two open spots, the last two spots in Rocky Mountain National Park. We secured the absolute worst campsite of the entire summer. Imagine McCarthy's *The Road*. The campground itself had no trees because of pine beetles, and across a skinny meadow were stands of skinny black posts, like giant charcoal pencils sharpened, that were once green forests. The trailer barely fit into the spot. The campground had a covering of ash and black dirt everywhere (which made for a clean trailer as we went in and out). But we did have a spot, and that long line of cars circling the campground did not.

There's no park like this. You drive in the peaks, the highest road of any park in the country. We have driven through, above, and just under the clouds almost any time we traverse the park. And that next morning, we drove through fog so thick, and no this is not a Johnny Carson setup joke, so thick that we pulled over several times because we could not see the car in front of us. We'd wait for a bit to see if the fog would lift, and it only got worse. We decided to risk plunging over the side of a precipitous cliff because, for somebody, it'd make a good story.

Mac does this one thing, and he does it weirdly well. He finds things. I like to think I'm unusually observant, as most writers are because we need filler for our stories, but Mac takes it to another level. One time we were camping in a field by the Gila River in New Mexico when he found a rock that was partially cracked. He opened it, and it was the prettiest purple crystal-amethyst like you see for sale in rock stores all over Colorado. He discovered a dead rabbit with missing feet along the Conejos. Found a 1950s Colorado license plate in the Upper Roaring Fork. He always finds the oddest things. He found a metal talisman on a chain in a grocery store parking lot this summer that he wears around his neck, even today. The silver talisman looks amazingly like a cross between an angry trout and a circling raptor,

You'll find big boulders and lots of pocket water on the Roaring River.

the trout's tail coming to a sharp nasty point. That talisman described his underlying mood for much of the summer. I could tell he was on percolate, that he had a lot of issues swimming around in his big Mac brain, but except for the nuptials-argument-over-fire, he was fun and funny.

We went to the Permit Office. If you hike back into the backcountry and want to spend the night, you must get a permit. The lady ranger was a local. She was pleasant and pretty, and we talked a bit.

"Do you know the story of the three Steves?" (see Estes Park chapter)

We got our camping permit, but there was nothing open at Lawn Lake. Instead, we'd have to camp a mile below, off some other trail, along some tiny creek. Great. Oh well. Another lousy campsite in Paradise.

The Alluvial Fan. Roaring River. Fall River. Lawn Lake. The Mummy Range. The names were romantic and wild, especially with the story of the Three Steves.

We hoped to fish our way up the trail, but the trail doesn't see the river very much of the hike. The rain and cold slowed us down, that and the numerous hikers coming down or passing us dayhiking on the way up. *Jeez some people are entirely too perky. Let'em strap on this pack I'm carrying and see how damned energetic they are.* This is a pretty darned steep trail. Not for sissies or people with bad knees like me. Six hours to reach camp. A tough six. I kept my knee pains to myself because Mac's not having any trouble and I don't want to get hoorahed about it.

I had to deal with my wife's crappy backpack. Amy doesn't backpack often enough to buy herself a high-end pack like mine. I found one on EBay a couple of years ago, and she had always used one of my old framepacks instead of this new "deal" I bought her. When Mac and I loaded up the Aliner back in May, I stuffed her new pack into the compartment and didn't pull it out till I realized I forgot to add my good pack. Big mistake. Always, always, always check your gear and test your gear before you hit the trail.

I overpacked. As cold as it was, not knowing how many days we'd be in the backcountry (three by permit, but if the fishing was good...). The left shoulder strap broke from the weight and from lousy engineering only a half hour up the trail.

The trail is full of long drop steps. Or when ascending, long up steps. Slippery when wet. The pack sat funny, twisting because I had to hold the left shoulder strap with my hand, pulling on it, so it hurt my shoulders, and my knee was acting up even more, and if that wasn't enough my lower back was acting like it does once a year when it goes out for five or six days. Not good.

I stayed up with Mac pretty good going up. Despite the cool weather and rain, we were both sweating. Mac was ahead about fifteen feet and found the second of two springs that cross the trail. We know better, but we are dumb-asses and like risks sometimes. We drank from the cold clear spring. I am positive that bottled spring water does not come from springs because this tasted heavenly, like angels, whatever they taste like. Not like bottled water, I'll tell you that.

We reached camp in the late afternoon a couple hours later than we had hoped or predicted. She was a cold hard little camp, fifty yards from a creek no wider than a ruler. The campsite was just plain weird and not well thought out. Tucked back into mountain lion country complete with the side of a mountain, big boulders, and what looked like a cave one hundred yards up. Seriously, you've seen those amazing backcountry photos in *Field and Stream* of mountain lions ready to spring at a deer and they're crouched on a big chalky rock. This was where they must stage those shots. The next site was a thousand yards downstream (if you can call that a stream, maybe downbrook). All this open meadow and they stuck us, complete with logs laid out delineating where to lay out the tents, in a little cocoon of overhanging crowded trees. Dead pine beetle trees that looked as though they might fall over in the night. One good thing with the cold, the fog, the rain—mosquitoes would not be a problem.

Mac talked me into hiking an hour back to the creek so we could drop a fly on the water. We both caught some small ones from the green clear water

Left: A beautiful greenback cutthroat trout from Lawn Lake
Above: The Roaring River near Lawn Lake

and hiked back in the dark on that precarious, steep trail. Mac was quiet and surly. *Hope the mountain lion gets him first.*

We were up early because the tent sites are hard pack dirt with a sprinkling of pointy rocks. Quick coffee, strap on the fishing pack, put the rod together, and off we go.

The stream is clear and cold but doesn't seem fertile, especially with the white soil and bleached boulders. The soil is loose, the rocks roll when you step on them. You can see the bottom of the stream, alabaster and rocky, so the idea we're going to catch big trout in here seems remote. Boulders sit in the oddest places and their composition and coloring are evidence that they were violently displaced by the flood twenty years prior. The boulders range in size from igloo to Land Rover, as if strewn by Titans playing marbles.

We are in primitive dangerous country. If something goes wrong up here, you can pay for it. I mean, we are fishing for the greenback cutthroat, and these primeval fish were once nearly extinct. Why do cutthroat get us so jazzed? Remember that the original trout in Colorado were cutthroats. In the waters all over the state, there were once no brook, rainbow, or brown trout.

Leap frogging up the small river, we catch fish after fish, sightcasting to most. We hide behind boulders, dap cast, land incredibly colorful creatures, 10 to 12 inches long and we release them without touching them. As we move up to the lake, the size of the greenbacks increases. Some large, some average, none small up toward the lake. We navigate through snow banks, leap from boulder to boulder, spot trout and then catch them. With each catch, *dude, take a look at the colors on this one!* Not many dry fly takers but then again, absolutely no hatches. We are using both beads and subsurface nymphs. The river's so shallow, too-shallow riffles and no fish, but bam and you have the deep-creviced one-foot, two-foot pools. We could not always see where they were lying in wait—we might have to cast and drift five times, ten times before we got a strike. Three hundred yards below the lake, the trout were all big, 15 inches the smallest we were seeing, catching. Others, 2 to 3 pounds. In a river not fifteen feet wide.

When we hooked up, we didn't always bring them to hand. Tight quarters, no way to wade the water, sharp rocks and big fish. The colors, damn man, the colors, and every fish differently colored, like explosions of a Sherwin-Williams factory. At the outlet, you can really see where the dam broke. A forceful faded photo of the three Steves. The boulders that sat sentinel were as big as cabins.

Mac found a large boulder, size of a tool shed, and laid prone, fishing to this one big fish I had lost thirty minutes before. We guessed 24 inches. The pool was the largest in this part of the Roaring River, maybe seven or eight feet deep and slotted, ringed underwater with wicked big rocks tumbled like a fallen Atlantis. He fished that turquoise pool for an hour or more while I hiked up and down the river, to the dam, back down again, catching 15 to 18 trout and discovering something we hadn't known before: in the canyon, no wind; on the lake, blustery was a mild description.

We're from Amarillo, so we know wind. This particular wind of Lawn Lake, on this particular morning, was a 30 to 40 mph steady gust that at times knocked us off balance. Made us take off our caps and stuff them in our packs. Neither of us could come close to making a forward cast into the wind. Lawn Lake is much lower now; like a bowl of chili, you can see where the chili used to be, a ring around the bowl. When I've seen this before, ten years later the river took back what it once lost. It seems to us the lake is doomed to keep shrinking, silt and soil destined to fill the lake.

The fish at Lawn Lake are hiders. We tried a few techniques until we found one that worked, and here it is: cast a wiggly fly like a Madam-X or a Stimulator with rubber legs to an edge. A dropoff, a submerged rock, around an exposed boulder. Let it sit. If no trout comes up, and they often do, twitch the fly. If no trout shows, short-strip your fly. If you do that, you will catch fish after fish after fish, even on a gale-force-windy-day. A word of

Stealth fishing on the Roaring River

warning—the Lawn Lake cutts don't aggressively take flies. They open their big white mouths and sip the fly. We overreacted and set the hook hard at first. The only hard strikes I had were when I was stripping wet rubber-legged flies deep through the inlet runs.

Like Trappers Lake, this lake is chockfull of 15- to 19-inch cutthroats. Mac went around one side of the lake, me the other. We normally don't split up—photo opps—but this was the way. Mac was pensive, almost sullen. I was windchapped and eager to explore.

I caught trout all along the shore. When the wind would let down (say, 15 mph), I'd see a rise or splash, occasionally a cruiser, but for the most part I was fishing blindly. Mac was moving slower up the other side, taking his time, landing trout. He came to this one bluff that butts up against the lake. Most of the lake is open with an easy gradient. The bluff was dramatic and unique, a sanctuary from the wind. Mac stayed at the bottom of the bluff for an hour while I walked around the lake to the inlets that spread out over the sandy valley. I fished these myriad inlets and had a blast. I got sloppy or lazy, I'm not sure which, and chose not to net the largest trout of the day. I pulled him up on the sandy beach, half in the water, and tried to snap a quick photo. *Leverage.* Gone in a flash. The trout had blood red gills, big spots, a blushing pink belly, and greenish hues on the side. In the water, he sparkled like a prism. I watched his strong form swim away from me confidently until he reached the dark, green, silent demarcation.

I waited for Mac to come around that side and meet me. I walked up-stream, back again, wondered if he had gone back to the outlet and stream. I

Another greenback cutthroat landed in the park

searched for him through the viewfinder of the SLR. When I was about ready to head back to the outlet, I saw a flicker of movement against the bluff. Mac. I didn't see him because he seemed a part of that bluff, camouflaged, minimal movement. He had one on. A splash showed it was another.

Mac had found something else. Himself. He had been on simmer all summer.

For a few hours, he had found a safe spot, a womb hidden from the wind, insulated from everything but the water and fish in front of him. Whatever ailed him vanished for those hours at the bluff.

Rocky Mountain National Park is simply spectacular. The wildflowers in the summer are a palette of color blanketing meadows and rolling hills. With fog hanging low over Big Thompson River as it flows through the meadows of Moraine Park, where an elk feeds near the banks, the scenes are as though you are on your very own postcard.

You don't go to Rocky Mountain National Park to catch big trout. (You can, but unless you are willing to hike a long way, you probably won't.) You go for the magnificent scenery. You go for the solitary angling. You go to catch the rare and beautiful emerald jewel, the native trout indigenous to the park, the greenback cutthroat.

The park can be crowded during the spring and summer, especially since it is such a short drive from Denver. Rocky Mountain National Park is a family vacation hotspot, with nearly three million visitors per year. But there are ways to avoid the crowds. Most folks stay at the popular access points,

Years later, you can still see where the Lawn Lake flood scourged the land.

A herd of elk in Rocky Mountain National Park

but if you get off the beaten path a bit, by walking a few minutes, by hiking, by backpacking, or by riding astride a horse, you can get away from all the commotion (amidst the park's 414 square miles, or 265,727 acres). The park holds over 150 lakes and hundreds of miles of rivers.

The 48-mile drive from Estes Park through the park to Grand Lake takes over 2½ hours depending on traffic and how long you stop to admire the views. The park has a diversity of terrain, from the junipers and pines of the 7,000-foot lower areas to the firs and spruce of the rivers, to the aspen of the high country to the alpine tundra of the even higher country, where peaks reach to the skies some 14,000 feet high. This is one of the prettiest places on the continent.

The great scenic road that cuts across the park, Trail Ridge Road, is the main artery through the park, but with all the crowds there are simply not enough roads for all the vehicles. This lack of access is a good thing for exploring anglers. It makes Rocky Mountain National Park ideal for hikers and backpackers willing to trek off the road to find trout, solitude, and pristine wilderness. Visitors can hike over 350 miles of trails in the park.

Anglers can catch four species of trout in the park—brook, brown, rainbow, and cutthroat. The Holy Grail of these four trout is the greenback cutthroat trout. Outside of Colorado, this colorful trout, whose range is the farthest east of any native trout, is hardly known. A great thing about Rocky Mountain National Park is that if you want accessible lakes and streams, you can find them right along the road or off an easy trail. If you want solitude, you can hike difficult, rarely hiked lonely trails leading to clear lakes and rarely fished trout hotspots. Trails are usually well marked. If you want to camp "out there," you will need to reserve one of the 250 backcountry campsites and get a permit. If you don't like hiking, contact a local livery and mount a horse to go exploring the backcountry.

So what can you expect from the fishing opportunities in the park? Anglers will encounter a diversity of water types that runs the gamut—winding little brooks with deep undercut banks and long slicks, choppy canyon water chockfull of pocket water and big pools, and the headwaters of major rivers like the Big Thompson where anglers fish in lush valleys under the sentinel of tall, snow-covered craggy peaks. We're talking majestic views.

Favorite Places to Eat

If you stay in the park, you'll eat at your site or drive out of the park to find food. Fix up something good at your campsite and holler at us. We're hungry.

Favorite Places to Stay

If you don't camp, you can find an amazing array of lodging at any of the area villages like Estes Park or Grand Lake. If you camp, you'll camp in one of five campgrounds in Rocky Mountain National Park: **Aspenglen, Glacier Basin, Moraine Park, Longs Peak, and Timber Creek,** with group camping at Glacier Basin. Reservations for summer camping in Moraine Park and Glacier Basin begin January 1 (800-365-2267). Campers have stay limits of 7

Mark fishes in the Big Thompson canyon

nights from late May through September. The limits extend to 14 nights at the year-round campgrounds the rest of the year. At all campgrounds 2 tents OR 1 vehicle and 1 camping unit (i.e., tent, RV, or trailer/tow vehicle) per site.

You can also stay outside the park, but nearby, at one of these locations: **Seven Pines Campground** (970-586-3809), Estes Park; **Marys Lake Campground** (970-586-4411), Estes Park; **Estes Park KOA** (970-586-2888), Estes Park; **Elk Meadow Lodge and RV Resort** (970-586-5342), Estes Park; **Paradise On The River** (970-586-5513), Estes Park; **Elk Creek Campground & RV Resort** (970-627 8502), Grand Lake; **Yogi Bear's Jellystone Park Resort** (970-586-4230), Estes Park; **Manor RV Park and Motel** (970-586-3251), Estes Park; **National Park Resort Camping & Cabins** (970-586-4563), Estes Park.

Fly Shops, Guides, and Tackle Stores

So many shops and guides serve the park, with outfits in Estes Park, Granby, Grand Lake, and other surrounding communities. **Estes Angler** (970-586-2110) and **Kirk's Fly Shop,** Estes Park Mountain Shop (970-586-6548) in Estes Park; **Angler's Roost** (970-377-3785) and **St. Peter's Fly Shop** (970-498-8968) in Ft. Collins; **Alkire's Sporting Goods** (970-352-9501) in Greeley; **St. Vrain Angler** (303-651-6061) in Longmont; and **Lyons Angler** (303- 823-5888) in Lyons.

Fishing Places Solid Choices near Home Base

Way too many to list. Your main fisheries include the Colorado, Big Thompson, Cache la Poudre, Fall and Roaring Rivers, and North St. Vrain Creek. The better lakes include Chasm Lake, Lake of Glass, Mills Lake, Peacock Pool, Lake Haiyaha, Loch Vale, Sprague Lake, Sky Pond, Lake Estes, Marys Lake, Fern Lake, Upper, Middle, and Lower Hutcheson, Pear, Ouzel, Sandbeach, Fern, Odessa, Spruce, Loomis, Lilly, Lawn, Big Crystal, Lost, and Husted Lakes. Kirk's Fly Shop has some secret special streams they'll share with you if you go in and talk to them, but we don't feel like we should write about them just yet. These are just some of the inventory of good fishing lakes. The park has 147 lakes but only forty-some-odd lakes hold self-reproducing populations of trout. Cold water temperatures and lack of spawning habitat prevent reproduction in high altitude lakes. Supplemental stocking is done only to restore native species to altered waters.

25 Saguache

Our first night out. Intolerably cold. Reminiscent of Apollo 13 when they must power down to conserve. Everything from our blood to our Spanish olive oil coagulates. By 2:00 a.m., riverfishing is absent from the mind and sleep is elusive. We imagine the streams frozen. Time, cast in ice. No ebb or flow. Only ice. Not really what we had in mind for all this. Sleep visits us in short cycles.

Stanzas from Canto XII of Dante's *Inferno* chilled me to the bone between dreams:

> *The place where to descend the bank we came*
> *Was alpine, and from what was there, moreover,*
> *Of such a kind that every eye would shun it.*

We believe in omens. Me more than Williams, but he knows I know. Signs point us in certain directions. The cold seems to chase our spirit away in the night, wondering if this is how it was to be.

I have pain emerging in my jaw on the right side just in front of my ear. I cannot bite down, nor open up all the way. Annoying, and unexplainable, all day this pain festers. Fistfuls of Ibuprofen prove pointless—a confounding affliction that seems to be the beginning of a summer-long plague. Williams taunts of Tetanus and lockjaw. I fear he could be correct.

We wake early to glistening frost in the daylight, and only espresso could change the disposition lingering from the night before. So we visit the town of Saguache.

Not much here in "Colorado's Gateway to San Luis Valley." A place where the post office still seems central to the town, and only a couple of carbon-copy gas stations exist. But they sell the beef jerky, trail mix, and miniature pecan pies we dig, so it's enough to resurrect some of our spirits.

There's Big Valley Motel. Another joint called Desserts First Coffeehouse, a place where wi-fi seems a futuristic theory, but evidently it exists even here, and we get our espresso fix on and steal their bandwidth from the parking lot to investigate the weather. Down the road a piece is the Gunbarrel Steakhouse, which we presume is a staple for the meat-eating Saguachians, young and old.

These few establishments seem as much a part of Saguache as Saguache seems a part of the outlying mountainous terrain—however, a truly *Divine Comedy* we thought upon first approach. *Could there be quality trout fishing within a day's journey of this place?* we pondered. Our books and maps seemed to indicate there was. And in maps we trust.

South of town is a mountain that resembles a breast like no other monument we've seen to date. (Williams dubs it Nipple Peak within seconds. Visit, and you'll see why.) It attracts our eyes, lures us in. Otherwise, nothing notable exists out southeast of town.

Trout seem implausible. But Nature has her way of forcing beauty out of the starkest earth. 'Tis such in Saguache, Colorado.

We move back west of town. The views on CO 114 are special. Wondrous. Mysterious. Not too many are savvy about this area. Not even devout Coloradoans. It's desolate. Isolated. Ancient. And the rivers are siblings, yet alone. As are we. Williams and I. And it's beautiful to be alone on the river. We're needing the solitude. And yet, this trip wouldn't be the same without the other guy. Such a strange dance.

Near Buffalo Pass Campground, where we've pitched camp, an eerie sensation arises from the landscape. Rocks arranged in thin layered piles— resembling giant molten blobules of petrified, layered dough. Explorers and photographers should follow Sheep Creek Road for the most geologically bizarre scenic drive north of Carlsbad, New Mexico. But do not travel too far down FR 810 locating fish, for Spanish Creek is too small, and Sheep Creek is covered with alders. We got lost here and escaped perhaps only through divine intervention. Nearly trapped. Wedgied between two trees in a steep, catastrophic way. But the mountain released us so that we might catch and release trout later that day.

Williams fell in love with Pauline Creek, a small dry-fly stream.

Favorite Places to Eat

The Gunbarrel Steakhouse on US 285, a.k.a., "the gun barrel," in the town of Saguache serves a "hearty meal in quiet, mountain scenery." 719-655-2264. **Desserts First Coffeehouse,** also on US 285, is an inviting stop for espresso and sweet tooth fixins. **Oasis** on Gunnison Ave. bakes great pies for after the meal, and has a gift shop attached.

Favorite Places to Stay

Big Valley Motel has remodeled every room and is very clean. 440 Gunnison Ave., 719-655-2524. **Old Cow Town** is brand new, with Old West-style lodging and an Old West feel. 36710 36 CC, 719-655-2224, http://oldcowtown. net/. **Saguache Creek Lodge** is an RV park and offers a few rooms as well. 21495 US 285, 719-655-2264.

CAMPGROUNDS: At 9,000 feet elevation and with 26 campsites, **Buffalo Pass Campground** is a solid choice for big game hunters and anglers in season. Also, mountain biking and 4-wheel driving on area roads is popular. From Saguache, go 28 miles west on CO 114, then 2 miles south on the access road. Season: May to September. No reservations.

OTHER STUFF: Since there is very little if any tackle in town, bring what tackle you'll need and don't expect to find guide services, unless you tempt one from Gunnison to take you in there. The beauty of fishing Sagauche is found in its untouched, unmolested desolation, so most anglers who home base here are do-it-yourself kinda guys.

There is so much more to fish here than what we had the opportunity to cover. Check your map and explore the wilderness rivers that lie southwest of CO 114, rather than spending too much time on the northeast side of the road. This is where the action is.

Fishing Places Solid Choices near Home Base

Cochetopa Creek: Anglers should venture to Cochetopa Creek first, as it is designated as Wild Trout Waters within the State Wildlife Area. Pronounced "Coach-a-tope" by locals, this river, especially near the Coleman Easement, cuts an even, snakey swath through the valley floor, resembling the infamously winding Highway 1 on the California Coast. On the upper Cochetopa, little to no riparian vegetation exists to foil a backcast. The banks are often feathered into the water or deeply cut, depending upon which side of the bend one stands.

A brown trout puts up a fight on the Cochetopa.

We pull out at a crossover on the Coleman Easement area and find the strangest, spongey, marsh-like terrain we've ever seen. Easy to turn or even break ankles crossing to the water, Williams nicknames the anomalous land-mass "Sponge-henge" before we decide we've had enough and turn back for easier access.

Heavy browns densely populate the length of the Cochetopa. We saw some as large as 22 to 24 inches. I land an 18-incher with my favorite 3 wt. and 7X tippet. The fish rips line from the reel, and spooks up an even larger 2 footer that slashes across the creek bottom in less than eight inches of water. Trout this size in this stream seems impossible, so don't pass over the shallows. Huge fish are there. We fished this two more times in the summer and did better each time. Maybe we got better. Maybe they did. I did lose at the last second before netting what Williams calls the Shadow Fish. She would have been the largest fish I caught all summer if that tells you anything.

Canyon section of Cochetopa Creek: The lower section of Cochetopa Creek offers more public access along CO 114. From downstream, begin at mile marker 12. About 5 miles of upstream public water flows through the canyon. A few picnic areas offer public access and parking along the river. Upstream from there, some signs read "State Stocked Water—Permission Required." Ask for permission to fish these areas, contact the Colorado Division of Wildlife in Durango, 970-247-0855. There will be high riparian vegetation, so short rods will remain the rule.

Lower Saguache Creek near the town of Saguache is mostly private.

Lower Los Pinos Creek: The lower Los Pinos is similar to Cochetopa. Almost twins, but Cochetopa is the prettier twin. Same rules apply when fishing either river with tackle, tactics, and regulations. Los Pinos also holds the same designation as Wild Trout Water within the State Wildlife Area.

Utilize 3 wt. to 5 wt. gear and an assortment of dries and nymphs. We fish a homemade beadhead with a yellow body and red collar tied about 16 inches below fat Stimulators. We dubbed the nymph pattern Big Mac since our very own "MacPhail" concocted it, and also because the colors are reminiscent of Mickey D's logos. But red Copper Johns and Beadhead Princes find the trout as well.

On the way to fish the lower Los Pinos, we spot a wolf for the first time in the wild. We both photograph it, but it appears as only a blurred blip against a grassy background. Amazingly, just around the bend from the "woof" (as my daughter Savannah calls them), we spy an oddly statuesque antelope. She won't move. I exit the Jeep with camera in hand. She allows me to come within ten feet of her before she bolts across the road and into the brush, luring us away from her calf, which we find when we glass the field from whence she came. Her baby lies there, crouched low in the grass, hiding. Mark reminds me that we are here to rodeo the trout in the Pinos, not to ride antelope.

Dome Lakes: After fishing the Pinos and Cochetopa, we stop to use the restroom at one of the Dome Lakes. Waiting for Williams, I cast the Big Mac into the drink a few times and get several rainbows to take hold in the process.

Mac fishes with his Big Mac fly on the Saguache.

Williams high-sticks on Pauline Creek.

This fly is the bomb here for browns, and we are intent on keeping the recipe a secret. By the way, these lakes are a great place for aging anglers and kiddos to rack up a limit.

For the Adventurer

Upper Los Pinos: Moving towards the headwaters of the Los Pinos pays off in ample dividends. The Pinos falls through a high canyon before slowing down in the valley flats. Up above, the brooks and cutts take over, and fishing small streamwater in the midst of alders proves challenging. But we pine over the Pinos because the ridiculous numbers of trout in this creek.

Tinkering in the upper Pinos, I find myself in an intricate series of braided waterways chock full of eager brookies. Strangely different aspen stands keep distracting me from fishing with full intent.

Pauline Creek: We travel south of the Dome Lakes, taking FR 794 to the culvert that crosses Pauline Creek. She is but a mile of lonesome, fishable stream, but her current is strewn full of cutts, brooks, and browns—absent only of rainbows, curiously enough.

Pauline Creek is hidden and desolate, and the fish are as wild as they come. Jumping across Pauline Creek is feasible at nearly all points. Williams and I both manage each side of the stream. And the deeply cut banks produce dark residential habitat for fattening up the trout that reside inside of her. Once more, the stream is only good for a half a day's fishing, no matter how diligent. So plan for angling somewhere else the second half of the day, or fish Pauline twice!

26 Salida

HOME BASE

*S*alida—the Spanish word for departure, or exit. Not a welcoming epitaph by any means for a friendly town in the West, despite the inviting landscape and its accepting people. We stepped upon the bank of the Arkansas, and Huck Finn's words seemed to slip out of the crackled, yellowed pages of my youth:

> *"So, in two seconds, away we went,*
> *a-siding down the river, and it did seem so good to be free again*
> *and all by ourselves on the big river and nobody to bother us."*
> —MARK TWAIN (*Huckleberry Finn*)

Salida, the word, may not seem too welcoming. But the town and the river that flows beside it are. The town of Salida has done just fine with its unfortunate name.

However, the word can be cause for a problematic visit for linguists and wordsmiths as well. Pronounce it "Saleeda" (as it should be), and you're liable to offend the locals. It's Salida, with a long "i," as in the word "wide." It's all a part of Colorado code to mispronounce Spanish town names such as Boona Vista,

Rafters and kayakers share the Arkansas River where it flows through Salida.

Del Nort, and Mont Rose (Buena Vista, Del Norte and Montrose, respectively).

Salida is an unpretentious beehive: eccentrics, adrenaline junkies, the Joneses—all collectively buzz about the place with singularity and individuality. It's a damn friendly place to play, for kids and adults alike. We are sitting in a restaurant overlooking the Arkansas River. Two girls are dancing around a water snake, squealing like piglets at dinnertime. A woman is reading her book while perched atop a huge rock as her husband does Eskimo rolls in a kayak just fifty feet away from her. We are enjoying icy pale ales and the warm temperate weather. It won't get much better than this the entire summer. Williams and I know it. So we're cherishing it.

Once, this was Ute Indian territory. The tribes have slowly been replaced by weekend warriors: kayakers, rafters, ATVers, and flyfishing fanatics. Grinning river floaters splash about on what some might call the Are-Kansas River. But by God don't call it that. Just say Ark-n-Saw. It's easier that way.

Favorite Places to Eat

Pull up a chair overlooking the Arkansas at the **Boathouse Cantina** and partake in some excellent fish tacos and a pint of your favorite ale. You'll find it at the very end of town. 228 North F St., 719-539-5004. **Moonlight Pizza** at 242 F St. wields a wicked slice of pizza at reasonable prices. **First Street Café** on 1st St. scores high marks with us for serving American food the right way! **Me Gusta** has bold *sabroso* flavor, particularly the spinach, goat cheese, and caramelized onion enchiladas. Crazy fiesta in the mouth. **The Butcher's Table** has something different going on—the Iron Chef Re-Deux Dinner at the Butcher's Table, with Chef Kurt Boucher.

OTHER PLACES TO EAT: Twisted Cork Café boasts warm ambiance when they turn the out-

The Arkansas River flows beside the Boathouse Cantina.

door lighting on at night and all things are perfect. Great salmon and reasonable wines. **Smokin' Jack's Pit BBQ** will make your mouth water with smoky goodness and sticky, lip-smackin' sauce. For more upper-echelon fare, **The Laughing Ladies** at 128 W. 1st St. serves international delicatessen cuisine, such as Cajun duck, duck spring rolls and grilled Halibut. And for an upper-crust pizza pie try **Amicas** at 136 E. 2nd St. The great salads and pizza are well worth the sometimes-lengthy wait.

Favorite Places to Stay

Lodging in Salida can be limited in summer, so book a stay early at the **River Suites Luxury Cabins & Villas** in Salida/Maysville, just 9 miles from town. Quiet peace right on the North Fork of the Arkansas River. 719-539-6953, http://www.riversuites.com/. Or visit the **Gazebo Country Inn Bed and Breakfast** right in the middle of town. 719-539-7806, www.gazebocountryinn.com.

The Cabins at Chalk Creek will not disappoint a discerning angler looking for a wicked-cool place for the entire family. Besides the natural hot springs just down the road to relax in, there are endless fishing opportunities,

hiking, biking, 4-wheeling, gold panning, rock hounding for aquamarine gemstones, rafting and float fishing, ghost town exploring, horseback riding, and creek side campfires to keep you entertained. Nathrop, CO, 719-395-2366 (cell), 719-221-4972, http://www.cabinsatchalkcreek. com/. **Creek Side Hot Springs,** sitting right on Chalk Creek, is an unbelievable stay—a furnished 3 bedroom, 2 bath home with a finished basement. TV with a DVD player and a variety of DVDs. Nathrop, CO, 15654 CR 289A, 719-395-2071, http://www. creeksidehotsprings. com/home.html.

OTHER PLACES TO STAY: **Days Inn,** 719-539-6651, www.daysinnsalida.com. **Aspen Leaf Lodge,** 800-759-0338, http://www.aspen leaflodge.com/. **The Bunny Lane Cabins,** Nathrop, CO, 17290 CR 291, 719-395-2800, http://bunnylanecabins.com/.

The architecture of Salida harkens back to a time when brick and mortar were wielded into works of art.

Fly Shops, Guides, and Tackle Stores

There are three area **ArkAnglers Fly Shops** that carry top-quality gear and the dudes there are great for tips, locations, and river reports. 719-543-3900, http://www.arkanglers.com/FlyShops.html.

Mac thumbs through his flies at O'Haver Lake, south of Salida.

OTHER STUFF: River rafters will by far out-number the anglers here. And if you're going to fish the Arkansas River, you are going to have to deal with them. I say, if you can't beat 'em, pop their boat with a hook and snag one of them by the eyelid with your fly! NO, JUST KIDDING! What I was going to say was, if you can't beat 'em, join 'em. If you've never rafted before, do it. I once rafted for a solid week. From the deserts of Utah all the way down into Colorado. No question about it, this is where I fell in love with the river. Not just that one, but all rivers. It's worth a shot, and the river guides in the area are some of the best in the country. Don't be scared. It ain't like "Shootin' the Chutes" with the MacLeans. You'll come home wet, but you WILL come home.

Fishing Places Solid Choices near Home Base

Arkansas River (Gold Medal Waters): Known for its trophy browns and world class rapids, the Arkansas slides wide and flows deep, falling north to south between the Collegiate Peaks and those others named by the Utes themselves.

Feeder creeks trickle into the Arkansas like feathers to the quill, bolstering the mother river along her journey. The town of Salida is finally starting to utilize the water as an attraction, as all river towns should.

While home based in Salida, definitely hit the Gold Medal Waters, a 28-mile stretch from the stockyard bridge just east of Salida to Fernleaf Gulch between Cotopaxi and Texas Creek. The 7.5-mile stretch of Gold Medal Water from the stockyard bridge to Badger Creek is restricted to two fish, 16 inches or longer, which you will manage if you have the diligence and proper presentation. All rainbows must be returned to the river, and anglers are limited to artificial flies and lures only. Try bushy Royal Wulffs, Stimulators, hopper patterns, and match the hatch flies as needed.

Beyond the Gold Medal Waters, a designation of Wild Trout Waters has been also been established. Artificial lures and flies will be the guide, but don't be surprised to find old jars of salmon eggs or worm containers on the banks. You may become as postal as we did when we found them.

Browns Creek is about 12 miles north of Salida. Since we both adore fishing for wild browns, Browns Creek seemed a logical choice. Against my instincts, I grabbed one of those nostalgic Coca-Colas in the slender ice-cold

Mark shoots his loops to trout on the Arkansas above Salida.

bottles made the old school way with the real cane sugar. God, that thing hit the spot! Mark scored a sticker for the Aliner, and northward we trudged, me burping and belching the entire way down the bumpy road.

Just south of Chalk Creek we ascended into the crack between Mounts White and Shavano. From US 285 we turned west onto 263 RD and worked our way to Browns, which we thought might be a little bigger than what it was. But since Williams and I are small stream enthusiasts, we high-fived and bolted for the water.

Williams wanted the first go at it, which is actually quite rare, so we pulled over at this picturesque pool where he dropped a Madam X looking thing on the water. He loves the buggy flies. We were both befuddled when he yanked a cutthroat from Browns Creek. We later read that Browns is good for native cutthroat trout, and at the headwaters there are large ponds and beaver dams ideal for flyfishing with light lines and dry flies. For an added scenic bonus, way in the upper basin is a rocky, shaded waterfall that's a must see if you're gonna go all this way. That trail is approximately 5 miles. Take provisions.

O'Haver Lake is close by and heavily stocked with rainbows. With walk-around access and plenty of camping area, families love it because it's close, easy to fish, and absolutely gorgeous, with spectacular views of Ouray Peak and the San Isabel National Forest. Try the beaver ponds and small streams on the way to O'Haver for brook and rainbow trout. We caught so many trout here on beadhead nymphs that we got bored and left.

But kids won't get bored here, so to reach O'Haver, leave Salida heading southwest on US 285 to Poncha Springs towards Poncha Pass. Turn right on CR 200, then right on CR 202, and follow the signs to parking.

For the Adventurer

The Pomeroy Lakes beg to be fished for large native cutthroat trout. But getting there is most of the fun! And if you think you're "Gonzo" enough, you'd do this on a rented mountain bike. We dare ya!

There is a campground remotely located behind Mount Shavano—North Fork Reservoir Campground. This is high-altitude camping, so bring layers, and lots of them. At 11,000 feet, snow is common in early spring and fall. From the junction of US 285 and US 50, head west for approximately 6.5 miles to CR 240. Turn north (right) onto CR 240 and travel northwest for about 10 miles to the campground. After passing the Angel of Shavano Campground, the road comes to resemble the moon's surface—pot holes, ruts and divots make travel slow. Low-clearance vehicles or vehicles towing trailers are not recommended for travel on the North Fork Road. Once you find the campground, you're not quite done. FR 240 continues north where TR 1437 allows hikers to travel by foot to Billings Lake, Upper Pomeroy Lake, and on to Pomeroy Lake where you can land 20-inch cutthroat with the proper presentation of beadheads like Prince Nymphs and red or black Copper Johns. Use hair-fine tippet and have your knots tied properly. Sometimes these fish will take lightly presented dries too, like #20 black gnats or mosquito patterns. Let them sit on the surface a while. Something's bound to happen!

> **Our Top 3 Favorite Fly Lines**
> - Monic MDT (no stretch, no memory, high floating and supple)
> - Sage Quiet Double Taper II (slick and thin with light presentation)
> - Rio Selective Trout II (slick, responsive, and unfurls naturally)

> **Top 10 Productive Flies in Colorado**
> - Stimulator
> - Yellow Humpy
> - Parachute Adams
> - Red Copper John
> - Copper John
> - Irresistible Adams/Wulff
> - Elk Hair Caddis
> - Beadhead Prince Nymph
> - Lime Trude
> - Beadhead Hare's Ear

27 South Fork

I fished Beaver Creek twenty years ago at the Campground and never again. Spotty, pressured, but great-looking water. I kept passing it by. What a mistake.

We didn't plan to camp and fish Beaver Creek. It was one of those situations where we got off later than we thought, stopped in Rainbow Lodge and Grocery, and realized that it was too late make a good camp up at Saguache. Why so much time wasted?

A recurring theme in this summer across Colorado was this (and we both repeated the mantra):

"I've got more than enough flies. Anything else I need, I spend a couple of hours tying before I go to bed."

Yeah. Right.

Going into early June, we both had enough flies to outfit the Mormon Tabernacle Choir. We don't lose many flies as a rule. But there's something about going to a new locale, to a fly shop, that inspires us to try unusual patterns or variations on a theme. *What if the one remaining #14 H&L Variant I have in my box is the only fly working, and I lose it!*

This is the kind of wild fishing you can find around South Fork.

For starters, if we plan to ask questions in the shop—how's the such-and-such creek fishing, tell me about the evening hatches on the big river, that sort of thing—we believe we need to patronize the shop. We're sure it's proper protocol for them to provide that information for nothing, but that's not the way we roll. You get something for something.

Rainbow Lodge and Grocery is the hub of tourism in South Fork, contrary to any chamber of commerce pronouncements. The place is a combination gas station, grocery store, lodge, fly shop, and overall mercantile store. Some of the flies in the thousands of bins might have been there since 1957, but if you need anything angling, camping, or recreating, Rainbow's got it. Plus they are a friendly bunch. "What's fishing best around here right now?" we asked the clerk. "Heard they're killin' 'em over on Beaver Creek." We each paid for our forty dollars of flies and headed a couple of miles south of town to Beaver Creek Campground.

We backed into a campsite and noted how empty the place looked (especially if the fishing was so hot). Campground host Bill sauntered over and motioned to us. "I've got this great spot right over there, overlooks the river, a mighty sweet spot." He motioned to us. "Follow me." So we did. Campground site number 10. Perfect.

The Aliner went up in twenty seconds, we spent ten minutes putting up our camp chairs, collecting firewood and protecting it, stringing up the rods. That pregnant suspicion we anglers get when we are putting on the vest, tugging on the wading boots, and peering at the river is maybe the real reason we go fishing. The anticipation that might become premonition. The *what if* factor. What if I catch the big one? What if I have one of those days that beats all others? What if, after all these years, these other rivers and creeks and lakes, what if here, on this water, there is realization?

Beaver Creek certainly looks like one of those rivers that could provide realization. Answers. We scrambled down the hill looking for answers. By the campground working your way upstream, one has to be in the river, slipping and sliding, boulder-hopping, keeping from stepping into deep holes. The water here is green and swirly, womblike pools ringed by gray comforting softly sculpted boulders, arm-wide runs that *chute* through openings, prone logs sleeping under tinted clear water. We caught a couple of browns and one

This nice brown trout came from tiny Cross Creek.

rainbow, but when the clouds descended, the shadows covered the canyon. And there were no trout. We were stealthy, casting our asses off, hitting all the lies with precision, switching out flies to match non-existent hatches, running beads under rocks and logs and banks. Four fish in two hours. We walked up a couple of miles easily and then hit the road and hiked back. No answers.

I had heard my buddy Denham talking about Cross Creek before, and when we drove upstream and parked at where it enters the reservoir we figured it must surely be a joke. Cross Creek is tiny. Not worth fishing. Small brook trout, the literature tells you. But because Denham had mentioned it, we at least needed to bushwhack a bit (because there is no trail) and see what it was like.

For 80 percent of the creek, you can't drop a fly on the water because of the brush covering the brown-tinted clear water. Every so often, you get a shot, especially at a pool. Our first pool was a revelation, hidden a 1/2-mile upcreek, no footprints, virgin three-foot wide pool dropping into another five-foot wide pool. This pool could definitely hold answers.

As an aside integral to the next fifteen minutes: Mac had gotten a new IPhone at the start of summer, and if you are an IPhone user you know how quickly you become dependent on these crazy things, how meaningful they become. Mac used his for the obvious, like communication and texting his kids and girlfriends, but he also used it for this one cool GPS tracking device that allowed you to monitor your trip or hike and take photos along the way.

Back to Cross Creek.

We decided Mac would cast first. This is a scientific method whereby one of us says "you go first" and the other one either goes first or says "nah, you go first," and the first Samaritan then casts. Easy. I offered, and he accepted. We did something we almost always do. We stayed out of sight, watched for trout, and discussed strategy. *If I can get my first cast dapped right by this rock... If you can bounce it off that bank and hit that one current... If you catch one in this tail,*

Just after he fell in with the iPhone, Mac displays his brown trout on Cross Creek.

get his head up so you don't spook the pool. And so on. That's fun to us. The chatter, the strategy. The realization of said strategy.

Mac had no room to backcast conventionally, but if he got on his knees, made a high 45-degree short backcast, he could swoop it in and land his #16 Royal Stimulator in the tail current and quickly mend line off the water. So he did. And out of the pool exploded a brown trout—orange fire—which smashed the fly. Head up, in net, then in hand while in water. I took pics with the Canon. A fine 12-inch wild brown.

"Here, get one of me with the iPhone so I can put it on the GPS tracker."

"You sure? You're out in the water. Be careful."

And he nodded at me like I was an idiot and then he slipped. Fell, feet in the air, right on his keister, in the creek. Like the Lady of the Lake offering up the sword to Arthur, the iPhone appeared in hand, held high above the water, Mac on his back in the water. He had saved his device.

I snapped a pic (too late because I was rolling on the ground laughing). He was drenched.

He offered me the next cast, but I was wiping tears from my eyes. Dammit. The next trout was the leviathan of the pool. Cross Creek Creature.

Answers.

Mac tried to pull its head up, but this trout was too large, too powerful for his 3 wt. to muscle it around. Seventeen inches is not a small fish, but when the fish is half the size of the pool and about as long as the creek is wide throughout, well, that's a *huge* fish. Size *is* relative.

Yeah, we took photos with both the Canon and the iPhone, but this time the Apple product stayed on the dry shore.

We struggled through vines and bramble and brush for another mile, catching fat wild trout wherever we cast, but after a while the reward didn't outweigh the hiking.

We found a gem. We knew that even if we wrote about it, few would go to the trouble to whack their way through this dense habitat. We found answers.

The rest of the story:

Williams fights a fish on Upper Beaver Creek.

The next day we fished the Beaver Creek headwaters. Like so many days that summer, gray wet clouds covered the horizon, a chill in the air. Easy access, right along the road, big wide valley ringed by green thick forests. Upper Beaver Creek winds through meadows and rushes through short canyons. Our fave is this one big long meadow below this one huge beaver pond/lake. We caught lots of trout, size 4 inches to 12 inches, brookies and cutts and rainbows, all colorful and wild and spunky. Mostly on dries, but sometimes when the rain/sleet thickened we'd have to drag beadheads through deeper pools.

Here's the funniest thing about those few days on the upper Beaver: We were way back in the meadow, smoking cigars and watching it sleet, when Mac had this one fly get taken by a radical brook trout, greener than an Irishman, spots so big we could see them from the banks. The angry brook trout dashed under a bank and wrapped the line around a submerged bush. Mac, for whatever reason, decided he couldn't just break off and tie another fly on, so he disrobes to his shorts and goes into this, the deepest pool in the whole 3 mile stretch and sticks his arm and head under the frigid water. He came up for breath and twice more went under, and on that last time he raised the brook trout out of the water. Mac's lips were blue.

While South Fork is growing up, progress is slow. This sleepy spread-out valley town is still reminiscent of Colorado twenty-five years ago. Rustic cabin resorts, wide open spaces devoid of condos, less-than-state-of-the-art grocery markets. South Fork sits at the confluence of its namesake river, South Fork of the Rio Grande, and its parent river, the mighty Rio Grande, built out of logging needs, located in the middle of thick green forests of spruce and fir.

The choices for digs and eats are lean. They tend to the do-it-yourselfer, the RV crowd. This is a rent-a-cabin, cook your own vittles kind of home base, and if that's what you're looking for, South Fork is as good as any in the state. Anglers have choices of over a dozen lakes within a fifteen to twenty minute drive from South Fork. You've got great camping options and myriad fishing choices—lake or river, big or small, lots of stockers or plenty of wild streams.

Favorite Places to Eat

The Hungry Logger (719-873-5504) has been around for a long time (Mark first ate there in 1989), but this roadside restaurant tends to lean to the pricey side. Their burgers are pretty good. **Chalet Swiss** (719-873-1100) is a great option, but we're not fans of the **Rockaway Café** (719-873-5581), though friends of ours love it.

South Fork is an outdoor wonderland.

Favorite Places to Stay

Palisade Campground on the Rio Grande right alongside CO 149 west of South Fork as you're going to Creede. Problem is that there are only 12 sites. **Beaver Creek Campground. Cross Creek Campground** (kind of exposed and very close to the road). **Beaver Creek Reservoir Campground. Upper Beaver Creek Campground. Park Creek Campground.** All managed by American Land &

Leisure, contact (800) 280-2267. Near Wagon Wheel Gap is **Cottonwood Cove Guest Ranch,** which has the tiniest little cabins ever, but if you need a place to stay on the river and don't need to break the bank, this is a decent choice. **Foothills Lodge and Cabins** are a nice choice for digs (719-873-5969).

Fly Shops, Guides, and Tackle Stores
Rainbow Grocery has a throwback tackle store (with some fly gear); **South Fork Anglers** (877-656-3474); **Wolf Creek Anglers** (719-873-1414).

Fishing Places Solid Choices near Home Base
Rio Grande: The act of fishing this classic, quintessential western trout stream is a tradition passed from father to son, family to friends. You meet folks on the river who've been coming to the Rio Grande for decades. Talk to families who have come to the Rio Grande for generations, and they'll talk about rustic cabins, fish frys, campfires, weenie roasts, burnt marshmallows on the end of coat hangers, meeting families from all over the country, crisp clear cold summer mornings, and the thrill of catching their first trout.

Above: The South Fork of the Rio Grande
Right: The method to float the Rio Grande

April to June on the Rio Grande is tough for flyfishing; spotty at best, too danged high at worst. Spinfishing is the ideal way to match the spring, high-water brawn. The fish are active, feeding after the long cold winter. And the Rio Grande is one of the first major rivers in the state to become fishable after runoff, and by early to mid-June the banks are clearing. One of the best spots is that stretch from Rio Grande Reservoir downstream to South Fork, an area loaded with an amazing amount of wild trout and unparalleled scenery.

Flyfishing is often an art, but we've seen it done badly enough that it's less art and more finger-painting. If you've ever watched someone spinfish who knows what they're doing, it too, can be an art. At the risk of hearing about this forever, Randy is one of those guys. We've flyfished beside him on this river while he flipped lures, and the guy is amazing.

Denham's grandfather fished the Rio Grande like so many of our grandfathers—with worms and salmon eggs, camped out for hours at a huge pool. Denham has tried all kinds of lures on the Rio Grande for over 45 years (I love writing that number about him), but nowadays has narrowed down his selection to Panther Martin choice #1 and Panther Martin choice #2. First choice is a PM #9 with black body, yellow dots, and gold or silver spoon. Second choice is a PM #9 with red body, red dots, and silver spoon. Killer consistency, says Denham.

The Rio Grande was once a typical put-meat-on-the-table kind of river, but progressively stricter regulations have been put in place to protect the river's trout. You won't likely catch a Frying Pan–size trophy trout, for those whoppers are far and few between. But you can catch lots of athletic, plump trout in the 10- to 16-inch range, trout that fight hard and run long. The mighty Rio Grande flows through the prettiest scenery in Colorado, and the section from South Fork up to the Rio Grande Reservoir is the most scenic of the river. The water is as clear as air, the air is clean, the mountains majestic, and the trout plentiful.

So you have a freestone stream in wilderness setting with numerous tributaries. This is beautiful and rugged country, where the nation's second longest river begins its southward trek, the river swelling with tributary after tributary, surrounded by interconnecting trails and alpine lakes. Deep runs, big pools, riffles, all kinds of water flowing through narrow canyons and broad valleys.

You're in some of the most primeval scenery left in the lower 48. One of the great things about this section of the Rio Grande is that despite its remoteness, despite its lack of angling pressure, the river is easily accessed by road and trail. Private water is marked and visible, and you'll be pleased by the dozens of miles of public water and roadside access from CO 149. Some of the more obvious public areas include Highway Springs Campground, Coller State Wildlife Area, Marshall Park, Palisades, and Fisherman's Access. The 23 miles of designated Gold Medal Water restricts anglers to flies and lures only, but read the regulations and signs because it seems like each year new restrictions are in place, especially regarding possession, slot limits, and catch and release.

Denham has seen many changes in and around the Rio Grande since he first visited the river in 1962. As much as this area has grown in population over the decades, settling in Creede, South Fork, Del Norte and Monte Vista, he maintains that "it's still easy to fish all day on the river without seeing another angler." He's right, too. You see the occasional drift boat. You drive along the river and only every now and again do you even see an angler in the water. Some days, you can drive for miles and never see anyone holding a rod. What other changes?

"It's been years since I've seen any cutthroats or cutbows caught in the Rio Grande," Denham confides, "but at one time, you'd catch them regularly. And after whirling disease hit the river in the 1980s and early '90s, the brown trout population has thrived even as the rainbow trout population declined."

His wife Vivian is now an avid angler, and she also loves the Rio Grande. Now, catching a true 20-inch trout is rarer than any avid angler would like to admit. It's all too easy to grant an extra inch or two to make a 16- or 17- or 18-inch trout grow to that mythical number. Denham, in a moment of honesty, confesses that in all the years on the Rio Grande, the largest trout he has caught is a true, measured, 21-incher. Vivien's largest? A hard-for-Denham-to-admit 22-inch brown trout. Nice legacy, buddy. See what honesty in fishing will do for you?

South Fork of the Rio Grande: We think the quality of the river has been declining for some time. While you would never catch many lunkers, you could always have a few takes in the obvious lies, but the scenery is so spectacular, the drop pools and deep-green runs so inviting, this was always one of our favorite rivers to fish. We fished the river three times this summer and were gravely disappointed. The water was lukewarm, shallow, and we saw few trout. We want to blame all the woes on Fun Valley upstream, but not all the problems are because of that absurd campground resort. The river gets pounded by the resort anglers and because it parallels US 160. Maybe we just hit it wrong three times this summer and it still fishes well except on those days.

Even though the river sees lots of fishermen (and many parts of the river are private but will allow anglers with permission), the river has 20 miles of easy access, and up until this last summer I can always seem to locate a nice hole or a set of productive riffles somewhere along the way.

Williams fishes Beaver Creek by the campground.

Beaver Creek Reservoir: Close to town (20 minutes tops) in the middle of the forest, 114 acres with all kinds of access, along the road, several species of trout (including kokanee salmon). Camping, steep banks, narrow and long, boat ramp. Brown trout can reach high teens or longer.

Big Meadow Reservoir: Family central. Great access for everyone, nice hiking trails, plenty of angling opportunities. Rainbow, brook, brown trout and kokanee salmon. Spans 110-plus acres when full, at 9,200 feet elevation. South of South Fork 18 miles. The small creek above and below it can surprise with some chunky trout. Good for bait and spin fishing, kayaking, canoeing. Great spot to make as a home base and camp.

Park Creek: One of Amy's favorite creeks in the area, south of South Fork about 15 minutes. Park Creek is where our fishing buddy Randy Denham fished with us twenty years ago and had on his hip a net better suited for Mackinaw than 10-inch trout. Let's just say he was an optimistic angler. Lots of campers and traffic, but if you fish right off the road before and just after the bridge, you'll have it to yourself. Nothing big regularly, but enough trout and the occasional fat one that this is definitely worth a day trip. Good for beginners, with lots of open water, easy casting from the road, and tons of pocket water. The deceptively wide canyon sections are the places to focus, especially the few dark deep pools.

Williams' nephew Will Brock fishes Park Creek.

Wolf Creek: Small creek worth more for the elven-like medieval-forest scenery than the great angling. Step-across creek with brookies and cutts. South of South Fork just on this side of the pass.

Million Reservoir (a.k.a. Millions Lake) is an up and down small lake near Beaver Creek Reservoir.

Shaw Lake: Near Lake Fork South Rio Grande, near Big Meadows Reservoir, a utilitarian lake with adequate fishing for brook and cutthroat.

Alberta Park Reservoir: State Wildlife Area just off US 160 on FR 391. Pretty setting in meadow, decent angling for rainbows, cutts and brooks, just a couple of miles from Wolf Creek Pass summit.

Hunters Lake: An 8-acre high-country lake with good brook trout fishing. Caught many 12 to 15 inchers here. Take FR 430 and then a short hike. Randy Denham and his son Sam ran into a bear with two cubs on the way to Hunter Lake when Sam was a kid. Young Sam had no clue of the danger involved. "That was one nervous hour as Sam and I waited for the bears to leave the trail," Randy confided. You guys be careful out there, okay?

Tucker Ponds: We don't get the fascination with these average-looking ponds, but they're always crowded. Only 4 acres total, Tucker Ponds has nice access, is good for kids, and for those who want to sit on the bank and leave the bobber bobbing. Handicapped accessible, toilet, docks, and camping.

Pass Creek and Pond: Not much parking but not bad fishing for stocked rainbow trout on this 5-acre lake. On US 160, the feeder to the lake, Pass Creek, begins below Wolf Creek Pass, fishes well to its east, and is small, clear, and worth fishing if you like catching small fish on dry flies. Brookies and cutts.

For the Adventurer

Race Creek and Crystal Lakes: A feeder to Beaver Creek, upstream from Cross Creek about 4 miles. You need a 4WD on FR 359 or you'll have to come over from Poage Lake. Crystal Lakes are at the headwaters of Race. The upper and lower (11,300 ft. elevation) are both good for rainbow, brook, and cutthroat trout.

Poage Lake: My cousin Billy Max fished here for three decades in the '70s, '80s, and '90s and swears he caught cutthroat over 20 inches and one close to 30 inches. He didn't take pictures, and he ate everything he caught. I've talked to others who swear the cutts grow to gargantuan sizes in Poage. As it is, standard reports come in where the cutts range from 9 to 12 inches (and rainbows about the same). Poage sits at the headwaters of Beaver Creek.

Archuleta Creek and Lake: This is wild country. If you want to fish here, fill up the backpack or hop on a horse because it's 6 miles up from the campground. Located at 11,720 feet, this 4-acre lake is chockfull of selective brook, rainbow, and cutthroat trout. We have both caught dark-bodied cutts in the mid-teens but we don't ever catch lots of trout. Fish the small creek on your way up, good for small cutts.

Lake Fork of the South Fork Rio Grande: A local fave, tributary to the South Fork from the west, 10 miles south of town. Scenic day getaway for lots and lots of brookies. Ideal for beginners.

Crater Lake: High elevation lake (try 12,700 ft.) that provides 10 acres of fishing for big bows and cutts. Access is by 4-wheel drive or a difficult hike.

OTHERS FISHERIES WORTH INVESTIGATING: Alder Creek, Spruce Lakes, Upper Piedra River, Bellows Creek, Cross Creek, Upper Beaver Creek, Weminuche Creek

Blue Ribbon Fisheries near South Fork

Piedra River
San Juan River (both in and around Pagosa and south in Aztec, NM)
Lake Fork Gunnison

28 HOME BASE
Steamboat Springs

For those who've never been, the name "Steamboat Springs" may evoke Twain-like images of Huck Finn and Jim. It always has for me. I can see them now, the two of them relaxing in some bubbling hot mineral spring, naked, side-by-side, by and by.

Shattering such a priceless mental image might be likened to the breaking of a stained-glass window at the Vatican. However, consider the image broken. There has never been a steamboat in this town. Instead, legend says that three French trappers thought they heard a steamboat "chug-chug-chugging" along a river. What they discovered was a bubbling spring, which still exists on the far end of town.

Another discovery one might want to visit in Steamboat is Fish Creek Falls, a three-hundred-foot waterfall a few miles east of town. We drop $5 to park in one of two lots, but the hike and site are worth it. Just don't leave your Jeep door open like touristy buffoons. Williams and I did that. Felt dumb.

Steamboat is a bustling river town with great shopping, mountains all around, exquisite eateries, and extreme sports galore. Not quite Aspen, not quite Breck, but more of a relaxed and livable town, like Austin, but at a higher elevation.

Williams drags huge streamers through deep, gushing runs on the Elk River.

Since childhood, I'd seen my brother's older buddies wearing t-shirts with "Steamboat Springs" on them, and every time, all the time, there was a graphic of a smoke-puffing steamboat on them, and I just knew I wanted to be there.

Favorite Places to Eat

Azteca Taqueria at 116 Ninth St. serves these shredded pork soft tacos with a cilantro lime vinegrette that flat out rocks! **Big House Burgers and Bottlecap Bar** is located at 2093 Curve Plaza. It's a build-your-own-burger sorta gig and they serve all local beef. Excellent! At the **Boathouse Pub** at 609 Yampa St. the cuisine appeared worthy of a four-star rating. Although we didn't eat a thing (this is where we drank pale ales and spied the waters from the balcony above), we passed the kitchen and saw several plated dishes awaiting their hungry patrons. Extravagant presentation and bar-none one of the finest smelling digs we went into. **Steamboat Smokehouse**—a true Texas BBQ haunt in a Rocky Mountain setting, the Smokehouse uses hardwood hickory to cook everything low and slow. Located at 912 Lincoln Ave., it's easy to find and a "must-try" kinda dig.

OTHER PLACES TO EAT: Freshies is a fav among locals for deliciously famous, gigantic, enormous freshly baked cinnamon rolls. Yes, they are wicked-fresh, so they live up to their name! Freshies is located at 595 S. Lincoln Ave. **Geek's Garage Internet Café** is a badass place kick it, grab a hot cuppa joe, and jump online with the laptop. They offer bistro fare and apparently have some people addicted to the chipotle bacon mayonnaise they spread on their "sammiches," as Mark and I call them. **The Ghost Ranch Saloon** is located at 56 Seventh St., Steamboat's newest restaurant and live entertainment venue. It's the Old West—AMPLIFIED. Their happy hour is a can't-miss with half-price Angus burgers and drink specials. **Saketumi** is located at 1875 Ski Time Square and makes some kickass sushi rolls. Sometimes a cold, light roll is perfect when it's hot and you still intend on fishing the second half of the day.

Favorite Places to Stay

The Inn at Steamboat near the ski resort is a fair place to stay. 3070 Columbine Dr., 800-551-2409. **Moving Mountains Chalets** features impeccable log structure with turret-looking rooms on the corners overlooking the magnificent Steamboat valley. 155 Anglers Dr., 877-624-2538, 970-870-9359, http://movingmountains.com/. **Strawberry Park Natural Hot Springs** can set you up with one of the most unique stays you've every experienced!

Sleep in a renovated train caboose, or covered wagon, or a rustic lodge, and even more options! 44200 CR 36, 970-879-0342, http://www.strawberryhot springs.com/2005/. **Trappeurs Crossing Lodge** has a wow factor of eleven! On a scale of ten! Very modern facility but with warm lodge house charisma. 970-819-6930, http://trappeurs-crossing.com/.

OTHER PLACES TO STAY: The Bunkhouse Lodge, 3155 S. Lincoln Ave., 877-245-6343, http://www.thebunkhouselodge.com/. **The Lodge at Steamboat,** 2700 Village Dr., 970-879-6000, www.steamboatresorts.com.

CAMPSITES: Yampa River State Park has 50 campsites; 35 are RV electric sites, 10 tent sites, and 5 sites for group camping. The proximity to US 40 makes this a nice home base for fishing around Steamboat. http://parks.state. co.us/Parks/yampariver.

Fly Shops, Guides, and Tackle Stores

Bucking Rainbow (888-810-8747, 970-879-8747, http://www.buckingrain-bow. com/yampa.htm); **Straightline Sports** (800-354-5463, 970-879-7568,

http:// www.straightlinesports.com/); **Steamboat Flyfisher** (866-268-9295, 970-879-6552, http://www.steamboatfly-fisher.com/).

Fishing licenses and some tackle and gear for fisheries north of Steamboat are available from: **Clark Store** (970-879-3849), **Steamboat Lake Marina** (970-879-7019), and **Steamboat Lake Out- fitters** (800-342-1889, 970-879-4404) in Clark.

OTHER STUFF: One of the coolest things about Steamboat is that there are trails to hike, you can take a relaxing dip in the Strawberry Hot Springs, you can hop on the back of a horse and trot the trails, climb into a wagon, or tube through the town of Steamboat down the Yampa River.

Mac netted this brown trout on the Elk River with 6X tippet and a 3 wt. rod.

The Tread of Pioneer Museum will thrust you into the past, or you can take that hike to Fish Creek Falls. There are endless activities for thrill-seekers, such as rafting, rock climbing, and racing the alpine slide down Howellsen Hill—a ski jumping hill directly across the river from the Nordic Lodge.

The Yampa River by Steamboat Springs

Fishing Places Solid Choices near Home Base

Yampa River: The Yampa drainage is made up of a slough of rivers and streams, some of our favorite digs. In town, the Yampa is crowded. Expect nothing less in any river town. Steamboat anglers will have to learn to actually dodge hot babes (fat guys, too) in bikinis (not the fat guys) floating inner tubes, drifting over your perfectly good trout lies. Stocked and hold-over rainbows and browns take flies here, but the trout are leery and only take the perfectly presented flies.

Stagecoach Reservoir: South of town in the Pleasant Valley area, anglers wade a tail water below Stagecoach Reservoir, a 3/4-mile public section of the Yampa River where rainbows get fat and colorful. And farther downstream on the Yampa is the Sarvis Creek State Wildlife Area where another 2-mile section of public water flows. We never made it this far because we got hung up drinking pale ales and watching the hotties and trout that were floating in the river.

Just south of town near Haymaker Golf Course, we watched a few anglers fish the Chuck Lewis State Wildlife Area, yet another public 2-mile stretch of the Yampa. It didn't interest Williams, so we drove north of Steamboat, where he'd read that just over a mile of public fishing existed on the Elk River where it slithers through the Christina Wildlife Area. We got there, pulled over, read the signage in the turnouts for details about boundaries and regulations, got confused, and decided we'd pass on this boring-looking section as well to fish far wilder waters.

Elk Creek: Elk Creek is our Steamboat Springs home base *pièce de résistance*. Where the Elk crosses the road on 64 RD northwest of town, we bank right, head in a northeasterly manner into the Routt National Forest (on FR 400) where the Elk flows from its headwaters. Williams and I have finally found a premier Steamboat-style river and set up camp in the Seedhouse Campground, where the campground hosts were intrigued by the Aliner, which they called an Uh-liner.

The Elk at this point is flowing deep, cold, and fast. Even in late summer. We pull up to a stretch across from some cabins that shall remain unnamed. However, if you go, you will see them off to the left about halfway between 129 and the Seedhouse Campsites. And when you do, don't fish across from them or you'll get "told." Even though there's no signage. Go figure.

Well, we got told. "Move along. This is private!" the killjoy commanded. And with a few choice words, we finally did so. Thank goodness this happened. Good always prevails over evil. Learnt this from *Star Wars,* and Mark Twain.

We put in about a mile upstream, where the Elk is broad. The sorta scary water where carrying a $1,200 camera seems fatuous, but we think not twice about it. Rocks are huge. Round. Slippery. Wet. Perfect for breaking SLRs, egos, and femurs.

Williams is on the left bank, manipulating overhanging trees for balance. He's older. Tired. Cantankerous. And mostly only taking photographs by this time. Conversely, I'm risking life and limb in the middle of a torrent. Fishing a 3 wt. and 6X. I haven't seen a fish yet. But I know what I know.

My fly drifts beneath overhangs on the far bank. Yellow Humpy over shade water. Dark and unlikely. I think, *maybe on the seam.* I present the fly…mend… drift…*SMASH!*

A take. I set, strip, and stabilize my weight. Balance here is key. Williams barks that it's big, though I'm never convinced till I hear the sizzle of bearings on my CFO. The fish is angry and heading upstream, fighting against a raging current and the stress of my line. Only now do I realize how big. *A hefty brown,* I surmise, *since rainbows nearly always leap.*

I feel confident, despite fishing an ultra-light Dorber full-flex rod. Williams, immobile and stuck on the edge, gives it all to God as I see an attempt to genuflect. Or perhaps he's just trying not to fall in as I am. He worries something's going to snap, my tippet, my rod, my leg…anything. He yelps feeble advice— the river is too loud. But suddenly, a plan occurs to me. *I remember…*

Against Williams' logic, horsing this trout towards me, I watch as it passes my legs, dark and heavy like a waterlogged railroad tie. Scarlet spots stare back at me like the many eyes of a spider.

I seduce her, coaxing her in where I want her to go, dropping and luring her into a foamy plunge—a still pool where I'd stood to cast only moments prior. I know if I can get her here, out of the current, I have her.

Williams waits with the impatience of an avalanche. I stagger, fall briefly, and rise again, reclaiming a taut line. Mark challenges my manhood with slicing words from the cuff, like a sushi chef dicing up tofu at Benihana's.

With a plunging swipe, I dredge deep with the net, forearm bursting. She falls in, heavy and tired. I raise her, as some might an offering to the gods, and we pay our homage. Not to God. Not to Steamboat Springs. But to her. This single fish. For allowing us the pleasure of catching, fighting, and holding her.

North and South Forks of the Elk

North Fork of the Elk: Pours into the main stem near the Seedhouse Campground on FR 64, which soon turns into FR 400. It crosses under FR 400, and a glance upstream will allow for an idea as to what you'd be in for if you choose to hike up and fish. There are lots of trees shading the stream, and the water is manageable and productive, with the brook trout becoming smaller but more plentiful as you climb.

South Fork of the Elk is a task to get to—drive down FR 400 to FR 443, where you will turn right and travel downhill into a small valley where

Mac lands a small brook trout on the South Fork of the Elk River.

the Middle Fork crosses under a bridge. Forget fishing the Middle Fork. Too much pressure. Keep trucking down FR 443, winding around the mountain and down the bumpy hill until you curve back south to a large flat area where there are several areas to park and put in. Watch for eagles and falcons in the huge meadow slough area off to the right. The South Fork water is icy cold, even in Late July, and there aren't tons of trout, but there are some, and it's worth fishing if you're in the area. Fish small dry flies like BWO, PMD, Irresistible Wulffs, and Caddis.

Pearl Lake State Park: Cutthroat trout and grayling swim about in this 167-acre reservoir. The best fishing of the year tends to be mid- to late May during ice-off and again in the fall. No bait is allowed, so bring your lures or fly rod, and a two-fish bag limit is enforced, with a minimum size of 18 inches. The lake is fishable during the winter months through the ice, but is restricted to flies and lures only. Check with the Colorado Division of Wildlife for more information.

For the Adventurer

Steamboat Lake State Park (Gold Medal Water): This mystical place is Gold Medal Water for a reason. Fishers can easily find themselves knee-deep in rainbow, brooks, browns, and cutthroat trout, and your chance of them being big is truly plausible. One may mistake the pinnacle of Hahn's Peak that looms over the northeastern shore for Olympus. Watercrafts come in handy for accessing the deepest sections of this 1,050-acre body of water. But if you're sorta timid about the waters, like Williams, fishing along the many miles of easily accessible shoreline is a popular and effective option. Leave Steamboat Springs traveling west on US 40 for two miles to CR 129. The lake will appear 26 miles to the north, long after Hahn's Peak steals the scene.

Top Ten Favorite Adult Beverages
- 5 Barrel Pale Ale (Boathouse in Salida)
- Early Times (everywhere)
- Three Rivers Malbec wine (Williams Reservoir)
- Dale's Pale Ale (Flat Tops)
- Third Eye P.A. (home in Durango)
- French Rabbit Pinot Noir in eco-friendly ePod container
- "Two Buck Chuck" from Trader Joe's (Trapper's Lake)
- Miller Lite on tap (bar in downtown Durango)
- Sam Adams (Hickory House BBQ in Aspen)
- Lindeman's Merlot (Taylor Reservoir)

29 Telluride

Three years ago, we were on our way back from a month-long fishing trip in Arizona and Utah, cutting through Moab and ending up in Telluride on the Fourth of July. We were tired, skinny, and ready for good cold beers and tacos at our favorite haunt in Telluride. We crossed the border and followed the San Miguel in from Norwood, Placerville, Vanadium, and into Telluride. We were in need of some strong coffee, so we dodged some detour signs, went around a sawhorse and turned onto Colorado Avenue, right into the middle of a traffic jam.

We had forgotten that it was July 4th. Neither of us knew because we hadn't seen a calendar in weeks, nor did we care to. We were in a parade with no way out. Hundreds of people lined both sides of the street. We were stuck behind a truck pulling a trailer, and as we passed by throngs on either side of the street waving flags and wearing red, white, and blue, we realized that we were now in the holiday parade, two anglers in a dirty Jeep, representing the fly-fishing brotherhood. The Jeep was dirty, and we had our fishing hats and shirts on with our rack loaded with fishing gear and ice coolers and wader bags and rod tubes. We looked like we were advertising for a fly shop or guide service.

We couldn't find a way to turn out of the parade and everyone waved and seemed to love our "float." We did all we could do. We drove slowly and waved.

We might enter again this year.

When Mac and I talk about Telluride, we always mention that first trip. In the summer heat, sitting toward the sidewalk, watching hot chicks wearing expensive next-to-nothing as they sashayed by the outdoor taco stand near the outdoor coffee cart where we were lazily eating and drinking. Entering the wine-liquor store and being amazed at how many quality wines and top-notch liquors the store held, more than what we usually see in a mountain town.

Parade summer. Mac's first time on the San Miguel. He didn't fare well, and he almost always fares well because he is one helluva fisherman. But I have this image of him on a big silver rock, fishing upstream to a big welled-up stormy pool. Nothing rising. No hatches. No rolling backs. But he is Brad Pitt shadowcasting. Arc of a diver. He had the predator lean goin on. He wasn't there. He was in that weird somewhere else place we all go when we are so focused, so into it, so there, that we aren't there anymore. That's where he was. *Prajñ. Pañ.* And then, when no monster rose from the depths, he wasn't there. He was here.

Mac works a pool on the San Miguel River.

You see Tibetan prayer flags strung across porches of many of the Telluride houses in town (not the multi-million-dollar luxury homes of Hollywood expatriates—not that I've ever been to their vacation homes, but I'm taking an educated guess). You see Tibetan flags (usually weathered) draped and drooping in the windows of certain retail shops in the mountain town. I am not going to pretend like I understand the meaning beyond some sort of wikipedia-meets-religion101 understanding. I do know there are five colors and they represent the elements—earth, wind, air, and fire. These flags promote wisdom, strength, peace, and so on. One purveyor of the flags told me, when I asked why leave them up when they are tattered and faded, "because they become one with the world." And this aging beatnik added that "I just add new ones alongside the old ones." A cycle. I get it, but I don't pretend to understand it. My point is that Telluride, even for all its money and celebrity, has a cool vibe, a mysterious serenity. American Beauty. In Telluride, you have all the ingredients for a transcendental experience. A box canyon, one-hundred-foot waterfall, isolation, one road in one road out. You know, without all the millionaires and hippies, this could be a European monastery.

I always chuckle when I read writers going on about the religious or spiritual nature of flyfishing. On the one hand, I think it's funny and silly to attach so much reverence to something so recreational and regular. On the other hand, I secretly agree. When I'm out there, not here but there, I feel something. I think about things I don't regularly think about. I think about things that become daydreams and, in truth, I meditate. I don't purposely meditate. Look, either you get that inner maudlin, sentimental, fuzzy feeling when you watch *A River Runs Through It* or you don't. You either feel a spiritual connection and slip into a meditative state when you're fishing in the wilderness or you don't. Mac and I don't always find that we're not "there." It only happens a few times a summer, those times when we're so into the moment, so into the concentration of fishing, that we lose ourselves in the moment. We don't know why it happens. Maybe it's euphoria from doing something very well. You can love fishing and not have those moments where you're not there. Maybe that place is simply grace. I don't know.

No need to go to Telluride and fish if that's all you plan to do—only fish. You need to play in town, eat great meals, enjoy the cool vibe, live it up. Otherwise, get a room in Ridgway or drive on over to Gunnison for lodging. Don't get us wrong, there is a fishing community in Telluride. You'll see some Telluriders and plenty of tourists who are Orvis-outfitted to their eyes, and then there's the hardcore fly anglers who look like they slept in their clothes, left their cap to a mountain lion to play with. Both can fish. Plenty of water for all. But there is a distinctness to the newbies

The San Miguel River

who just walked out one of the fly shops, dropping thousands in the process. We're not going to sit here and tell you to plan a fishing trip to Telluride. What we are going to suggest is that if you are in Telluride for a vacation, you take a day or two and fish while you do all the other stuff you were going to do.

San Miguel River is the only game in town if you're coming to Telluride looking for a close by fishing destination. The fishing community is willing to drive a couple of hours to other blue ribbon waters—Black Canyon Gunnison,

Dolores, Uncompahgre. So many anglers have it stuck in their minds that the only good fishing around Telluride is the San Miguel River. Wrong. In a way.

Amy and I spent a lot of time in Telluride the last decade, but especially this last year because we were writing a book about the town, *Top 30 Things to Do in Telluride*. We found a lot more than 30, but that's the series' name. Since we were there during each month, we got to fish each month. The diversity and quality of the fisheries is overwhelming. Your choices range from small creeks that meander through wildflower-covered meadows, high-country lakes, big reservoirs, Gold Medal rivers, and tail waters that require technical ability in order to tangle with large trout. You'll find all kinds of angling types for these rivers—spin, bait, and fly—but flyfishing is the most common way for those who fish rivers. In fact, many rivers have sections with regulations that allow for fly only, or fly/lures only. We highly recommend hiring a guide to get to know these waters and how to fish them.

Telluride doesn't have the big reputation for trout fishing.

Telluride has the elite rep, the luxury mountain village thing, but you'd be surprised how inviting and friendly the town can be. Great places to grab breakfast, excellent coffee shops, a laid back vibe all the way. Ideal to take the wife and get brownie points or perfect if you like to 4-wheel-drive to your fishing locales. Probably the prettiest scenery in Colorado.

This is a community with many personalities. On the one hand, there's no denying that there is a reason for outsiders to sense a closed mentality, an us-against-the-world frontier attitude driven as much by its pioneering spirit and isolation as it is the real money of this area. On the other hand, there's a genuine

The San Miguel River winds through this mountain valley.

fun, festive, thumb-your-nose-at-authority, hippie vibe. Telluride has funky charm even though it's a world-class ski resort. Rich folks everywhere. Regular folks too, gawking at celebrities and wishing they were rich folks. And the hippie-types who look at the rich and regular and then go about their business. You find clapboard fronts, Queen Anne-Victorian architecture, and luxury vehicles.

You get it all in this dualistic town: world-renowned festivals such as Bluegrass, Jazz, Wine, Film, and Blues & Brews, blue-ribbon flyfishing, horseback, jeep, and river rafting trips in thousands of acres of national forest and wilderness areas (much of which is accessible from either downtown Telluride or Mountain Village), hiking, biking, and rock climbing, hundreds of miles of old jeep and mining roads to explore, ghost towns, and the tallest free-falling waterfall in the state just minutes from downtown Telluride.

Two more aspects of fishing around Telluride: 1) What about winter? Swish and fish. Ski in the morning, catch trout in the afternoon. The Dolores, San Miguel and Uncompahgre Rivers are viable, healthy trout fisheries even when the snow is coming down. 2) Lots of quality private angling opportunities in the area.

Above: Telluride has a unique atmosphere.
Left: Shops on Colorado Avenue in Telluride

Favorite Places to Eat

Great town for quality dining, everything from affordable comfort to high-end eating where you don't know which fancy fork to use first. **Maggie's Bakery and Café** (970-728-3334) for a quick hearty breakfast. **Baked in Telluride** for lunch or bakery goods. (Late note: we just read that it burned to the ground. Talk is, they will rebuild.) Go upscale for dinner at either **Cosmopolitan** (970-728-1292) or **Allreds** (970-728-7474)—Amy's favorite spot—or go local at **Brown Dog**

Pizza (970-728-8046) or **Fat Alley BBQ** (970-728-3985). Mac and I always eat tacos at **Cocina de la Luz** (970-728-9355). The list is long and you can't go wrong.

Favorite Places to Stay

Amy and I have stayed in lodges, hotels, bed and breakfasts, and, our favorite, camping in **Town Park.** You get the San Miguel right in your front yard, ballfields and showers and trees and vistas, with town across the street. Other options include **New Sheridan,** the pricey but awesome **Inn at Lost Creek** (970-728-4351), and **Mountain Lodge at Telluride** (866-368-6867). We haven't had bad lodging in Telluride, but it will cost you more than you're used to. Unless you're rich, of course.

Telluride in spring

Fly Shops, Guides, and Tackle Stores

Black Canyon Anglers (970-835-5050); **BootDoctors/Further Adventures** (800-592-6883, 970-728-8954); **RIGS Fly Shop & Guide Service** (888-626-4460, 970-626-4460); **Telluride Flyfishing & Rafting** (800-294-9269, 970-728-4440); **Telluride Angler/Telluride Outside** (800-831-6230, 970-728-3895, www.tellurideoutside.com); **Telluride Sports Adventure Desk** (800-828-7547, 970-728-4477); **San Miguel Anglers** (800-828-7547, 970-728-4477).

Fishing Places Solid Choices near Home Base

Town Park: This small pond located in town is ideal for families to take kids fishing, age twelve and under. Good for fly or spin fishing. Stocked with trout.

San Miguel River Trail: This in-town fishing locale is an ideal fishing spot if the wife is fishing or to take the kids or to teach someone how to fish (esp. flyfishing). The water is sometimes skinny, always clear, so here are a few keys to success in fishing this 2.75 mile stretch: 1) Don't walk right up to the edge because the trout will scurry to hiding places; stalk, sneak up, be stealthy; 2) look for deeper waters, especially if you are spin fishing; 3) fish to edges like seams, foam, where the fast water meets the slower water, around rocks and limbs.

San Miguel River: One of the classic western freestone streams in the Southwest, the San Miguel is a blast to fish. The undammed San Miguel is full of personality and verve. At first glance, the San Miguel looks like a river made up of all riffles and fastwater, but if you're patient and observant, you'll find the slow runs and deeper pools. If you do, you'll have a better chance to tie into the bigger rainbows and browns. Even still, the river is chockfull of trout.

The San Miguel River gets great press, and rightfully so, because if you like riffles, dramatic scenery, and feisty 12-inch trout that like dry flies, this is your stream. But the diversity and quality of the fisheries is overwhelming. Dry fly anglers love this river. Fishers of all ages and skill levels will love that the San Miguel is fishable all year long. Anywhere there is public land, anglers can access the river. Some of the better-known accesses include: South Fork/Ilium Valley Road, River Road, Mary E, Tram Site, Placerville Park, Specie Creek Road, Saltado Creek Road, Silverpick Road, Beaver Creek.

This lovely mountain stream flows past Jurassic and Triassic red sandstone canyon walls. Over 50 miles of the San Miguel drainage holds excellent trout fishing. Access is not a problem to the main river or its forks, since roads generally parallel the drainage. Pre-runoff fishing is great in spring, and good fishing lasts into November. To reach the river follow CO 145 west out of Telluride; the river follows the highway.

Lake Fork San Miguel: This smallish river originates under one of the most recognized natural landmarks of southwestern Colorado, Lizard Head Peak. Lake Fork parallels CO 145 after it leaves Trout Lake. FR 626 off of CO 145 will take you the upper reaches of this brushy stream.

South Fork of San Miguel: Make sure you don't overlook this sleeper stream. Uncrowded, easy access, and the trout aren't selective. South Fork has good fly water, rife with runs and pools and riffles. Ilium Valley Road follows the river on its east side. There is some nice water at the Nature Conservancy Preserve.

Uncompahgre River: This high-desert tail water is shallow and rehab-improved, slightly theme-park-y but loaded with heavy-bodied, strong trout. Located 1 hour from Telluride, just below Ridgway Reservoir, eight miles north of Ridgway, the Uncompaghre River is the best winter fishery in this part of the state, ideal for those times when other rivers are frozen or are in runoff. The prime water flows through Pa-Co-Chu-Puk State Park, a little over a mile of green water buttressed by instream rehabilitation and weirs, forming excellent trout habitat. You reach the Uncompahgre River from US 550.

For the Adventurer

Upper Dolores River: Amy's favorite drainage to fish in southwestern Colorado, and with good reason, too. The upper main stem of the Dolores holds mostly rainbow with some brown trout and has good access, with CO 145 running right beside it. Anglers will find good fishing above Rico, from the headwaters at Lizard Head Pass down to the town of Dolores. Between Lizard Head and the town of the Dolores, the watershed is fed by a dozen feeder streams descending from alpine basins. The Main Fork and West Fork offer more than 75 miles of trout water. Willing fish and magnificent scenery make the Dolores a Colorado trout-fishing classic. The Upper Dolores is a checkerboard of public and private water.

West Fork of the Dolores River: This interesting stream is located about 15 miles northeast of the town of Dolores. FR 535 parallels the West Fork (more or less) for 30 miles and offers excellent access. This gem is a narrow feeder stream with rainbow, brown, brook, and the occasional cutthroat trout. Great dry fly stream. There are four campgrounds along West Fork of the Dolores River. All four campgrounds are on the river and are seldom full. Travel south on Highway 145 about 15 miles and take FR 535 west. The road will take you past Dunton as the road twists and turns alongside the river southwesterly until it meets back up with Highway 145 several miles south of where you turned off.

Alta Lakes: You get a ghost town and high-country scenery and good fishing in three lakes. Don't think about going here unless you have a high-clearance vehicle (and we recommend a 4WD). You'll end up driving over 10 miles round trip from your turn off, and it's 6 miles south of Telluride, so you'll be in your vehicle a good amount of time. No need to go any earlier than late June, when the lakes usually ice out. Concentrate your angling on the lower lake. These lakes are above timberline and form the headwaters of Turkey Creek. Travel 6 miles south of Telluride on CO 145 to Alta Lakes Road, staying on the main road for 4 miles. Turn right at the old town and follow the signs to Alta Lakes.

Woods Lake: This high-country lake is one of the most gorgeous settings in the area. Woods Lake sits at 9,400 feet, at the base of thirteeners and fourteeners. This 29-acre alpine lake surrounded by forest is stocked with rainbow trout, but also holds cutthroat and brook trout. Travel west on CO 145 for 10 miles just after Sawpit. Take a left (south) on Fall Creek Road (FR 618) and drive for 9 miles to Woods Lake. Fall Creek is the feeder to the lake. Anglers may use artificial lures and flies only.

Bear Creek: Feeder creek to the San Miguel River with pretty good angling in its short water, even if it's challenging fishing. Bear Creek runs about eight feet wide, has lots of streamside vegetation, and is quick on the draw. The creek holds brook and stocked rainbow. Ideal for fly-angling small-stream aficionados. It's a 4-mile round trip from the trailhead to the falls. Start the trail from the end of South Pine Street and follow Bear Creek up the canyon.

Galloping Goose Trail: Really, you're not gonna fish this part of the South Fork unless you're hiking, backpacking, or biking. So this is a corollary angling trip to your main trip. Small stream, small wild trout, wild country along the historic route of the old Galloping Goose Trail.

Navajo Lake: This high alpine lake sits under El Diente Peak (14,159 ft.) and Mt. Wilson (14,246 ft.) and is one of the more scenic lakes in the region. The lake in the Lizard Head Wilderness is set in a beautiful alpine basin of verdant meadows and white-trunked aspens. The lake sees heavy use from campers, hikers, and anglers. There are other trout fishing opportunities in the Lizard Head Wilderness— small streams, small lakes.

Priest Lakes: The biggest lake is 10 acres and sits at 9,568 feet elevation. Priest Lakes are situated above Trout Lake, off of the Lake Fork San Miguel River, and are surrounded by aspen, fir, and spruce and grassy meadows. Accessed from CO 145.

Trout Lake: Located at the base of some of the more dramatic mountains you'll see, Trout Lake provides great photo

The area southwest of Telluride has numerous free-stone streams like this.

opportunities with its high-country scenery and solid angling. The lake is typically at 150 acres and is located south of Telluride 12 miles on CO 145. Trout Lake holds brown, rainbow, brook, and cutthroat trout. Despite the pressure the lake sees during the summer, it tends to hold up well, and the fishing can be frenetic at times when the fish are biting. Super for family outings.

Deep Creek: For serious hikers or for fishers who ride bikes. Tricky, challenging stream with lots of forks. One way to access Deep Creek is to use the Jud Wiebe Trail to reach Deep Creek Trail.

Silver Lake: Long, steep, moderately difficult hike that covers nearly 6 miles and takes about four hours round trip means you won't find many other anglers at this scenic high-country 6-acre lake. Start your hike from Bridal Veil Falls.

Lizard Head Creek: This productive little stream runs into Snow Spur Creek in the Dolores drainage. Travel south on CO 145 from Trout Lake. The creek snakes across green meadows.

Snow Spur Creek: Decent angling for cutts, browns, and brooks in this small high-country stream that feeds the upper Dolores near Lizard Head Pass. Flows in view of CO 145 south from Trout Lake. See the Dolores chapter for more info.

Blue Ribbon Waters not far from Telluride

Dolores River (tailwater): The high-desert countryside below McPhee Reservoir, 2 hours away from Telluride, is rugged and looks nothing like a setting for a trout stream. This river was originally named Río de Nuestra Señora de los Dolores (River of Our Lady of Sorrows). The Dolores River, with its nice riffles, horseshoe bend pools, undercut banks, and deep runs, is a pleasure/nightmare to fish. The Dolores can often force anglers into technical fishing, similar to bigger tail waters. In many places, the Dolores acts like a big, clear spring creek, with transparent pools showing off green beds of algae and moss teeming with insect life. Great choice in winter.

Black Canyon Gunnison River: The 14 miles of the rugged Gunnison Gorge is a trophy trout destination. Gold Medal water ideal for fly and spinner alike. While you can hike in on a few trails, if you've never fished it before, hire a guide and either float it or walk in with someone who knows what they're doing. The Gorge is no place to make a mistake. Since this is one of the top angling trips in the country, do it correctly and increase your chances of landing one of those huge browns and rainbows.

McPhee Reservoir and Recreation Area: McPhee Reservoir (6,924 ft. elevation) is similar to Ridgway Reservoir in that it is fully loaded with family activity opportunities and services. Over 140 campsites, most with hookups, restrooms, showers, boat ramp, dump station, marina. Fish for trout, bass, walleye and kokanee salmon. Spanning 4,470 acres at pool, this reservoir is located in a river canyon and is the second largest body of water in Colorado. Located 65 miles southwest of Telluride, near Dolores and Cortez.

Miramonte Reservoir: This big lake (405 acres) sits at 7,700 feet elevation 20 miles south of Norwood on the Dolores-Norwood Road. Miramonte holds stocked rainbow trout. Lots of boat traffic, water-skiers. There is camping at the lake as well as a boat ramp.

Ground Hog Reservoir: A sleeper lake, and a big lake (668 acres) stocked with trout. The lake has a rough road access its last 5 miles and at one time enjoyed a big-time reputation for producing big fish. Ground Hog Reservoir (8,718 feet) lies 32 miles north of Dolores on FR 526 to a rough gravel road, FR 533 (Dolores-Norwood Road).

Gurley Reservoir: Located near Norwood. The lake holds 363 acres with an average depth of fifteen feet. Stocked with brook and rainbow trout, and they get pretty big. Travel southeast from Norwood on CO 145 to Norwood-Dolores Road (44Z Road), turn right (south), and travel about 7 miles.

Top 10 Favorite Campground/Campsites
- La Jara Reservoir "Grassy Bowl"
- Ridgway State Park
- East Fork Hermosa Creek
- Haviland Lake Campground
- Taylor Reservoir
- Beaver Creek Campground (South Fork)
- Ma and Pa Kettle's Del Norte Campground
- Trujillo Meadows Campground
- Weller Campground near Independence Pass
- Spring Creek Campground

We've always passed through Vail or camped near Vail when I fished the local waters—the Colorado, the Eagle, Gore Creek. We've caught lunch in Vail, went for drinks in Vail. But we've never done Vail the right way. This summer, we stayed in Vail proper and we'll confess, Vail ain't as snooty as we thought.

The first time we camped in Vail this summer, I took Amy instead of Mac (who was off taking quick care of some business). We had a difficult time getting off the freeway to get to the campground. We found it after several misfires but it was frustrating because the exit to take was not the exit the GPS told us we needed. This part of the interstate is lacking in exits, so if you miss one you'll drive a ways. We had to drive to upper Eagle, turn around at Minturn, go back to Exit 180, turn right at this funky road then follow two miles to kind of a dead end.

It's rare that we camped in any place nearly this wild and still got any 3G for i-Phone or wireless for the laptop—we did here. That is good (I could research, tend to emails, update the website) and bad (nature should be natural.)

Amy high-sticks a dropper fly rig through a Gore Creek pool.

The campground was ideal. We could fish Gore Creek a hundred-yard walk from our site. In less than five minutes, we could be parking in Vail proper.

In Vail, on the river, at the cafés, we are in love and we talk about those things we don't always talk about, like my dream of moving to Spain for a year or two, or to the Caribbean for a few years. How I can't wait to finish my next novel. How she wants to write her own book. This won't be DiCaprio and Winslet. No dashed American dreams for us. We are living our dreams.

Life is not just adequate. Life is great, life is good. This is as good as it gets. And it's very, very good. But at age 50, is this the summit? Traveling all summer, fishing and soaking up the mountains and streams, and writing a destination fishing guide? Loving my teaching job, but wishing I was in my study in some other location, writing my next book? The thought crosses my mind more and more all the time. Age 50. I am who I am. I may not become who I thought I would be. And that's angst or sentimentality or something. Because sometimes, it's all so good with a cigar and a friend as we sit and talk on my sun porch. A great Cormac McCarthy book I devour in one sitting. A new wine in a new country. I would like

Grouse Creek

to move to Costa Brava for a year. Maybe longer. What if I get old and I miss all the bucket list items that to me are terribly important?

These qualms I have with my success are minor. Temporary. Fleeting. They come and go. I am, by any measure, happy. Daily. Monthly. These bouts of foggy gloom are here one day, gone for months. Triggers? Rejection on a novel. An agent turning me down with a generic letter. (Twelve books and a thousand articles isn't enough for a freakin' personal email or call?) Why reject me or my proposals?

Gore Creek in its stretches by the campground holds no monsters. An unsightly overpass shadows overhead—the water is narrow but deep enough. Under the overpass, you have the tall grass and beer cans and expired makeshift fires where locals in cars congregate to drink and shoot the shit.

We walk Princess (half Blue Heeler, half Corgi) and Piper (purebred Weimaraner) a few miles down and then put in and fish back up. The dogs listen, are on their best behavior, wanting to be wild but knowing that being in the wild requires them to be tamer than normal. Piper runs circles around us but when one of us approaches the water to cast, she stops, sneaks to our side, overlooks the bank, watches. They know trout. They smell them and try to lick them when we present them after the catch.

Amy has her new fishing shirt on and she looks like an Orvis calendar girl. A statuesque beauty who not only can flyfish, but is good at it. She writes books, teaches school, and stayed young looking. Man, am I a lucky guy. With the hot sun on our backs, we fish and the water is cool.

I catch another trout. This one was a tough cast on a creek with few tough lies. This is one easy river to fish. But I pulled it off, a sidearm cast with little backcast. I had to stop the fly under an overhanging branch and let it drop, softly or it would have gotten caught up in the bush. The brown jumped, tail-smashed it, and I saw it in slow-motion, waited till he turned back on it and only then set the hook. I couldn't have done this twenty years ago, but I do fish a lot.

I present Amy and the dogs with the yellow-bodied brown trout and then gently release it into a small pocket, where it darts back to the bush. Gore Creek is not a challenge, so I am in meditation mode even though Amy and the dogs are there. The beaver pond configuration is interesting because of the way the river runs between the pools, full and clear, not yet silty. That's where I'll find the fish. The answers. My mind flits back to movies. The lost dreams of *Revolutionary Road*. Two hours. I didn't catch a damned thing.

Williams lands a nice brown in Gore Creek near the campground.

We liked Vail. We fished Gore Creek downstream, upstream, in town. We fished at one of the bridges, near the gondola. We ate at sidewalk cafés. We zipped along the interstate to Minturn to Eagle to Edwards. And back.

Here's a weird thing from that trip: Amy and I, with the dogs, rode the gondola up the mountain, free. Piper was her typical weird self, struggling to fit under the seats in the air-car. Princess was over-friendly with the two other couples. We got out, mingled, oohed and aahed at the views (Mount of the Holy Cross is hard to impossible to see except when snow frames the image), then began a long hike down the Berry Picker Trail. As trails go, it's not all that difficult, but it has a few spots where the trail disappears and turns into foot-drops and slick spots and tree roots. We managed these tough spots in the trail and were in sight of the bridge back into Vail when Amy's feet slipped on the gravel and she fell and skinned her knee. Pretty deep, rocks embedded and lots of blood. We cleaned her up in the river, and it wasn't twenty feet before she slipped and fell again. Same knee, same result. Weird enough, right? Back at camp that same night, walking on the road to pick up firewood, she fell one more time. Same knee. To this day, this fall, she still has tiny rocks under the scar.

Gore Creek outside of Vail

We cooked meals on the stove of the Aliner, on the barbeque grill at the base of the hill at our site. One minute we are listening to coyotes or hearing from campers about a bear in camp last night and fishing in the cold rushing creek catching primitive creatures, and then we hop in the car and in a few minutes we are shopping in a boutique and eating a gourmet breakfast and talking to some folks from Denmark. A dream home base.

I like Vail a lot. But Vail was the one place, because of what it is, of who is there, that inspired me to wander in and out of doubt. Success. Not just money, although I am not against money. Vail has that thing, that thing that says come ye that have seen success. And in Vail, I measure myself.

I think about Dad from time to time, but less than before. The note he wrote me before his death asked me to do two things: one, forgive him for not being the father he could have been and, two, think of him when I am in the outdoors, fishing. Unfair. I spent three decades feuding with him, and in a swoop of the pen he gets to erase years of inconsiderate behavior? Dad was born without a lot of money, worked hard, started his own company, made a lot of money, and his success was a thorn in our relationship for thirty years. He didn't like the jobs I chose, the money I made, how I left his company, even how I wore my hair or the eyeglasses I selected. That's just Dad.

He fished with me once in all the time I was writing about the outdoors. He hated it. Tolerated it, hated it, whatever, said after fishing all day and not catching a thing that it would be his last time ever. He was true to his word, too.

Dad shopped at Wal-Mart even when he had lots of money, but he and Mother sure liked to travel. All over the world. He didn't care much for mountain vacations, and maybe it was because of my outdoors writing thing—he would have liked Vail though, a lot. And that's why I think of him here. I don't want to, but for some reason Vail is one emotion-tugging mountain resort town. Mom sure likes it, her husband Don sure likes it. Amy likes it. I guess I do, too.

The last year, when Dad was dying of cancer, he bought new tools, and he already had more tools than anyone I've ever known. These tools were specialized, small, requiring a magnifying helmet to do the work for which they were designed. Dad, in his last year, collected and bought clocks. He fixed clocks, trying, even as he knew his death was coming, to fix time, to somehow delay the gray steady click of the hands of time. Roman philosopher Seneca once said that "time discovers truth." As Dad repaired clocks, I write. No difference. Just looking for answers.

Walking around Vail

Vail is understated and self-contained in a womb-like way, like the village in M. Night Shyamalan's *The Village*—isolated, warm, sequestered. East Vail, Golden Peak, Vail Village, Lionshead Village, Cascade Village, and West Vail. This is a world-class resort, so the money is not just the noveau riche or pretend rich. This place has real money, blueblood money, too. Palm Beach, Beverly Hills dough. There's a bit too much faux European architecture. You have nature in the midst of sidewalks and gardens and cubbyholes, arched bridges over a creek, umbrella-tables outside quaint cafés, all with the the Gore Range looming in the background of this verdant valley. Nearby winter flyfishing options are the big surprise, and even more of a surprise: we're talking high quality. You can shoot west or east on the I-70 Corridor from Vail to Avon to Wolcott to Eagle. Minturn is only a few minutes away. You can fish in the Eagles Nest Wilderness, Holy Cross Wilderness, White River National Forest.

Favorite Places to Eat

Meals don't have to cost an arm and a leg, and while you can pay a lot, it's not that way for all Vail restaurants. **Westside Café and Market** (970-476-7890), **Up the Creek** (970- 476-8141), **Terra Bistro** (970-476-6836), and **Sweet Basil** (970-476-0125) are fantastic, and we enjoyed our meal at **Old Forge Pizza** (970-476-5232). Not all places are equal—we had one average lunch, but enjoyed being on the sidewalk looking out at the mountain and the river and the people walking by. So it was fine.

Favorite Places to Stay

Staying in Vail is expensive, several hundred dollars a night in most places. You can contact the chamber to find rental properties and often save them there (and you can visit offseason, which is a lot cheaper). I asked friends who have stayed in Vail (because I've only camped in Vail) and

Vail, as seen from Gore Creek

they like **Lions Square Lodge** (970-476-2281), **Arabelle at Vail Square** (970-754-7777), which is incredibly expensive, but this friend has crazy money, and **Nine Vail Road.**

Fishing Places Solid Choices near Home Base

Gore Creek: You may not even notice it sometimes, but this pretty river flows right through the middle of the Vail Resort on its way to meet the Eagle River at Dowds Junction. We've mentioned that the Gore above Vail is small and the fish unpicky, but the trout you'll approach in Vail proper are wickedly selective and seemingly unfazed by your flies, or presence, or much of anything. Sight fishing is the norm, and, honestly, if you want to learn how to fish better *and* catch these Gore Creek trout, hire a guide for a half day and learn more. They know the hot flies and latest techniques. Gore Creek is ideal to finally get the wife to learn how, a fine place to teach the kids. You can even fish in winter, and that's one of the great things about Vail as a home base.

Fishing a beaver pond near Vail

For the Adventurer

Homestake Creek and Lake: Brown, brook, and cutthroat trout swimming in a wild trout stream that, while technically a tail water below the namesake lake, acts just like most freestone streams. Homestake is back in the wilds, even though it's not far at all from Vail. You probably won't run into another angler, and if you do, you can still find a mile all to yourself. Amazing scenery, snow still on Homestake Peak, which keeps watch over the river.

Homestake Creek's rainbows are copper-green with a million jet-black spots and neon pink gill plates. Chunky as your baby pictures. If you've tired of fishing shoulder to shoulder on the Pan or the Fork or the Eagle, wished for wilder settings than Gore Creek, drive on over to Homestake for a medium-river treat. You can wade up the river, fishing dries in choppy riffles, attack the cutbanks, stopping to work the pool-runs more closely, then move up to the next unfished section. Travel west on I-70, turn south on US 24. You'll pass through Minturn and go about 10 miles. Turn west on FR 703 (Homestake Road). You can start fishing from the bridge upstream, but watch for private water. We had to nymph to get most strikes, but when the hatches were on or the sun shaded by clouds, we got voracious takes on dries. Dropper rigs work best.

Blue Ribbon Fisheries not far from Vail

Eagle River
Blue River
Colorado River
Roaring Fork
Frying Pan River
Crystal River

Pocket water on the Eagle in Minturn

Fly Shops, Guides, and Tackle Stores

Gore Creek Fly Fisherman in Vail Village (970-476-3296), www.gorecreek flyfisherman.com; **Minturn Anglers** in Minturn (970-827-9500), www. min turnanglers.com; **Alpine River Outfitters** in Edwards (970-926-0900), www. alpineriveroutfitters.com; **Fly Fishing Outfitters** in Avon (970-845-8090), www.flyfishingoutfitters.net; **Eagle River Anglers Fly Shop & Guide Service** in Eagle (970-328-2323).